LIBERTY IN HUME'S *HISTORY OF ENGLAND*

ARCHIVES INTERNATIONALES D'HISTOIRE DES IDÉES

INTERNATIONAL ARCHIVES OF THE HISTORY OF IDEAS

130

N. CAPALDI and D.W. LIVINGSTON (editors)

LIBERTY IN HUME'S *HISTORY OF ENGLAND*

LIBERTY IN HUME'S
History of England

Edited by

NICHOLAS CAPALDI

and

DONALD W. LIVINGSTON

Kluwer Academic Publishers
Dordrecht / Boston / London

Library of Congress Cataloging-in-Publication Data

Liberty in Hume's History of England / by Nicholas Capaldi and Donald
W. Livingstone, eds.
    p.   cm. -- (Archives internationales d'histoire des idées ;
130)
    ISBN 0-7923-0650-3 (alk. paper)
    1. Hume, David, 1711-1776. History of England. 2. Hume, David,
1711-1776--Views on liberty. 3. Great Britain--Historiography.
4. Liberty--Historiography.   I. Capaldi, Nicholas.
II. Livingstone, Donald W.   III. Series.
DA30.H93L53   1990
942--dc20   89-71718

ISBN 0-7923-0650-3

Published by Kluwer Academic Publishers,
P.O. Box 17, 3300 AA Dordrecht, The Netherlands.

Kluwer Academic Publishers incorporates
the publishing programmes of
D. Reidel, Martinus Nijhoff, Dr W. Junk and MTP Press.

Sold and distributed in the U.S.A. and Canada
by Kluwer Academic Publishers,
101 Philip Drive, Norwell, MA 02061, U.S.A.

In all other countries, sold and distributed
by Kluwer Academic Publishers,
P.O. Box 322, 3300 AH Dordrecht, The Netherlands.

printed on acid-free paper

Printed in The Netherlands

TABLE OF CONTENTS

PREFACE

LIBERTY IN HUME'S *HISTORY OF ENGLAND*

In his own lifetime, Hume was feted by his admirers as a great historian, and even his enemies conceded that he was a controversial historian with whom one had to reckon. On the other hand, Hume failed to achieve positive recognition for his philosophical views. It was Hume's *History of England* that played an influential role in public policy debate during the eighteenth century in both Great Britain and in the United States.

Hume's *History of England* passed through seven editions and was beginning to be perceived as a classic before Hume's death. Voltaire, as an historian, considered it "perhaps the best ever written in any language." Gibbon greatly admired Hume's work and said, of a letter written by Hume in 1776 praising the *Decline and Fall of the Roman Empire*, that a compliment from Hume "overpaid the labor of ten years." After Hume's death on August 20, 1776, the *History* became a factor in the revolutionary events that began to unfold. Louis XVI was a close student of Hume's *History*, and his valet records that, upon having learned that the Convention had voted the death penalty, the King asked for the volume in Hume's *History* covering the trial and execution of Charles I to read in the days that remained. But if Louis XVI found the consolations of philosophical history in the Stuart volumes, Thomas Jefferson saw in them a cause for alarm. Jefferson believed Hume's *History* threatened to subvert constitutional liberty in the new republic and to "spread universal toryism over the land." He, accordingly, worked to suppress the *History* in America and had it banned from the University of Virginia. It remained, however, the standard history of England for nearly a century, when Macaulay's began to replace it around 1849. Still, Hume's *History* went through at least 175 posthumous editions and imprints and was published regularly into the early part of the twentieth century. Winston Churchill learned English history from a student's edition of it, and one such edition was published continuously from 1858 to 1910, with some imprints issuing in well over 100,000 copies. Hume

N. Capaldi and D.W. Livingston (eds.), Liberty in Hume's History of England. vii–xii.
© 1990 *Kluwer Academic Publishers. Printed in the Netherlands.*

is still classified in the British Museum Library as "the historian."

By 1913 the pendulum began to swing in the other direction. It was said in *The Cambridge History of English Literature* that "No one now reads Hume's *History*." Today David Hume is generally acknowledged to be the seminal figure in the Anglo-American philosophical tradition. Hume is remembered and seriously studied as a philosopher, but amongst philosophers in the twentieth century his historical works were rarely read. More widely known and read are Hume's political essays and ethical writings. Here at least some philosophers, historians, and political scientists come across common ground. Nevertheless, until recently Hume was read by and large by philosophers first and foremost on narrow epistemological grounds. Hume's so-called "literary" productions were philosophically marginalized.

All of this has changed dramatically since the mid 1960's with the revolution in Hume scholarship that has sought to understand Hume, his work, and his context from a much broader perspective. Part of the new focus has been on the Scottish Enlightenment, and as a result the academic division of labor has been altered. The entirety of Hume's philosophical project, and the relation and coherence of the different genres within which he worked, is now the center of a rich and growing body of interdisciplinary scholarship. It is therefore fitting that Hume's *History of England* should be reexamined both in its own right and for its general relevance to Hume's other writings.

The conflicting images of Hume as historian and philosopher reflect not only peculiarities of Hume's life and subsequent intellectual developments but a much older debate. It was Aristotle who first denigrated history because it dealt with particulars and who praised poetry for being much more philosophical because it dealt with universals. In opposition to this austere notion of philosophy there developed what has been called a rhetorical tradition. Going back to Cicero, the rhetorical tradition has always stressed the importance of maintaining and strengthening the community. Since the community is defined by its history, history emerges as *magistra vitae*. As such, it is history which serves as the morally foundational discipline and from which philosophy itself takes its meaning. Given that Cicero was Hume's favorite author and given Hume's philosophical rejection of universals, it is easy to see that for Hume history would be viewed in a far more favorable light and that philosophy and history would have to be closely bound.

Hume's *History* is, of course, a mammoth work, and so we have made no attempt to cover or even to mention all of the things within it which are of interest and continuing importance. Rather we hope that our modest treatment will encourage others to read, reread, and pursue the many topics which the *History* suggests. Instead we have focused on one concept that we find is at the heart of Hume's *History*, and of much of his philosophical writing. That concept is the concept of "liberty". We seek to bring to the attention of an interdisciplinary audience the larger conceptual significance of one of Hume's primary historical and philosophical interests.

Modern liberty, as opposed to liberty in the ancient world, first emerged in institutional form in Great Britain. We are naturally led to wonder why and how this was possible. Moreover, in the eighteenth century debate in Britain between Whigs and Tories, the first modern political parties, the concept of liberty was central. Were there ancient liberties enshrined in an ancient constitution or was liberty, or the liberties of Englishmen, of more recent origin? How one understood the history of England determined how one interpreted the concept of liberty, and how one interpreted the concept of liberty influenced if not determined how one understood British parliamentary government, the role of political parties, the monarchy, the future of liberty, etc. Given this framework, it would be surprising if there were not an intimate connection between Hume's *History of England* and his political philosophy as a whole.

If there is a close connection between the *History* and the political essays then no serious student of Hume's political philosophy can ignore the *History*. Moreover, if there is a close connection between Hume's political philosophy and his ethical writings, then no serious student of Hume's ethics can ignore the *History*. The same can be said for Hume's philosophy of religion. Finally, if Hume's philosophy is of a piece, with close connections between his normative and epistemological views, then familiarity with the *History* becomes crucial both as a way of throwing light on Hume's treatment of normative and epistemological issues and as a way of illustrating the treatment of those issues. It is our hope that the publication of these essays on liberty in Hume's *History* will lead to a reconsideration and more careful examination of Hume's position on normative issues, epistemological issues, and their interconnections.

The first two essays in this anthology attempt to place Hume's *History* into methodological perspective and raise the question of how that work should be read. This is brought out by Peter Jones' focus on the relationship of the *Essays* to the crucial Stuart volumes of the *History*. In his essay,"On Reading Hume's History of Liberty", Jones sees Hume's *History* against the background of the eighteenth century Scottish Enlightenment and touches on a wide variety of issues such as the notion of "sentiment". Jones also deals with Hume's conception of himself as an historian and how this relates to Hume's conception of himself as a philosopher.

Craig Walton, in his essay,"Hume's *ENGLAND* as a Natural History of Morals", advances the thesis that Hume's *History* is modeled along the lines of a Baconian natural history, as well as spelling out how Section I of the *Enquiry Concerning the Principles of Morals* could be read as a program for the History. In addition, Walton draws some important parallels between the *Natural History of Religion* and the way the *History of England* was written as well as the treatment of religion in the *History*.

Eugene Miller's essay, "Hume On Liberty in the Successive English Constitutions", is a careful detailing of Hume's own view of how liberty evolved in successive English constitutions. In itself this is an invaluable summary and running analytical guide and commentary on the *History*. Miller begins with England before the Norman Conquest, moves into the period from the Conquest to Magna Carta, the second feudal constitution, and the Tudor monarchy. Miller exhibits Hume's treatment of the "Present Plan of Liberty" by isolating three phases: 1603–1641, 1641–1660, and 1660–1689. Of particular importance are Miller's discussion of Hume's understanding of "conquest," Hume's use of Spelman and Brady in his account of feudalism, Hume's conception of the "mixed constitution" and its bearing upon the relationship between law and liberty, and Miller's analysis of Hume's purposes in periodizing the era 1640–1689.

Having seen the intimate connection between liberty and history, we come to Donald Livingston's essay "Hume's Historical Conception of Liberty". Livingston provides a philosophical analysis of Hume's developing concept of liberty not only to clarify what liberty means but also to show that Hume's conception of critical philosophical reflection represents a rejection of speculative theorizing. As is to be expected, Livingston focuses on the role of convention in Hume's narrative and the importance of tradition and custom in Hume's understanding of liberty. Livingston also draws a connection between the *History* and the *Enquiries*. If Livingston is correct, then Hume's philosophy as a whole is a profound reorientation, a Copernican revolution in how we are to think about the social world. By examining this intrinsically historical Humean perspective in a specific work, the *History of England*, with a specific focus, liberty, Livingston brings this revolutionary philosophical perspective to life. Of special interest is the concluding section where Livingston discusses the conceptual destruction of liberty by false philosophy.

John Danford's essay, "Hume's *History and the Parameters of Economic Development"*, *focuses on the early volumes of the History* in which Hume gives an account of the emergence of modern commercial societies and his explanation of the disintegration of the feudal order in England up to the Tudor period. Danford shows how Hume's *History* is a defense of emerging commercial societies against the claims of its eighteenth century critics and how that defense has contemporary relevance for those committed to the importance of liberty. Danford's essay exhibits how Hume's historical analysis provides a basis for drawing normative conclusions. Specifically, Hume's account of the replacement of the feudal order is still relevant to developing countries who seek a genuine civilization as constituted by "the rule of law with an independent judiciary, personal liberty, and commerce." Danford draws our attention to Hume's relationship to eighteenth-century republicanism and the significance for Hume of the science of jurisprudence. Finally, Danford notes the importance of the notion of development informing the *History*, what Hume called the "moral cause" of social transformation.

In the concluding essay, "The Preservation of Liberty", Nicholas Capaldi attempts to do two things. First, he draws together the remarks Hume makes about liberty in the *History* so as to construct a coherent account of how Hume himself thought that a better understanding of the history of liberty would lead to a better understanding of those institutional arrangements that support it. One of the primary objectives of the *History* was a defense of liberty understood as a crucial but fragile achievement of civilized, commercial societies. Capaldi articulates four general sets of conditions for sustaining liberty: legal, political, economic, and intellectual. Capaldi's second objective is to show how Hume's *History* is consistent with Hume's overall political and social philosophy and how that consistency suggests a unified view of Hume's philosophy, one that stresses the primacy of practical knowledge and the fundamentally historical and secularly conservative nature of that philosophy.

The essays in this volume grew out of a Liberty Fund colloquium held at the Huntington Library in October of 1985. The idea of the conference originated with J. Charles King, Vice-President of Liberty Fund. The organizer and director of the conference was Nicholas Capaldi. Initially, four papers were prepared, one each by Eugene Miller, Donald Livingston, Nicholas Capaldi, and Peter Jones. Also present at the conference as discussants were O.M. Brack,Jr., Joseph Cropsey, Ronald Hamowy, Robert S. Hill, James T. King, David Levy, Leonard Liggio, Ian Ross, M.A.Stewart, C.N. Stockton, William B. Todd, the editor of the Liberty Classics edition of Hume's *History of England*, and Craig Walton. The four papers were subsequently represented at the Scottish Enlightenment Conference held in Edinburgh during August of 1986. We are grateful to all of the foregoing individuals and institutions for contributing in innumerable ways to the clarification of the ideas presented and for bringing these ideas to the attention of scholars in many disciplines.

Note on Contributors

NICHOLAS CAPALDI is Professor of Philosophy at Queens College, City University of New York. JOHN DANFORD is Professor of Political Science at the University of Houston in Houston, Texas. PETER JONES is Professor of Philosophy and Director of the Center for Advanced Studies in the Humanities at the University of Edinburgh in Scotland. DONALD LIVINGSTON is Professor of Philosophy at Emory University in Atlanta, Georgia. EUGENE MILLER is Professor of Political Science at the University of Georgia. CRAIG WALTON is Professor of Philosophy at the University of Nevada, Las Vegas.

PETER JONES

ON READING HUME'S *HISTORY OF LIBERTY*

The first section of this paper is devoted to a brief discussion of the problems of reading Hume's works appropriately, and of his views on the nature and tasks of "history." Sections II and III consider Hume's references to "liberty" in the political *Essays* of 1741–42 and 1752, and in the Stuart volumes of the *History* of 1754–56. The final section offers a brief summary and suggestions for further studies.[1]

I

It is a sign of our uncomprehending distance from the eighteenth century that we too often fail to grasp the import and range of issues covered by Buffon's remark that *"le style est l'homme même."* Hume, following his mentor Cicero, explicitly endorsed such a view on many occasions. For style, to such writers, was not a detachable ornament, but was constitutive of the whole moral stance of a human being, embracing his attitude towards himself as well as towards others and the natural world. This feature of classical humanism is important to remember when trying to establish the load-bearing elements in Hume's works. Precisely because the context of an observer interlocks in varying ways with the context of the thing observed, as he emphasized in the Introduction to the *Treatise* and the first section of the first *Enquiry*, it is necessary to ask what I call the "seven first questions" about context twice over. Of a given text, we ask: who wrote it? for whom? about what? how? when? where? why? And of critical discussion or interpretation of that same text, we must also ask: who wrote it? for whom? about what? how? when? where? why?

Such reflections are important when we ask ourselves which of his "speculative," "political," "moral," and "historical" maxims Hume

N. Capaldi and D.W. Livingston (eds.), Liberty in Hume's History of England. 1–23.
© 1990 *Kluwer Academic Publishers. Printed in the Netherlands.*

seriously regarded as re-applicable in different contexts, appropriately identified: how universal was "universal"? By and large Hume's *Essays*, published anonymously, in the first instance, and the *History* stand, and can be read, as self-contained works. Because most contemporary readers of them were presumed ignorant of the author's other efforts, no references to those efforts are made. We would be foolish, however, to set aside *our* knowledge of the philosophical work, or reflection on the influence it might have exerted on the other writings. We would be wise, also, to recall the setting for Hume's initial work on the Stuart volumes of the *History*. In a city rocked to the core by the '45, a discussion of the Commonwealth and Restoration was no more taken to be of merely antiquarian interest than a discussion of Roman rites or Greek mythology was mistaken as addressed to merely classical scholars. More locally, Scottish thinkers divided quite sharply over their notions of "moral philosophy" because of different responses to Natural Law; different attitudes to science, particularly Newtonianism in its various forms, reflected, and in turn influenced, attitudes to moral and political issues; regional theological differences between Episcopal Aberdeen, Evangelical Glasgow, and Presbyterian Edinburgh influenced political views after the '45. William James, whenever he wished to stress his Humean inheritance, was fond of quoting a remark he had heard in connection with Kierkegaard: "we live forward, we understand backward."[2] James, Proust, and Collingwood, over a span of some 50 years, all sought to develop this view, which they explicitly traced to Hume.[3] An exact contemporary and acquaintance of Hume, James Hutton, the founder of modern geology, devoted a large part of his own philosophical reflections to the problem of causation. He argued that, on a Humean account, a cause is strictly "only known by means of effect; and effect is only known by means of action and order in change."[4] Four points can be usefully separated: firstly, we can only know about causal connections after they have occurred, only know, in this sense, the nature of an event after it is complete; secondly, the temporal processing of sensory and intellectual data alike means that we can only achieve understanding of what is passed; thirdly, such interpretation, as temporal events themselves, are subject to subsequent re-interpretation; fourthly, earlier and later events illuminate each other reciprocally, just as knowing the end of a story throws earlier episodes into relief, revealing their significance. These points are important both for a grasp of Hume's view of historical understanding, and for the interpretation of Hume's works themselves.

Hume discusses problems of interpretation in a long footnote of

Section III of the first *Enquiry*.[5] He argues that events in "narrative compositions" must "form a kind of unity which may bring them under one plan or view, and which may be the object or end of the writer in his first undertaking." An agent "seldom acts or speaks or thinks without a purpose or intention" (E, 33), and knowledge of these "necessary" principles is a condition of understanding what a man does. Hume's view of the nature of historical writing and understanding rests on two fundamental tenets: agents usually know their intentions, but are doomed to mere foresight of their outcome; observers after the event are blessed with hindsight of the outcome, but are doomed merely to conjecture the intentions necessary for understanding it. The unbridgeable gap between foresight and hindsight, the asymmetrical views of "actor" and "spectator," as Hume refers to them (H, XI, 138), sometimes baffles the most diligent enquirer. Hume explains his position in the following way. "Mens' views of things are the result of their understanding alone: Their conduct is regulated by their understanding, their temper, and their passions" (H, IX, 222). By definition, that is, the spectator uses his understanding alone for determining the nature of another person's actions; an agent himself, however, although assisted by his understanding, can never be motivated by it. But even if a spectator uses his own understanding, that does not require him to explain another's actions solely in terms of understanding. Hume might reply that spectators typically emphasize the agent's understanding both because the motivating passions are unknown and because it is mainly by reference to the understanding that actions become intelligible. This aside, Hume insists that spectators have access to data denied to agents, namely the long term consequences of their acts and the different evaluations made of them from different perspectives. Re-interpretation – or, at least, re-evaluation – is always possible in the light of succeeding events, and this is a major reason behind the need for each generation to write its own histories, although Hume primarily cites the accumulation of "monuments" (L, I, 284). He gives several examples where the "event" shows the views of one party to have been "better founded," even though the rival views "ought beforehand, to have appeared more solid, more safe, and more legal" (E, 500; cf. 347, 366). "Time, by introducing new subjects of controversy" enables posterity to see events in relation to factors unknown to the agents themselves; that is why "after the event … it is commonly easy to correct all errors" (H, IX, 232; X, 290).

There are several issues that Hume never fully articulates. On his own account of causation there could be only one true historical interpretation of events, namely the one giving the causes. The reason that different evaluations become possible in the light of later unforeseen consequences is that different sets of events are being considered; since, on his partly casual theory of evaluation, no single cause can have different effects. Sometimes Hume remarks that a historian, finding no reasons, must restrict himself to causes of certain actions. One implication here is that, in retrospect, the participants can be seen only as material bodies passively reacting to external forces (cf. H, IX, 236). It is worth observing that in the domain of taste, Hume does not allow for legitimate multiple interpretations of works of art. His main reason is that the first requirement of a critic is to discover the artist's own intentions, goals, aims, expectations, and the potentially definitive answers to these were taken as over-riding changes in the spectators' contexts.

Hume is insistent that the historian must exercise the greatest care in his analysis: "what is most probable in human affairs, is not always true; and a very minute circumstance, overlooked in our speculations, serves often to explain events, which may seem the most surprising and unaccountable" (H, IX, 222; XII, 81). To take one example: "if we are left to gather Cromwell's intentions from his instrument of government, it is such a motley piece, that we cannot easily conjecture, whether he seriously meant to establish a tyranny or a republic" (H, XI, 95). Even though we find "habits, more than reason ... to be the governing principle of mankind," "those, who are curious of tracing the history of the human mind," must study the "minute" circumstances which may inflame or animate the passions, in order to decide "how far its several singularities coincide in different ages" (H, IX, 88, 200).

A central them in Hume's historical reflections concerns the unavoidable struggle between liberty and authority. In 1741 he writes: "in all governments, there is a perpetual intestine struggle, open or secret, between AUTHORITY and LIBERTY" (E, 40). In tracing this theme through his writings, it is necessary here only to remark that Hume offers no formal definitions or analyses of these "notions," nor would they be proper to the works in question. As we shall see, he is primarily concerned with liberty under the law, and with constraints upon it exercised by various kinds of authority; to a lesser degree he considers limits on personal liberty imposed by habit or education, but he is not concerned, in the *History*, with philosophical problems of "freedom and determinism." He simply assumes, as a matter of common-sense morals, that we are morally responsible for the thoughts and passions, intentions and willings, that function as the causes of our actions; and that we are generally not responsible for the causes of those mental events themselves, nor of external events which may impede us.

II

Hume's essays on what he regards as practical philosophy concern the whole tenor of life: a discussion of liberty is not ultimately separable from a discussion of virtue and thus of how to live as a social being.[6] "The spirit of the age," he writes in 1752, "affects all the arts; and the minds of men, being once roused from their lethargy, and put into a fermentation, turn themselves on all sides, and carry improvements into every art and science":

> But industry, knowledge, and humanity, are not advantageous in private life alone: They diffuse their beneficial influence on the *public*, and render the government as great and flourishing as they make individuals happy and prosperous.... Laws, order, police, discipline; these can never be carried to any degree of perfection, before human reason has refined itself by exercise, and by an application to the more vulgar arts, at least, of commerce and manufacture. Can we expect, that a government will be well modelled by a people, who know not how to make a spinning-wheel, or to employ a loan to advantage? Not to mention, that all ignorant ages are infested with superstition, which throws the government off its bias, and disturbs men in the pursuit of their interest and happiness. (E, 271–73)

"General virtue and good morals in a state," Hume insisted, "must proceed entirely from the virtuous education of youth, the effect of wise laws and institutions." That was one reason behind his claim, later disputed by Adam Ferguson, that "the first place of honour seems due to LEGISLATORS and founders of states, who transmit a system of laws and institutions to secure peace, happiness, and liberty to future generations" (E, 54).[7] By contrast, the real enemies are the founders and fanners of factions: "Factions subvert government, render laws impotent, and beget the fiercest animosities among men of the same nation, who ought to give mutual assistance and protection to each other" (*ibid.*). Aside from personal factions, Hume distinguishes what he calls three kinds of "real" factions: those which arise "from *interest*, from *principle*, and from *affection*." Of these, by far the most dangerous are "parties from *principle*, especially abstract speculative principle," since they are typically "the origin of all religious wars and divisions" (E, 56–60). Although they are not alone in their achievement, Hume claims on many occasions that "in all ages of the world, priests have been enemies to liberty": "Liberty of thinking, and of expressing our thoughts, is always fatal to priestly power, and to those pious frauds, on which it is commonly founded; and, by an infallible connection, which prevails among all kinds of liberty, this privilege can never be enjoyed, at least has never yet been enjoyed, but in a free government" (E, 66). "Separate interest" must be constantly checked in order to safeguard against "faction, disorder, and tyranny"; "the force of laws" is independent of the "peculiar interests and present temptations," "the humours and tempers of men" (E, 43, 38, 16). A "free" government might thus be characterized as

> that which admits of a partition of power among several members, whose united authority is no less, or is commonly greater than that of any monarch; but who, in the usual course of administration, must act by general and equal laws, that are previously known to all the members and to all their subjects. In this sense, it must be owned, that liberty is the perfection of civil society; but still authority must be acknowledged essential to its very existence. (E, 41)

A practical problem which confronts both the historian, reflecting with all the advantages of hindsight, and the legislator facing an unknown future, is that "'tis difficult to penetrate into the thoughts and sentiments of any particular man; but 'tis almost impossible to distinguish those of a whole party, where it often happens, that no two persons agree precisely in the same maxims of conduct." Hume is inclined to think that "those principles or causes, which are fitted to operate on a multitude, are always of a grosser and more stubborn nature ... than those which operate on a few only." Accordingly, "the domestic and gradual revolutions of a state must be a more proper subject of reasoning and observation, than the foreign and the violent, which are more commonly produced by single persons" (E, 613, 112). One problem with which Hume is grappling here, and which exercised contemporaries as diverse as Adam Ferguson and James Hutton, concerns the proper identification of events to which levels of macroscopic and microscopic causation apply. In 1752 he rather impatiently asks: "why should the case be so different between the public and an individual, as to make us establish different maxims of conduct for each?" (E, 351). Hume is loathe to consider *groups* of men as agents, in the strictest sense: *individual* men are agents, motivated by their passions rather than by reason and reflection, but the extension of the notion of agency to groups immediately challenges us to identify their "actuating principles." "The social passions are by far the most powerful of any," Hume holds (E, 620): "Interest and ambition, honour and shame, friendship and enmity, gratitude and revenge, are the prime movers in all public transactions; and these passions are of a very stubborn and intractable nature, in comparison of the sentiments and understanding, what are easily varied by education and example" (E, 97).

In this context, two features of the ancient Greek city-states in their prime attract Hume. Their municipal laws were "few and simple" and issues were decided by "the equity and common sense of the judges." By the middle of the eighteenth century, on the other hand, the "study of laws" had become "a laborious occupation ... incompatible with every other study or profession" (E, 102). This last remark about specialization and the division of intellectual labour was already a topic for debate in the 1730s and a major concern of Ferguson's in the 1760s. Hume's view is that the law should not aim to meet every contingency it might be called upon to cover; the advantages of general laws far outweigh their disadvantages and, by definition, they cannot possibly be framed to cater for exceptions: "All general laws are attended with inconveniences, when applied to particular cases; and it requires great penetration and experience, both to perceive that these inconveniences are fewer than what result from full discretionary powers in every magistrate; and also to discern what general laws are, upon the whole, attended with fewest inconveniences" (E, 116). Municipal laws can be improved only by trial and careful observation, since, wherever arbitrary power reigns a people so governed "are slaves in the full and proper sense of the word." But law is necessary not only for justice: "from law arises security: From security curiosity: And from curiosity knowledge" (E, 118).

Hume bases his second commendation of the Greeks on this last point. "Divisions into small states are favourable to learning, by stopping the progress of *authority* as well as that of *power*." He even wonders whether "interruptions in the periods of learning, were they not attended with such a destruction of ancient books, and the records of history, would be rather favourable to the arts and sciences, by breaking the progress of authority, and dethroning the tyrannical usurpers over human reason. In this particular, they have the same influence, as interruptions in political governments and societies" (E, 123). The other "tyrannical usurpers," of course, include the debilitating inertia which results from the habits to which all human beings succumb.

Although "man is a very variable being, and susceptible of many different opinions, principles, and rules of conduct," at the level of generality on which the nature of law is considered, Hume holds that human nature must be taken as more or less uniform and unchanging (E, 256; 468). A "moral" philosopher, on the other hand, studies the *mores* of man, that is, the distinctive character, conduct and customs, manners and morals of individuals and groups, as determined by themselves. That is why Hume says he is not interested in "physical" causes of behaviour, in, say, the influence of "air, food, or climate"; he is interested in the "moral" causes of agency, understood as those within a person's potential cognition and control. In brief, "moral" causes are "all circumstances, which are fitted to work on the mind as motives or reasons, and which render a peculiar set of manners habitual to us" (E, 198).

Hume is keen to emphasize the gradual development of human institutions, and the relatively slow transitions to which they are subject; so slow, normally, that they can be discerned only in retrospect. Law, for example, is "the slow product of order and of liberty," and even the "great revolutions" from agricultural to commercial society require "a long course of time" and are the result of "a variety of accidents" (E, 124, 260). It is precisely because of such variety, and because the public good "depends on the concurrence of a multitude of causes" that "philosophers" and "politicians" alike should make it their "chief business" to "regard the general course of things" with a view to determining the "general principles" which operate (E, 254). What such reflection discovers is the causal inter-dependence of factors often thought to be unrelated. For example, an increase in commerce "by a necessary consequence" increases the number of money-lenders, which in turn secures low interest rates, which in turn generates industry (E, 302). Or, a different example: "knowledge in the arts of government naturally begets mildness and moderation, by instructing men in the advantages of humane maxims above rigour and severity, which drive subjects into rebellion and make the return to submission impracticable, by cutting off all hopes of pardon" (E, 273). Philosophically, the mutual influence of individuals is explained by the principle of sympathy: "there is a moral attraction, arising from the interests and passions of men," and "a single man can scarcely be industrious, where his fellow-citizens are idle" (E, 313, 329). Emulation, encouragement, and competition also operate at a national level, and can be of great mutual benefit "where an open communication is preserved among nations, it is impossible but the domestic industry of every one must receive an increase from the improvement of the others" (E, 328). Indeed, a nation can succumb to a form of self-induced slavery to its own ignorance, resulting from the domination of primitive passions such as jealously or revenge. Thus, jealousy in France led to "innumerable barriers and obstructions upon commerce" and no gain whatsoever (E, 315).

Although "all general maxims in politics ought to be established with great caution," there can be no doubt that "the safety of the people is the supreme law"; moreover, "a power, however great, when granted by law to an eminent magistrate, is not so dangerous to liberty, as an authority, however inconsiderable, which he acquires from violence and usurpation" (E, 366, 489, 374). Of course, a magistrate "aims only at possibilities" (E, 280), and Hume reminds us of the important distinction between what it is reasonable and prudent to plan to do and what, in the event, may be forced on us. "To trust to chances and temporary expedients, is, indeed, what the necessity of human affairs frequently renders unavoidable: but whoever voluntarily depend on such resources, have not necessity, but their own folly, to accuse for their misfortunes, when any such befall them" (E, 351). The stability and structure of society depend on the upholding of law, and society faces its greatest peril when resistance to existing law is proclaimed as itself "lawful or commendable": "in reality, there is not a more terrible event, than a total dissolution of government, which gives liberty to the multitude." For this reason, and also because its beneficial long-term consequences were due to "fortune and accident," the English Revolution cannot function as a proper "precedent" or model (E, 472, 477). As a matter of principle and as a matter of public policy, "one would be better employed in inculcating the general doctrine, than in displaying the particular exceptions, which we are, perhaps, but too much inclined, of ourselves, to embrace and extend" (E, 491). The bulk of mankind are "governed by authority, not reason," in both a literal and a metaphorical sense: on the one hand, men are governed by magistrates, on the other by habits and passions independent of reason. "To tamper, therefore," with the principles and instruments of government, "merely upon the credit of supposed argument and philosophy, can never be part of a wise magistrate" (E, 512); or, it might be added, of a wise philosopher.

Two related conclusions follow from these reflections, of importance for policy and practice, on the one hand, and for historical understanding, on the other. First, as human society is in perpetual flux, one man every hour going out of the world, another coming into it, it is necessary, in order to preserve stability in government, that the new brood should conform themselves to the established constitution, and nearly follow the path which their fathers, treading in the footsteps of theirs, had marked out to them. Some innovations must necessarily have place in every human institution, and it is happy where the enlightened genius of the age gives a direction to the side of reason, liberty, and justice: but violent innovations no individual is entitled to make: they are even dangerous to be attempted by the legislature: more good than ill is ever to be expected from them: and if history affords examples to the contrary, they are not to be drawn into precedent. (E, 476)

Hume carefully contrasts here "innovation" and "violent innovations." Change is inevitable, and innovation is necessary in order to control the institution and prevent it from ossifying: "all human institutions are liable to abuse, and require continual amendments, which are, in reality, so many alterations" (H, XII, 90). The task for the magistrate is to introduce change "by such gentle alterations and innovations as may not give too great a disturbance to society" (E, 514). But "if subjects must never resist, it follows that every prince ... is at once rendered absolute" (H, XI, 244). The proscription of violence is justified on prudential and probabilistic grounds; a very peculiar state of affairs might warrant it, but the likely difficulty in recognizing the case justifies the proscription. It is logically possible that a future revolution would be justifiable, just as it is logically possible that if I leave my purse of gold on the pavement at Charing Cross it will remain untouched after an hour. But practical philosophy is too important and urgent to trifle with such closet fictions: they become "dangerous novelties" (E, 36; cf. 568). As he says on another occasion, "the question is not concerning any fine imaginary republic, of which a man may form a plan in his closet"; rather, the question is "what kind of republic we have reason to expect" (E, 52). Similarly, "it is needless to enquire, whether such a government would be immortal.... The world itself probably is not immortal"; "It is a sufficient incitement to human endeavours, that such a government would flourish for many ages" (E, 528–9). Plans and policies are best formulated, therefore, in the light of our knowledge of man and his actual practices and institutions; not on the dubious premise of a reformed human nature.

There is a further point associated with the fact that "all human institutions, and none more than government, are in continual fluctuation." It is this: "All political questions are infinitely complicated, and ... there scarcely ever occurs, in any deliberation, a choice, which is either purely good, or purely ill. Consequences, mixed and varied, may be foreseen to flow from every measure: And many consequences, unforeseen, do always, in fact, result from every one" (E, 507).

III

Almost all of the observations recorded above from the *Essays* re-appear in the Stuart volumes of the *History*, although with even less overt philosophical or theoretical explanation. Thus, "it is to be considered, that revolutions of government cannot be effected by mere force of argument and reasoning: and that factions being once excited, men can neither so firmly regulate the tempers of others, nor their own, as to ensure themselves against all exorbitances" (H, IX, 322). Hume's observation, from a philosophical standpoint, is potentially confusing. He holds that factions result from unmoderated passions, and that passions can be neither caused nor quelled by "mere force of argument." Demonstrative reasoning only is inert in the same that, as a purely reflective endeavour, it cannot by itself influence actions. But, of course, thinking or reasoning in a more general sense does, and Hume has to define belief in such a way that it can function as a cause. Accordingly, he classifies belief as a *sentiment*[8], since only sentiments function as "actuating principles" or "motives to action." Sentiments, taken as feeling and judgment compounded, bridge, or fudge, the gap between the intellectual and the passional, between the allegedly inert and the uniquely actuating. Hume, therefore, is not denying that factions are caused by argument, nor that the rival claimants have beliefs.

Throughout the *History* Hume observes that personal inclinations, political interests, and religious zeal are constant threats to society; it is "not enough for liberty to remain on the defensive," not least because, however "carefully framed," no laws could "possibly provide against every contingency" (H, VIII, 309, 238). Religious sects and schisms have constituted a danger to law and civil government for several reasons. During the Stuart period "religion was the fatal point about which the differences" arose; "and of all others, it was the least susceptible of composition or moderation between the contending parties" (H, X, 266). Hume holds that religious hypocrisy "is of a peculiar nature; and being generally unknown to the person himself, though more dangerous, it implies less falsehood than any other species of insincerity" (H, XI, 198). His contrast here is between individual religious zeal, which Hume takes to be grounded in ignorance both of oneself and of the social matrix in which religions function, and institutional zeal orchestrated by priests and collaborating rulers. In the *Essays*, and with greater concentration in his *Natural History of Religion*, Hume had aligned himself with Cicero's view that religions have their roots in ignorance of causes, and fear for the future; such fears feed, and are in turn fed by, pseudo- explanations which are systematized and propagated by groups seeking power – we must never forget "the appetite for power inherent in human nature" (H, XII, 310). Hume suggests three reasons why Christendom, in particular, became "the scene of religious wars and divisions": the authority of the priests, the separation of the ecclesiastical and civil powers, and the alliance of an outmoded speculative philosophy with "traditional tales and fictions" (E, 62).[9] Hume explains man's natural impatience towards opposing views by reference to psychological and social needs for agreement within social groups, and the mutually re-enforcing effect of such agreement. As we have seen, he holds that "liberty of thinking, and of expressing our thoughts, is always fatal to priestly power" (E, I, 135). This is because organized factions result from attempts to limit thought by making habitual those passions which inhibit it and can survive without it. Three points are worth making in this connection.

Hume always held that "scholastic learning and polemical divinity retarded the growth of all learning" (H, IX, 82): they are predominantly *a priori* in form, dogmatic and authoritarian, and lead to that fanaticism which is "no less destructive of taste and science, than of all law and order." "Gaiety and wit," "human learning," and "freedom of inquiry" all suffer (H, XI, 210). The second point follows: "an unlimited *toleration*, after sects have diffused themselves, and are strongly rooted, is the only expedient which can allay their fervour, and make the civil union acquire a superiority above religious distinctions." In fact, however, because the effects of such policies take time and become detectable only gradually, "vulgar politicians" are apt "to have recourse to more hasty and more dangerous remedies" (H, XII, 131). Hume believes that "the paradoxical principle and salutary practice of toleration" (H, IX, 48) arose, not as a result of positive policy but, from a slow recognition that attempts at fierce repression had merely fanned opposition and stiffened resistance. Such facts, if they are facts, are contingent, and Hume holds neither that toleration must always win through nor, conversely, that repression could never be total under some conditions.

The third point focuses on the dilemma facing Hume: the dilemma of upholding moderation, and of stabilizing the unavoidable tension between liberty and authority. He frequently reports occasions when opponents express their demands in ways that are "beyond all reasonable bounds," thereby exciting equal and opposite reactions. In the 1628 arguments over the Petition of Rights, for example, "extremes were very often affected, and the just medium was gradually deserted by all men" (H, IX, 143). And reflecting generally on Charles's lack of "vigour and foresight," Hume remarks that "the spirit of enthusiasm being universally diffused, disappointed all the views of human prudence, and disturbed the operation of every motive which usually influences society" (H, IX, 173). Hume is well aware that "no one will ever please" vehement opponents "by moderate opinions" (H, XIII, 122), but he does not grapple with the problem he identifies.

The problem here is not the general problem of casuistry, namely, the application of principles to particular cases; but the specific form of that problem as it confronts any moralist who follows "the experimental method" in "deducing general maxims from a comparison of particular instances" (M, 8). Moderation is a relational property, definable only by reference to limits to either side. There can be no criterion of moderation independent of a particular context with determinate boundaries; there can be no fully intelligible principle of moderation independently of cases. In an asylum for the insane, even the moderate remain insane. A related problem is how an attitude of moderation can motivate anyone at all – let alone those with deeply engrained habits one hopes to displace. It can be argued that Hume himself is not legislating for an unknown future, and that his references to moderation should be understood within the precise historical contexts within which, and also about which, he was writing. It can also be held that verdicts about moderation are essentially spectatorial verdicts, after the event, and not features of present engagement – precisely because being moderate in one's judgment would lessen one's passional motivation to do anything, and because the temporal limits of one's actions (their consequences) are unknown at the time.

On a more general note, it must be acknowledged that the leaders of the Scottish Enlightenment, almost all of them "moderates" of one kind or another, did nothing to defuse or forestall the vehement opposition that was mounted against their successors. It was as if they did not appreciate the complex nature of their own, often individual, achievements in rebutting fanaticism; did not grasp that the essentially sceptical frame of mind it required was an attitude requiring unremitting self-consciousness and effort; and failed to understand that the social conditions favourable to the acquisition of such attitudes did not yet exist. Almost despairingly Hume writes of the period prior to the summoning of the Long Parliament in 1640, that "one furious enthusiast was able, by his active industry, to surmount the indolent effort of many sober and reasonable antagonists" (H, IX, 261). And it is worth noting here that Hume rebukes those historians of the 1640 period who simplify the issues, and who "still represent the civil disorders and convulsions as proceeding from religious controversy, and consider the political disputes about power and liberty as entirely subordinate to the other." He holds that both sides of the bitter disputes at the time well "knew that no established government could be overthrown by strictly observing the principles of justice, equity, or clemency" (H, IX, 284–85). Strafford, for example, whatever his private advice, never failed to argue publicly that "if any inevitable necessity ever obliged the sovereign to violate the laws, this licence ought to be practiced with extreme reserve, and, as soon as possible, a just atonement be made to the constitution, for any injury which it might sustain from such dangerous precedents" (H, IX, 318). Up to that time "Charles dreaded no opposition from the people," partly because they "always take opinions in the lump," partly because they "are not commonly much affected with consequences, and require some striking motive to engage them in a resistance of establish government" (H, IX, 212, 113). Nevertheless, as early as 1628, the commons had no difficulty in listing their grievances against the king: "forced loans, benevolences, taxes without consent of parliament, arbitrary imprisonments, the billeting of soldiers, martial law" (H, IX, 133).

Hume observes that "by removing the star-chamber," so "unintelligible in a limited constitution," "the king's power of binding the people by his proclamations was indirectly abolished." He adds:

It must, however, be confessed, that the experiment here made by the parliament, was not a little rash and adventurous. No government at that time appeared in the world, nor is perhaps to be found in the records of any history, which subsisted without the mixture of some arbitrary authority, committed to some magistrate; and it might reasonably, before- hand, appear doubtful, whether human society could ever reach that state of perfection, as to support itself with no other control than the general and rigid maxims of law and equity....

And in the event it has hitherto been found, that, though some sensible inconveniences arise from the maxim of adhering strictly to law, yet the advantages over-balance them. (H, IX, 320–21)

When he discusses the debates between royalists and parliamentarians of 1641, Hume adopts his favorite device of singling out acceptable premises from each side, in order to contrast his own moderate judgment made with hindsight, with the inevitably limited foresight of the participants. We should recall his remark that "mens' views of things are the result of their understanding alone: Their conduct is regulated by their understanding, their temper, and their passion" (H, IX, 222): this precisely captures one difference between spectator and agent. Hume claims that the royalists based their arguments less "on opposite principles of government" than "on opposite ideas, which they had formed of the past events" of the reign. They denied that the king had formed a "system for enslaving his people"; and they insisted that "authority, as well as liberty, is requisite to government; and is even requisite to the support of liberty itself, by maintaining the laws, which can alone regulate and protect it." The parliamentarians emphasized that "governments, especially those of a mixed kind, are in continual fluctuation: The humours of the people change perpetually from one extreme to another," and advantages must be pressed in order to establish the security of the laws and constitution (H, X, 31–35). Hume's own position is clear. Inconvenience is never alone a sufficient ground for resisting or suspending a law; the great danger of "the sweet sound of liberty" is that it encourages "a giddy search after more independence" with the attendant risk of "abandoning all law and order" (H, X, 54, 66). In their "too eager pursuit of liberty" the parliamentarians failed to foresee the "slavery" to which they consigned the nation; for what they achieved was "a people without government and without liberty, a parliament without authority, an army without a legal master" (H, X, 233, 238); they expected "by the terror of the sword, to impose a more perfect system of liberty on the reluctant nation" – a "delusion" "the most contrary to common sense" (H, X, 243). And, in 1649, they "established a principle, which is noble in itself, and seems specious, but is belied by all history and experience, *That the people are the origin of all just power*" (H, X, 276). Above all, they disregarded the virtues.

Among the generality of men, educated in regular civilized societies, the sentiments of shame, duty, honour, have considerable authority,

and serve to counterbalance and direct the motives derived from
private advantage: But, by the predominancy of enthusiasm among the
parliamentary forces, these salutary principles lost their credit, and
were regarded as mere human inventions, yes moral institutions, fitter
for heathens than for christians. (H, X, 222)

Hume insists that "illegal violence, with whatever pretences it may be
covered, and whatever object it may pursue, must inevitably end at last in
the arbitrary and despotic government of a single person." Moreover, "a
government totally military and despotic is almost sure, after some time,
to fall into impotence and languor" (H, XI, 75, 103). A leader whose
power base is provided by the army faces the unending problem of
governing those whom he nourished on fanaticism: either he seeks to
defuse the fanaticism, and loses his power base, or he feeds the
fanaticism and jeopardizes his government. That is why "all military
government is precarious; much more where it stands in opposition to
civil establishments; and still more where it encounters religious
prejudices" (H, XI, 119). Ultimately, "no character in human society is
more dangerous than that of the fanatic; because, if attended with weak
judgment, he is exposed to the suggestion of others; if supported by more
discernment, he is entirely governed by his own illusions, which sanctify
his most selfish views and passions." No tyrant can ensure "that tranquillity which it belongs to virtue alone, and moderation, fully to ascertain"
(H, XI, 158, 146).

   Tranquillity, here, refers to a state of mind: it does not militate against
decision making. On the contrary, it is only with tranquillity, and the
"composure and mutual confidence which is absolutely requisite" for
government, that the most urgent matters can be dealt with effectively
(H, XI, 259n.; XII, 48). Aside from issues over which the law maintains
a "prudent silence," legislatures should not distract themselves over how
to formalize what to do in cases of extreme necessity; in the first place,
"no laws could beforehand point out a proper remedy," and in the
second, "no man, on the approach of extraordinary necessity could be at
a loss, though not directed by legal declarations, to find the proper
remedy" (H, XI, 245; XII, 90). On such occasions, discretionary powers
assumed by a magistrate supervene the existing laws. Thus, after the Fire
of London, the king insisted on certain street widths and forbad the use
of lath and timber in construction, but the "necessity was so urgent, and
the occasion so extraordinary, that no exceptions were taken at an

exercise of authority, which otherwise might have been deemed illegal"
(H, XI, 291).

<h1 style="text-align:center">IV</h1>

It will be convenient to summarize Hume's views on the obstacles to
liberty, and to supplement those reflections by briefly referring to
Ferguson.

For Hume temporality is the condition of existence, and historicity the
condition of its understanding; and, if the pun is permissible, accidents
constitute the essence of society. His warning that "it seems un-
reasonable to judge of the measures embraced during one period, by the
maxims which prevail in another" (H, IX, 199) is not a proscription upon
understanding, but upon moral judgment in advance of understanding.

The practical obstacles and threats to liberty usually stem from errors
in judgment resulting from fundamental theoretical or philosophical
misconceptions. On the economic front Hume saw the national debt, with
its attendant taxation levies, together with the prospect of nationalization
of property, as especially dangerous. "The source of degeneracy, which
may be remarked in free governments, consists in the practice of contracting debt, and mortgaging the public revenues, by which taxes may, in
time, become altogether intolerable, and all the property of the state be
brought into the hands of the public" (E, 95; cf. 360). Low interest rates,
controlled labor costs, competitive pricing are all essential to ensure
successful foreign trade and a buoyant home economy which motivates
the work force (E, 263–65, 283, 286, 294, 306). Arbitrary and penal
taxation alike, undermine liberty, and "pensions and bribes" are expedients which "cannot be too carefully guarded against, nor too vehe-
mently decried, by everyone who has a regard to the virtue and liberty of
a nation" (H, XII, 192). Realities, however, must be faced. "The continual fluctuations in commerce require continual alterations in the nature
of the taxes; which exposes the legislature every moment to the danger
both of wilful and involuntary error. Any great blow given to trade,
whether by injudicious taxes or by other accidents, throws the whole
system of government into confusion" (E, 358).

The economic obstacles, by and large, result from political and social
circumstances. All "abuses of treasures" are dangerous, but "abuses of
mortgaging" are worse, in Hume's view, since their consequences are
"more certain and inevitable; poverty, impotence, and subjection to
foreign powers." The contracting of debt is an attractive expedient to

politicians keen to avoid unpopularity. But "to mortgage the public revenues, and to trust that posterity will pay off the incumbrances contracted by their ancestors," save in cases of "necessary" wars, is profoundly misguided (E, 350–51): by constraining the capacity of our successors to deal with their own immediate problems, it is likely to diminish their own respect for the traditions to which they are heir, and make them adopt a more cavalier policy with regard to their own, unknown, posterity. In brief, the historical structure of society is undermined by irresponsibly bequeathing one's debts to later generations. Unfortunately,

> though men are commonly more governed by what they have seen, than by what they foresee, with whatever certainty; yet promises, protestations, fair appearances, with the allurements of present interest, have such powerful influence as few are able to resist. Mankind are, in all ages, caught by the same baits: The same tricks, played over and over again, still trepan them. The heights of popularity and patriotism are still the beaten road to power and tyranny; flattery to treachery; standing armies to arbitrary government; and the glory of God to the temporal interest of the clergy. (E, 363)

If exorbitant taxes "destroy industry, by engendering despair" – Hume advocates taxation of luxury consumption, "as least felt by the people" – so does extreme inequality of wealth: "a too great disproportion among the citizens weakens the state" (E, 635, 345, 265). Diversification may be necessary when an economy rests on single staple commodities, because such an economy is vulnerable to decreasing demand, and to successful competition from elsewhere (E, 330). One consequence of a buoyant commercial, as distinct from agricultural, economy is that people flock to the capital cities.[10] But "enormous cities are ... destructive to society, beget vice and disorder of all kinds, starve the remoter provinces, and even starve themselves, by the prices to which they raise all provisions" (E, 401; cf. 314, 271).

The separable political obstacles to liberty have been characterized sufficiently, perhaps, above. The exercise of arbitrary power, the influence of faction, whether resulting from interest, principle or affection, the use of military force, disregard of parliament, but above all attempts to suspend the law: all these have been noted. Hume remarks that "all human institutions are liable to abuse, and require continual amendments, which are, in reality, so many alterations. It is not indeed possible to make a law which does not innovate, more or less, in the government" (H, XII, 90). The philosophical point is simply that, in an important sense in which they are analogous to moral principles, laws are abstractions from particular cases; their fate is to be re-applied to new particular cases that, by definition, differ. Hume frequently draws a distinction between a principle or even an idea which, "in itself," has merit, but which in context and in practice is inappropriate. "Liberty" is no exception: "a regard to liberty, though a laudable passion, ought commonly to be subordinate to a reverence for established government" (H, XIII, 122). And, "for the full security of liberty and a limited constitution" a standing army cannot be permitted (H, XII, 193). Aside from being a tool dangerously available to a tyrant, the nature of such a force is inimical to the delicate balance between liberty and authority that is a perpetual challenge to magistrates. "In the same manner as excessive severity in the laws is apt to beget great relaxation in their execution; so their excessive lenity naturally produces cruelty and barbarity. It is dangerous to force us, in any case, to pass their sacred boundaries" (E, 415).

In the end, economic, social and political obstacles to liberty are traceable to mistaken philosophical views. Hume barely mentions this point in the *History*, although it is a condition of the intelligibility of his account, and is explicit in his so-called "philosophical" works. In the *History*, it emerges implicitly in his discussions of religion and its institutions, and in his remarks on the influence of habit, ignorance and the passions. Religions, in Hume's view, trade on and consolidate man's passions, and in so doing effectively inhibit that free inquiry which alone secures genuine fulfilment. There are, however, other and greater obstacles to knowledge of oneself and of others, and even of the external world, because all the sources of knowledge are liable to distortion or misinterpretation. The majority of our knowledge claims derive, not from our own first-hand experience of what we are talking about, but from what we have heard from other people who, themselves, learned it from yet others. Education, in both the formal and informal senses, is a principal source of our beliefs and thus of the actions informed by those beliefs. In the *History*, as elsewhere, Hume regards education as a genuine obstacle to liberty. In the past, this has been because education has been dominated by religions, in unholy alliance with scholastic philosophy; but, more abstractly, education essentially involves habit-forming which, itself, is intrinsically dangerous. Hume is not talking about the life-preserving habits such as sleeping and eating, on the one hand, or expecting the future to resemble the past, on the other: these he regards as entirely natural, and beyond either the beneficial or harmful influence of education. He is concerned with social conditioning, because man's whole existence as a social being, from the family upwards, makes him an easy victim of unscrupulous indoctrination. The herd instinct, along with the desire for agreement, approval and acceptance, may be necessary, at some level, for survival, but they represent essentially malleable characteristics. Hume does not really escape from the Platonic ideal of knowledge as transcendent, a-human, a-temporal, in spite of his assertions to the contrary; Proust, for example, recognised very clearly that in Hume the defining characteristics of man turn out to be also the fundamental obstacles to knowledge. The passions which motivate man, and to which reason is subordinate, are themselves a threat to the whole human enterprise. Hume could claim a commonsense view of politics and of history, derived from his commonsense morality; as such, it is deeply sceptical, profoundly conservative, and unavoidably pessimistic.

Commenting on Davenant's protection of Milton, Hume remarks that "men of letters ought always to regard their sympathy of taste as a more powerful band of union, than any difference of party or opinion as a source of animosity" (H, XI, 212). This is not a remark about aesthetics. It is about a style, and thus about the nature, of a life. Hume's own deeply moral concern emerges, for example, in his condensed reflections on "the standard of taste."[11] The necessity to practice critical discrimination over a wide range of similar and dissimilar cases is not a recipe for aesthetic judgment alone. In a famous passage, he states that "the constant habit of surveying ourselves, as it were, in reflection, keeps alive all the sentiments of right and wrong, and begets in noble natures a certain reverence for themselves as well as others, which is the surest guardian of every virtue" (M, 96).

We can now see that the study of history is the social analogue of the personal "survey … in reflection," whereby a nation can review itself with hindsight and, by the same token, learn to contemplate its present in an impartial and disinterested manner. Hume's study of the Stuart period was thus neither intended nor taken as merely an inquiry into an earlier age: it was intended to say something about his own. But if one is ignorant of a vocabulary, one is denied access to the language that uses it.

Hume's friend, William Robertson, Principal of the University, felt it important to declare, unequivocally, what the consequences for Scotland were of the Stuart period, even though his *History of Scotland* only goes to the Accession.[12] Adam Ferguson, on the other hand, Hume's successor as Librarian to the Advocates, and later Professor of Moral Philosophy, was more interested in the philosophical style and theses adopted by Hume. Ferguson holds that "wealth, commerce, extent of territory, and the knowledge of arts, are, when properly employed, the means of production, and the foundations of power."[13] However, although "peace and unanimity are commonly considered as the principal foundations of public felicity; yet the rivalship of separate communities, and the agitations of a free people, are the principles of political life, and the school of men."[14] Ferguson constantly stresses the gap between theoretical speculations about history and society, formulated in the study, and the sheer accidents and contingencies of reality. Mistakenly,

> we ascribe to a previous design, what came to be known only by experience, what no human wisdom could foresee, and what, without the concurring humour and disposition of his age, no authority could enable an individual to execute.... Men, in fact, while they pursue in society different objects, or separate views, procure a wide distribution of power, and by a species of chance, arrive at a posture for civil engagements, more favourable to human nature than what human wisdom could ever calmly devise.[15]

Whatever mistakes we make about the origins and history of society, however, "the dangers to liberty ... can never be greater from any cause than they are from the supposed remissness of a people, to whose personal vigour every constitution, as it owed its establishment, so must continue to owe its preservation."[16] Vigilance is necessary, but not enough:

> Liberty is a right which every individual must be ready to vindicate for himself, and which he who pretends to bestow as a favour, has by that very act in reality denied. Even political establishments, though they appear to be independent of the will and arbitration of men, cannot be relied on for the preservation of freedom; they may nourish, but should not supersede that firm and resolute spirit, with which the liberal mind is always prepared to resist indignities, and to refer its safety to itself.[17]

Ferguson is writing, here, a decade after Hume, and one detects a note of urgency which appears in Hume's letters of the same date. To the

Comtesse de Boufflers he complains that "the frenzy of liberty, has taken possession of us," and insists on his own "due regard to magistracy and established government" (L, II, 191). Over the Wilkes affair, Hume writes of "this inundation of the Rabble" (L, II, 245), and four years later, in 1775, he tells his nephew David: "One great Advantage of a Commonwealth over our mixed Monarchy is, that it would considerably abridge our Liberty, which is growing to such an Extreme, as to be incompatible with all Government. Such Fools are they, who perpetually cry out Liberty: and think to augment it, by shaking off the Monarchy" (L, II, 306).

Hume aimed at a complete philosophy of man, for man. In this, Cicero was a principal inspiration, and Hume intended to support, and supplement when necessary, almost all of Ciceros epistemological, political, moral, rhetorical and religious conclusions. The main task was to provide an analysis not only of the nature of man himself, but of man in the context which enabled him to be distinctively human: society. In the century before Hume, jurisprudents had attempted something similar, and had offered epistemological grounds for their philosophy of action, but their theories were theologically based and spoke to a social order that was on the verge of radical change. Hume's goal was to provide a philosophy that harmonized with and was testable by common experience and our most natural beliefs: it would be modestly sceptical, and rigorously secular, and it would be rooted in a study of the traditions of society. Hume's *History* is part of that study.

A fuller analysis of the historical and political writings requires careful consideration of the context in which he was writing, and the work of contemporaries such as Kames, Smith, Millar. In addition to the established and evolving views on jurisprudence, which were part of the context, the writings of Robertson, Ferguson and Steuart, together with those of Montesquieu, require re-examination in the light of our growing understanding of Hume himself.

Notes

1. Page references and abbreviations are of the following editions:

E *Essays, Moral, Political, and Literary*, ed. Eugene F. Miller (Indianapolis: 1985).

H *The History of England* (London: 1793–94).

L *The Letters of David Hume*, ed. J. Y. T. Greig (Oxford: 1932).

M *An Inquiry Concerning the Principles of Morals*, ed. C. W. Hendel (Indianapolis: 1957).

U *An Inquiry Concerning Human Understanding*, ed. C. W. Hendel (Indianapolis: 1955).

2. William James, *A Pluralistic Universe* (New York: 1909), p. 244, and elsewhere.

3. I have discussed these matters in: "Knowledge and Illusion in *A la recherche du temps perdu*," *Forum for Modern Language Studies* 5, 1969; "A Critical Outline of Collingwood's Philosophy of Art," in *Critical Essays on the Philosophy of R. G. Collingwood*, ed. M. Krausz (Oxford: 1972); "William James," in *American Philosophy*, ed. M. G. Singer (Cambridge: 1985).

4. I discuss this in "An Outline of the Philosophy of James Hutton," in *Philosophers of the Scottish Enlightenment*, ed. V. Hope (Edinburgh: 1984).

5. I explore this at greater length in *Hume's Sentiments: Their Ciceronian and French Context* (Edinburgh: 1982), especially Chapter 3.

6. For further discussion see my "'Art' and 'Moderation' in Hume's *Essays*," in *McGill Hume Studies*, ed. D. F. Norton *et al.* (San Diego: 1979).

7. In fact, Hume thinks states evolve much more gradually than this implies: see E, 40, and 465 ff., "Of the Original Contract."

8. See *Hume's Sentiments*, p. 59 f.

9. See *Hume's Sentiments*, pp. 76 ff.

10. Hume also notes the disruptive effects on families, and particularly on children, of divorce and polygamy. Although he talks about the adverse consequences of large concentrations of people, there is no reference to over-population, as such.

11. *Hume's Sentiments*, Chapter 3, pp. 106 ff.

12. William Robertson, *The History of Scotland*, 4th ed. (London: 1761), especially II, 293 ff.

13. Adam Ferguson, *An Essay on the History of Civil Society*, 1767, ed. D. Forbes (Edinburgh: 1966), p. 58.

14. *Ibid.*, 61.

15. *Ibid.*, 123, 237.

16. *Ibid.*, 223.

17. *Ibid.*, 266.

CRAIG WALTON

HUME'S *ENGLAND* AS A NATURAL HISTORY OF MORALS

I. Introduction

Above all things (for this is the ornament and life of Civil History), I
wish events to be coupled with their cause. I mean, that an account
should be given of the characters of the several regions and peoples;
their natural disposition, whether apt and suited for the study of
learning, or unfitted and indifferent to it; the accidents of the times,
whether adverse or propitious to science; the emulations and infusions
of different religions; the enmity or partiality of the laws; the eminent
virtues and services of individual persons in the promotion of learning,
and the like.

Francis Bacon, *Of the Advancement of Learning,* (II/IV)[1]

Although it was long neglected by philosophers, Hume's History of
England[2] began to be taken more seriously due to the 1965 publication of
David Fate Norton and Richard Popkin's *David Hume: Philosophical
Historian.*[3] In that study and since, the question has been raised as to
whether, and if so, how the *History* might relate to Hume's overtly, or
traditionally, *philosophical* works: Did he give up on philosophy in order
to pursue literary *fame* (where a history could offer such)? Or did he turn
to history as a repository of examples to illustrate his already-formed
moral philosophy? Or did he find employment for his "experimental
method of reasoning" about moral subjects here, in a more expansive
way than, or as a consequence of what he had done in, his *Essays Moral,
Political and Literary*? Was there something about his philosophical
maturation that justifies – or even requires an historical approach?

As philosophers' standards of interpretation and judgment are
heightened by a more comprehensive reading of a predecessor, Hume
begins to intrigue and challenge us far beyond the boundaries earlier set

N. Capaldi and D.W. Livingston (eds.), Liberty in Hume's History of England. 25–52.
© 1990 *Kluwer Academic Publishers. Printed in the Netherlands.*

by those who saw all things Humean in (and only in) Bk. I of his
Treatise. For example, Peter Jones has investigated Hume as Ciceronian,
and in the light of Malebranche and Bayle;[4] M.M. Goldsmith in the light
of Mandeville's *Fable of the Bees*;[5] Donald W. Livingston in the light of
Hume's concepts of the 'common life' and the activity of narration;[6] C.
N. Stockton in the light of economic history and method;[7] Duncun
Forbes on Hume as part of the natural law revival of the Enlightenment[8]
and Nicholas Phillipson has studied Hume as social and constitutional
historian[9] – to select only a few who exemplify this heightened and more
comprehensive standard.

Indebted to these authors and moved to aim toward the same standard,
I would like to attempt another widening of the frame of discussion in
what follows, by considering the early modern development of the idea
of 'natural history', and how Hume appropriated it to his (historically)
philosophical purposes. Increasingly, philosophers are re-assessing the
relationships between rhetoric, history, and philosophy. The occasion is
particularly ripe, then, to re-read Hume's *History* not so much in light of
its subsequent fame, influence[10] and later replacement as the standard
history of England, but in light of what Hume took to be his method in
this art: what were the philosophical reasons for, and findings during, his
thinking it through and writing it as he did, during some ten of the most
mature years of his life? Did he see it as a 'natural history of morals', in
a way in which that concept is philosophically substantial?

To forward my effort, then, I shall focus on the question as to whether
Francis Bacon's reformulation of the idea of "natural history" sheds any
light on what Hume is doing: to what extent might we better understand
Hume's introduction of "the experimental method of reasoning into
moral subjects" if Hume meant that method to be a Baconian 'natural
history'? Investigating what this meant to Bacon, and how it illuminates
Hume's *History*, may well add to our understanding of what Hume saw
as the task, method and achievement of "experimental" moral
philosophy, emphasizing how and why it is to be historically done.

II. Baconian Natural History

For in [a natural and experimental history], and in this way only, can
the foundations of a true and active philosophy be established; and
then will men wake as from deep sleep, and at once perceive what a

difference there is between the dogmas and figments of the wit and a true and active philosophy, and what it is in questions of nature to consult nature herself.

Bacon's *Preparative* (VIII/355)

Bacon's own awakening from the "deep sleep" of dogma took him well beyond his contemporaries' use of 'natural history'.[11] Though he credits Pliny the Elder with the phrase and the first example, he finds little help in that and other ancient collections of curious stories – they are usually "an undigested heap of particulars" because not yet "cast into method" (V/155). As Bacon's nineteenth century editor, Robert Ellis put it, "men delighted in nothing more than collections of remarkable facts; the more remarkable, so they did not become incredible, the better" (V/144). Nor was Bacon satisfied with the more recent examples, which he found to be done "for knowledge of particulars" – because though that knowledge is necessary, unless it is selective and organized, it cannot become the stuff of "true induction" (VIII/355).

In the original plan of his "Great Instauration", Bacon had intended natural histories to become "tables of discovery" – collections of observations, organized topically under specified headings, so as later to be subjected to his new, "true method of induction". These tables come under three general topical regions of nature: (1) some information was to be taken randomly from natural occurrences when any example is the same as any other; (2) some is to be selected just for uniqueness, since "monsters" or rarities, as negative instances ('negative' vis-a-vis our minds' anticipations of what is normal), may be more informative than the items under (1) which confirm our 'anticipation' or belief; and finally, (3) there is information we gather from carefully "vexed" circumstances, so that it is brought forth by using mechanical or liberal arts, and thus belongs in a category of its own (the first two having been provided by nature without our help). These three areas of evidence, then are to provide the beginnings of an eventual systematic science of all nature. This all-encompassing program was possible because it was based on Bacon's all-inclusive notion of nature as the "Book" written by God and given to man to "interpret" – a book ranging as it did from the most typical of her works to her monsters to all fruits of nature made by man's mechanical and liberal arts.

Bacon defines all 'arts' as "nature with man to help" (VIII/410). He places the mechanical with the liberal arts, under the one larger rubric, 'arts', for that reason – because they have in common their foundation in man helping nature. From this reasoning, for Bacon, the scientific place of the arts is within *natural* history as, by this point, it has been defined.

Now it becomes apparent why "Civil History" is, for Bacon, part of *Natural* History. As he sometimes explains it, his "Natural and Experimental History" must include two *sub*-topics, the natural and the civil. To explain this category system, Bacon first notes that there has been an opinion that man's artifices are other than nature, so people do an account of plants and animals, and stop – omitting the mechanical arts, even though they are a part of nature. But it is an error to think of any of the arts as merely *assisting* nature, as if they were of little philosophical interest once nature is known: that sort of approach is the counsel of "doomsayers", because they imply we cannot act except on the periphery of things, whereas, to Bacon, we are able to change, to "fundamentally alter nature". If we do not believe that, then we adopt "a premature despair in human enterprises" (VIII/410). The artificial does differ from the natural, but *not* in the form or essence. Rather, it differs only in the efficient cause. That is, by our arts all we can do is move things, put things together or take them apart, as with gold, or with a rainbow made by rain or by "a jet of water" in a fountain (ibid.) But these movings are actions which produce real changes.

His second reason for including the arts and civil history within *natural history* is the observation that man's activities can be sorted out as coming under all three of the areas of natural evidence just explained: (1) much of what men do is done as members of one species, where one example is as good as another in helping us reach understanding. For example, the civil history of laws and ecclesiastical thought is similar to the general or specific distinctions about plants and animals. But (2) when an act or person exemplifies a unique effort, we may learn as much – or even more! – by studying them, as we do from studying more common ones, just because our belief or anticipation of how such things usually happen is here given a pointed counter-instance, such that our science is challenged, expanded, and improved. Finally, (3) since both the common *and* the unique fruits of our arts are, still, work by us in nature, we must include both sorts in what he calls his "natural *and* experimental history" (emphasis added) if we are to achieve our goal. The three areas of nature overlap, and may be found together.

Bacon realizes his contemporaries will hesitate to take seriously his call for the study of mechanical arts, the "operative" parts of the liberal arts, and of those crafts not yet "grown up" to arts. As Dewey observed much later (in his *Quest for Certainty*) and as we see today, there is supposed to be a higher intellectual or spiritual status attached to work not requiring manual or mechanical skills, so that those kinds of skills are less esteemed and, implicitly, what needs to be known about them or what they entail of man's practical relationship to nature is less worthy of attention than are the activities we take to be more aloof from nature (in Bacon's time, the Schools; in ours, perhaps the fine arts and sciences). Yet these arts – the mechanical – are "of the most use", because they lead us to understanding of practice: "the vexations of art are certainly as the bonds and handcuffs of Proteus, which betray the ultimate struggles and efforts of matter" (VII/363). It may seem that investigating such matters is "mechanical and illiberal". But, "daintiness set aside", they deserve from us "the greatest diligence" (*ibid.*)

Lest his focus be lost, Bacon reiterates that the purpose here is not only to perfect the arts, as such, but to know them as "streams" which all "flow" to "true *and active* philosophy" [emphasis added], to understand nature as a whole, with all her parts considered. Philosophy is not "speculative" knowing; it is active, concerned with principles of operation, how things work, so that everything concerning *both* "bodies *and* virtues" is to be "numbered, weighted, measured, defined" (VIII/365f.)

Tackling all available evidence both from nature and artifice is a daunting task – the problems of probative value and of assessment of support for knowledge claims come to the forefront of attention. In order to begin, Bacon makes three general distinctions: First, some of this evidence will declare itself "simply", without controversy; second, some, not so clear, will be qualified as, for example, 'it is reported that....', with the source and its detail to be given in important cases to flag these claims as needing evaluation of the merits of the reports in question; then third and finally, that which the natural and civil historian judges to be false, should be "proscribed", and named as false, "overtly" (VIII/366ff.) Bacon likens this threefold approach to sorting evidence to the work of an attorney – our way of approaching putative evidence will be like examining a witness, deciding relevance and merit "upon interrogatories" *ad hoc* (VIII/371).

For several generations of Bacon studies, the view has circulated that his "Great Instauration" of the sciences – however eloquently launched by Part I of his *New Organon's* exorcising "the Idols of the Mind" – ultimately fails because he never managed to tell us how his "method of true induction" works. How are we to make the judgment passing from these carefully gathered and sorted "tables of discovery" to "middle axioms", and thence to universal laws of nature?

However, Bacon may not have 'failed' to deliver. Recent studies of Bacon and his predecessors suggests that a somewhat different logic opens up if we read his early and later works is the light of the history of reformers of philosophy via rhetoric, in the tradition from Cicero to Vives, Valla, Nizolius and Peter Ramus.[12] Paolo Rossi has emphasized that Bacon did not undertake so much to replace Aristotle, as to revise his historical approach to philosophy by bringing to it not one, but a large number of cooperating researches, in "a *civic* base for the advancement of philosophy" (186 ff.) These reformers do not omit the syllogism as pattern of deductive inference. Bacon discusses it; but he limits it to cases where the "form" of a thing is known, and thus usable as an apodictic premise. He hopes, at least early-on, that his new organon will work its way up to such premises about God's forms or "nature-engendering natures". But in the meantime, a century or so of skeptical doubts had shown him that there are few of these apodictic intuitions available. This is because our claims to know a universal form are themselves often unwarranted flights toward generalization 'produced and directed', one might say, by our minds' "idols of the theatre". He therefore shifts attention to a larger frame requiring that we inquire into the culture in which our "interpretation" took place, and into our own proclivities via self-examination. As I shall explain below, he may have abandoned the search for one whole pyramidal structure from lowest "tables" to highest axioms, in favor of the plan for natural and civil histories. He may not have. But in any event, he does not abandon all deductive reasoning. Deduction stays, but in a more yeoman role. What can be seen in his later years is increasing attention to the 'what' and the 'how' of making natural and civic histories.[13]

Bacon borrowed several concepts from classical rhetoric: the invention/judgment distinction, the doctrine of memory, and its discussion of modes of discourse. But he departed from classical rhetoric when he distinguished the invention of arts from the invention of "arguments". His "interpretation of nature" collapses the Ciceronian 'invention'/'judgment' distinction by tying invention *to* judgment in a continuous, dialectical process. The effect of this is to set up two problems – first the problem of evidence, and then the problem of assessment of evidence as support for possible higher levels of knowing. *Both* problems therefore contain gradations or degrees of quality – of evidence assessment in the first, of support assessment in the second.

This is neither a theory arguing solely from particulars to generalizations, nor one arguing from an hypothesis to test procedures thought

likely to confirm or disconfirm that hypothesis. Rather, as Jonathan
Cohen explains (citing Bacon favorably), it is a third task, that of
providing a logic for the three kinds of evidence ("simple" naturally
occurring, nature "vexed" experimentally, and events or things man-
made), and the fullest possible range of degrees of support these might
offer toward our understanding of things or events. Its kind of probability
is not Pascalian mathematical, but "Baconian inductive". And this logic
applies equally to moral and historical problems, and to those such as
astronomy where experimental controls cannot be applied, as it does to
more accepted laboratory circumstances of controlled gathering of
evidence. Bacon's work, Cohen remarks, puts him in a position to
vindicate Hume's thesis that 'probability or reasoning from conjecture
may be divided into two kinds, viz. that which is founded on *chance*, and
that which arises from *causes*' [*THN* I/II/xi]. The natural and civil
histories are the latter sort of "conjecture".[14]

It seems to me that in the last five years of his life, after his "fall" due
to the bribery conviction[15], Bacon did not so much despair of explaining
what is the "true method of induction", as set out virtually to replace it
with something else: He admits that the *Organon* and the *Natural
History* are not complete (IX/373) – a hard admission, as they had
seemed so likely of achievement in 1603. But, of the two, he decides that
the Natural History needs his greatest attention in his remaining (five)
years. His reason for this change is that the Instauration of the sciences
will advance more with Natural History than with the Organon. And he
does complete some of it – for example, his *History of the Reign of
Henry VII*, later used by Hume, is part of the civil history.

One central part of Bacon's new solution of the problems of evidence
assessment is his treatment of the art of memory; another central part is
his treatment of imagination. We need to recall that he is not simply
seeking universals, but "works", the understanding of an "active
philosophy". This means, not only that we seek warranted generalizations in the new science, but also that we need to know significant
exceptions, unique individual acts or beings; and perhaps most of all, we
need to understand the craftsmanship of all the arts, mechanical *and*
civil. Arts are not well-explained by (what we might call) the positivist
model of philosophy or of science. For there, they are seen "merely" as
"applications" or derivations, not cognitively or conatively significant for
science. But to Bacon, study of the arts reveals as much or more about
"nature-engendering natures" as do generalizations *or* particular
naturally-occurring instances. Therefore how we remember, and what we

remember, are vital to our choice and action just as well as to knowledge's level of universality. That is, the planting of the memory foretells how well we shall *use* what we know, embody it or create with it. And memory, in its turn, is affected by our imaginations both for good and for ill. Thus method, Bacon thinks, must bring memory and imagination into account (as well as this or that subject-matter). It is this line of reasoning which leads him to his "civic" interpretation (and to the thick mix of kinds of evidence he wants there).

All arts are "works"; one well- or poorly-done instance of a work may teach us more than a hundred more "run of the mill" instances could teach; it must not be averaged. Its significance is not confined to the topological status of counter- or negative instance (which it would be, by reference to averages). Moreover, the work of the observer and of the artist, both in expectations before the act, and in grasp of the concrete task during the act, cannot be glossed over with a pretended neutrality. To Bacon, our agency in observing or doing is itself part of what we are studying. The characteristics of the knower and doer, if masked by the four "idols", cause incorrigible superstitions. When they are unmasked, and their own roles are made to show "face up" along with the evidence of the thing being studied, "true and active philosophy" stands to gain.

Bacon's treatment of memory brings us back to why he finally preferred Natural History over the Organon: these histories are not only to be read or to record. They are to fix the sorts of and assessments of the evidence in memory, to stay with us *for use*. They belong to the art of memory because natural history both provides the selection and the significance of what we need in order to extend or to use "true and active philosophy". In the examples we have from these last years, he shifts his focus from his earlier habit of separating off abstraction and highest axioms, at the end (as *last* "vintage"), to integrating warranted judgments into the body of the account itself, at their appropriate places – that is, *along with* their evidence and their context. This way we both see more clearly why and whether they are supported, and keep in mind their significance and limitations *with* their evidence. Hume, we shall see below, follows this practice in his "Appendices" to the *History*. Without the checks imposed by the demands of practice upon our use of knowledge, our tendencies are to fly to ever higher levels of generalization, as if those were more and more true. But, getting back down to earth, each subject-matter needs "its own topics".[16] Though not taking up the classical tradition of rhetoric on its own grounds, Bacon reworks "topic" and "critic" to fashion a distinct alternative to the apodictic rational syllogism as model of scientific understanding.[17]

III. Hume's *Natural History of Religion*

For the mind of man is strangely eager to be relieved from suspense, and to have something fixed and immovable, upon which in its wanderings and disquisitions it may securely rest. And assuredly Aristotle endeavours to prove that in all motion there is some point quiescent; and as he very elegantly interprets the ancient fable of Atlas, who stood fixed and supported the heaven on his shoulders, to be meant of the poles or axletree of heaven, whereupon the conversion is accomplished; so do men earnestly desire to have within them an Atlas or axletree of the thoughts, by which the fluctuations and dizziness of the understanding may be to some extent controlled; fearing belike that their heaven should fall.

Bacon, De augmentis (IX/94)

For Bacon, our wish for an "axletree of the thoughts" accounted for the grip of the "Idols" on our minds, causing us to "anticipate", pre-judge, and overly-generalize, rather than to "interpret" experience. In his view, the institutionalized version or chief carrier of this disease was the logic and metaphysics of the Schoolmen. But some 150 years later, the Schoolmen by then largely defeated, for Voltaire and Hume the chief carrier of this disease was organized religion, particularly Christianity in its Catholic ("superstitious") or Protestant ("bigoted") versions, offering men that axletree of thought by which dogma (seemingly) relieves us of the uncertainty of philosophy. Because of the centrality of two questions, separable but sometimes connected – that of our human nature insofar as it longs for answers not yet available, and that of our religions' helpful and harmful roles in our work toward civilization, the relationship between Bacon's and Hume's concepts of natural history leads inevitably to examination of Hume's 1757 *Natural History of Religion*.[18]

Probably completed by 1751, and notorious before publication (not to mention since), Hume's *Natural History of Religion* prompts several observations suitable to our theme: first, some failings: in anything like a strict Baconian sense, it is not a natural history at all, for the sort of evidence Bacon thought useless or dubious in 1624 is here used almost exclusively – viz., uncritical observations of the ancients, and whatever subsequent tales of travel or philosophers' or historians' asides, uncon-firmed rumors or wild stories happened to come to hand suitable to Hume's theme. In that sense, it is more a diatribe of some considerable style and force, with a serious moral purpose, than a sifting of historical evidence for an anthropology of religious psychology and institutions. Christianity comes off worst in every comparison. No information about China or India is used, though since the first returns of Jesuits from China in the late 16th century, there had been considerable discussion, even controversy about oriental religions and what Europe could learn from the comparisons (as we, and Hume, had already learned from Voltaire). Unlike his later treatment of religion in the *History*, none of the stabilizing or elevating potentialities of the more recent, scriptural religions is given credit here. From these observations, then, one might conclude that though, for deep personal philosophical reasons, somewhat similar to those of Voltaire in his war against "superstition", Hume kept this work in print without major substantive revision, it still could be assessed in his life, and in a larger view of his work, as itself youthful (completed by about age 40), and less representative of his reflections on religion than are those in the *History*.

However, there is a bit more to add, if we undertake to consider these issues from Hume's, rather than our own perspective: the work is a natural history of morality in at least the two senses that (1) it takes a clinical, nonsectarian and virtually neutral attitude to its subject, for the first time since Carneades and Lucretius; and (2) that it reaches, some-what cautiously, to the level of principles and causes in the way Bacon would urge, via observation of natural human processes and the way they vary in time and social and material context. Not unlike some mystics of the *via negativa*, Hume distinguishes between what God or perfect being would be, on the one hand, and what our words and actions exhibit about ourselves and God, on the other. By doing this, Hume undertakes a moral pathology – and it can not be dismissed as out of date (one thinks of Hoffer on "true believers", and the several "holy wars" now ravishing some countries directly and most of us indirectly). We may well add – as indeed Hume did add in the *History* – that political faction produces its won moral pathology, equally destructive both of civility and of any real liberty. But for many of us today, the immediate violence of religious strife has receded from the scene, replaced with wide agreement on the value of religious toleration. We owe more of that to Voltaire and Hume than we may readily sense – remote, now, as they are in time. How did they argue for such tolerance? To Hume this was a philosophical question, of method as well as of substance. By "enlarging the view", Hume makes it more possible to esteem religious experience and action of the calmer sort, without necessarily connecting it to the violent passions and swings of temper we see in his (would-be) historical sketch.

Closer to Bacons' plan, and even more "Baconian" than Bacon in achievement, Hume examines the relationships between religious feeling, personal and institutional action, and common morality. Here perhaps is the strongest harbinger of the *History*, and the strongest tie to a natural history of morals: the religious sentiment is natural to us; it might have calm, benign or even beneficial consequences; but it can be and has been implemented to destroy human bonds, vital restraints, and mental balance. As perhaps the major psychological force other than natural morality in our moral lives, its natural history must be undertaken. Hume's deserves to be seen at least as a starter.

One final comment: whatever might be its fairness or present value as a philosophical anthropology or psychology of religion, this work must be read as Hume's mid-life undertaking of a natural history of the moral life as it is affected by that within us which gives rise to religions. As such, it has two findings – (1) that we tend to swing between extremes in religious passions as we do with the other violent passions, and (2) that reason is in the weaker, vulnerable position of needing the sceptic's philosophical art of observation and judicious balancing, if it is not to be gulled into giving its own horrible contributions to extremism. As with Montaigne, Hobbes, Pascal and Vico before him, Hume sees clearly that (what Vico called) the "barbarism of reflection",[19] once unleashed, is more violent, more lasting, more cunning and resolute in its destruction than were any of the ancient "barbarisms of sensation". It lends its dissociating, abstracting and unbalancing power to the destruction both of the inner spiritual bonds of sanity and the interpersonal bonds of humanity. Ironically, 'religion', when thus tapping into the roots of credulity and the farthest swings of our passional propensities to extremism, – far from being "religious", ie. a binding together – has its worst effects in unbinding our minds, our bodies and our ties to each other. With full respect for Pascal before him, and William James since, I think no one has so broadly and deeply explored these pathological relationships between natural morality and religious fervor. And Hume, with Bacon, attributes the therapeutic, philosophically stabilizing force of this study to its character as a natural history. It is by virtue of the *way* he "enlarges our view" and plants it in our memory for use, that we are able to benefit from its gift to our weak and needy arts of reasonableness. Thus, already by 1751, something is brewing in his mind as to where this might lead him in his work as a moral philosopher.

IV. Hume's England

> Civil History is beset on all sides with faults; some (and these are the greater part) write only barren and commonplace narratives, a very reproach to history; others hastily and disorderly string together a few particular relations and trifling memoirs; others merely run over the heads of events: others, on the contrary, go into all the minutest particularities, and such as have no relation to the main action; some indulge their imagination in bold inventions; while others impress on their works the image not so much of their minds as of their passions, ever thinking of their party, but no good witnesses as to facts; some are always inculcating their favorite political doctrines, and idly interrupting the narrative by going out of the way to display them; others are injudiciously prolix in reporting orations and harangues and even in relating the actions themselves; so that, among all the writings of men, there is nothing rarer than a true and perfect Civil History.
>
> Bacon, *De augmentis* (VIII/421f)

In 1751, the year he finished the *Natural History of Religion* and the year before he began work on the *History*, Hume opened his *An Inquiry Concerning the Principles of Morals* by observing that when we disagree on moral issues, no logic "which speaks not to the affections" can hope to resolve our dispute. Thus it is in vain to do moral philosophy on the grounds of pure reason – it can never even move us to act, much less to the act of agreeing with each other. In the long run, he tells us, reason and feeling are not really at odds: "*reason* and *sentiment* concur in almost all moral determinations". But in order for us to *make* that long run, we need the right philosophical growth or preparation: how do we insinuate what is to be blamed and praised into our feeling, to reach to our deepest sentiments, without at the same time triggering the violent passions which alienate or wildly react? Hume's response is that,

> [although] the final sentence depends on some internal sense or feeling which nature has made universal in the whole species...in order to pave the way for such a sentiment and give a proper discernment of its object, it is often necessary, we find, that much reasoning should precede, that nice distinctions be made, just conclusions drawn, distant comparisons formed, complicated relations examined, and general facts fixed and ascertained....As this is a question of fact, not

of abstract science, we can only expect success by following the experimental method and deducing general maxims from a comparison of particular instances....Men are now cured of their passion for hypotheses and systems in natural philosophy, and will hearken to no arguments but those which are derived from experience. It is full time they should attempt a like reformation in all moral disquisitions and reject every system of ethics, however subtle or ingenious, which is not founded on fact and observation".[20]

This counsel, at the opening of the second *Inquiry*, could just as well be read as the philosophical prologue to, and program for Hume's *History of England*. In the final section of this paper there will be occasion to reflect on how this 1751 discussion compares to the work done by Hume between 1752 (when he began) and 1761 (when he completed his *History*). At this point it is enough to consider the hypothesis that these prescriptive remarks illuminate his philosophical purpose in that larger work.

But this is not Hume's only reflection on the tie between moral philosophy and history. Other indications, one earlier and one later than the *Inquiry*, strengthen the philosophical connection between Hume's purpose in his *History* and Bacon's broad idea of natural and civil histories. First, in his 1741 "Of the Study of History": "A man acquainted with history may, in some respect, be said to have lived from the beginning of the world, and to have been making continual additions to his stock of knowledge in every century". Unlike abstract ethics, "History keeps in a just medium betwixt these extremes [of the 'interested' viewpoint of the businessman and the 'cold and unmoved' viewpoint of the philosopher in his closet], and places the objects in their true point of view. [That is,] The writers of history, as well as the readers, are sufficiently interested in the characters and events, to have a lively sentiment of blame or praise; and, at the same time, have no particular interest or concern to pervert their judgement".[21]

Again, much later – in his "My Own Life" (published, in some editions, as preface to the *History*), Hume looked back and described the *History* as neglecting "present power, interest and authority, and the cry of popular prejudices".[22] Again with Bacon, Hume did not see his purpose quite so much to be that of unearthing original materials (though he *does* do some of that[23]), but of comprehending, of creatively synthesizing, enlivening and unifying the otherwise disconnected and ponderous works of many others. He downplays the difficulty of this mammoth task. But he does see it as work *for a philosopher*: "The philosophical spirit, which I have so much indulged in all my writings, finds here ample materials to work upon"; with Bacon, his criteria for history are, "style, judgment, impartiality, care", he tells us in this brief autobiography.

Let us consider some of these issues as treated in the *History of England*, in the order in which it was written:

(1) Volumes V [1754] and VI [1757]: James died in 1625, leaving Great Britain on the verge of civil war. Yet in all of history, Hume notes, it would be difficult to find a reign less illustrious, yet more unspotted and unblemished: "all his qualities were sullied by weakness and embellished by humanity" (V/122). Hume here sounds, for the first time, a chord to be heard over the next ten years of his work – the distinction of, and thus the discussion of the interplay between, the virtues and vices of a person's moral character, on the one hand, and the harms and benefits of public policy decisions or results, on the other. In this instance, James' character leant only its weakness to the public realm.

Writing the first of what were to become nearly-regular "appendices", Hume explains what he will do in these apparent overviews ('apparent' because they do considerably more than just summarize, introducing new information as well as higher-order reflection). He tells us that he will survey government, manners, finances, arms, trade, and learning, because "Where a just notion is not formed of these particulars, history can be little instructive, and often will not be intelligible". With Bacon, he links coinage and revenue, trade, laws, the military, agriculture – all the mechanical and liberal arts into one whole story of what he often calls "the situation" of a reign or a time.

Turning to what we might call a bit of natural history of moral psychology, Hume observes that, unlike the 1750's, in the time of James there was less division between people due to luxury and money, less distance between rich and poor, but more division by ceremony, status and titles. This is significant because, while a large difference in wealth gives one no reason to approach one's inferiors, the differences of titles and ranks are largely imaginary, so that different people become familiar or at least acquainted. This implies a difference in the character of civil society, of ruler-ruled relationships. After pointing out this curious relationship, Hume implies that the difference is significant, for any society.

(2) Volumes III and IV (1759): Bacon had done his *History of Henry VII* after 1621, as one part of his "natural and experimental history", and included there his assessment of whether Richard III had committed the murder of the princes, his nephews. Hume refers to Bacon's investigation as "elaborate and exact". He concludes that Thomas More's contemporary account of the murders was accurate (III/Note A, 465–469). He adds that English history is beholden chiefly to four men – More, Bacon, Clarendon, and Whitlock.

For its philosophical bearing both on the Reformation and our subsequent moral history, this last observation requires expansion: Hume explains that "nothing more forwarded the first progress of the [Protestant] reformers" than their submitting all religious doctrine to private judgment. "They fancied they were exercising their judgment", whereas instead they actually opposed ancient prejudices with "more powerful prejudices of another kind". This same private judgment seemed to the sovereigns of the time to be dangerous, because it seemed to destroy implicit obedience, on which the civil magistrate is chiefly founded. But this is only an early reflection.

In fact, the reformation did not lead to a breakdown of civil society, Hume continues, because even though the liberty of private judgment was tendered to them, "it is not in reality accepted of". That is, what the people did, instead, was to "acquiesce implicitly in those establishments, however new, into which their early education has [sic] thrown them" (III/212).

(3) Volumes I and II (1762). The character and reign of Alfred may be favorably compared to any prince in any age – he was the model of perfect character. He established the counties, tithings, and mutual responsibility via his decennary system of administration (as in Hume's "Idea of a Perfect Commonwealth"?), thereby "reducing the people to law and government". These institutions, especially his administration of justice, favored their freedom – for example, by creating the first juries. He formed a body of laws, now lost, which probably were the origins of the common law. It is not that Alfred invented these institutions – rather, more likely, "like a wise man", he reformed and extended previously-established Saxon institutions. Hume admires the sentiment Alfred left in his will – that the English would remain as free as their thoughts. This testament was not an idle comment: it was rooted in Alfred's understanding that "good morals and knowledge are almost inseparable, in every age, though not in every individual, [that therefore] the care of Alfred for

the encouragement of learning among his subjects was another useful branch of his legislation...."(I/79).

Hume concludes his first two volumes with a comprehensive and climactic essay, written after ten years of work far more penetrating and pregnant for us when read at the end of our study of the six volumes in the order written. We have pursued the history of England through many barbarous ages, he begins, in order to reach [by 1485] "the dawn of civility and science". As for Bacon, so for Hume civil and military history cannot be severed from that of the mechanical and liberal arts and sciences – they are "intimately connected" (II/519). Every event, of whatever kind, in order to be weighted and interpreted, requires that we assess the full span of human understanding at that time: "the events of no particular period can be fully accounted for, but by considering the degrees of advancement which men have reached in those particulars [the arts and sciences]".

To conclude section IV, it would be helpful to consider what it is about Hume's work that might be more understandable if viewed as a Baconian "natural and experimental history". In Section V of the paper I shall then turn to how his *History* relates to the rest of his moral philosophy, in order to complete my discussion of it as a natural history of morals.

I have not attempted to present a microcosm of Hume's six volumes. I have not brought in a representative amount of his discussions of how money was evaluated, how battles were won or lost, and how political strife arose, came to a head and to some resolution – to name only some areas relatively neglected. There is no substitute for reading the original, not only for the arousal of interest Hume promised, but for the detail and strength of his observations, their frequent fairness and moral acuity. Readers unfamiliar with Hume's *History* may get some hint of these qualities from the foregoing.

In the epigram to Section I, we saw that Bacon requires that his 'natural historian' would have (a) to connect events to their causes; (b) to discuss the character of a people; (c) to consider the state of learning; (d) laws; (e) the effect of religion; and (f) the services of individuals. Let us review Hume's *England* by these criteria.

As for (a), linking events to their causes, Hume fills the bill: To recall just a few, he shows a causal link between "imaginary" social rank and the willingness to approach supposed inferiors, vs. rank based on wealth weakening that willingness to enter in to civil relationships; he brings out the links by which seizing convents and monasteries led, eventually, to higher prices for common people's needs, and the complex linkages between the abolition of entails and retainers, on the one hand, and the fostering of trade, arts and the rise of a "gentry" or middle rank of society, on the other.

(b) He discusses the character of the Germans, the Anglo-Saxons, the Roman invaders, the Norman invaders, the Roman Catholic and the Protestant followers, and the later Court and Country parties – each time eliciting that about their group character which flows from, interacts with or gives rise to the events in question, how their predominant beliefs or established customs and practices operated, for good, ill or both, sometimes predictably, sometimes unpredictably, but always in terms of the character of that people or subculture.

(c) Though materials have already been presented to illustrate Hume's consideration of the state of learning in an age, and what that had to do with laws, peace, commerce, the arts, and individual liberties, I suspect a detailed and rich story is yet to be told on that heading, if one were to investigate it: Hume clearly links learning to the virtues, and to progress in all mechanical and liberal arts, as well as to the stability or instability of the society as a whole. In the darkness of superstition or religious frenzy, learning is punished or inhibited, or, by contrast – when someone as level-headed as King Alfred exemplifies and honors learning, – others tend to emulate and benefit by its presence (even if not particularly learned themselves). Not only in his *History*, but from the *Treatise* to the *Essays* and *Inquiries*, Hume not only linked learning to its benefits, but also links commerce, trade, all the arts, and the safety or peril of the learned, to their chances of achievement. And – entirely Baconian – he clearly recommends public institutionalization of learning, the founding and keeping of academies, to promote and then to disseminate the fruits of learning.

(d) The quality and effect of laws is a theme one could trace throughout the *History*, even viewing the whole of it, perhaps, as most-well organized on that theme, above all others – because, as Hume argued, it is law which provides the security without which no other art can flourish; perhaps more importantly, law provides the model of judgment we need in civil life. Then, in turn, the flourishing of the arts and sciences and of civil life, give rise to significant individual liberties. It would be hard, on reading Hume's *History*, to miss the centrality of this train of reasoning from security to law to cultural and personal goods.

(e) No one can doubt that Hume considers religion as an inherent part of what he is studying. Unlike his *Natural History of Religion*, here he notes that Medieval Christianity kept alive some of the learning of the ancient world. More importantly in view of the importance of law in the overall making of the moral life, the church had revived, studied and spread the art of law after discovery of the *Pandects* – even if all for religious reasons. The Crusades disrupted all of Europe and caused untolled slaughter, in a mixture of rapture and bloody barbarism never, to Hume's day, superceded. The Reformation apparently unintentionally gave a boost to the cause of liberty, though its emphasis on private judgment had effects varying all the way from a new submissiveness to new tyrants, to zealously praying while being burned alive, or while burning others alive.

In fairness to Hume's critics, we can see that he finds little of merit in contemporary Catholicism – the memory of Bloody Mary is real, and deep. And though emphasizing the vital role of natural bonds or ties in the moral life, Hume never praises the ties of worshippers to each other in parish or synagogue, or those to mankind under their view of humanity as children of God. But in fairness to Hume, he explains when and how religion is stabilizing, and when, in its calmer customs and influence, it combines with law and learning to benefit society.

These brief remarks do not exhaust the topic of religion and morality. Hume clearly links religion with moral principles, showing how and when it is destructive of them, when it opposes them, and how and when it is supportive; this aspect, alone, deserves further study. Between the *Natural History of Religion* and the *History*, there is much on this topic yet to be explored and evaluated. But for the present, it is enough to note that his natural historical account of religion is far more accurately done in view of current documentary evidence, and historically integrated with other factors, in the *History*, than it was in the earlier work. It is more carefully presented, in a more balanced way, and yet is still done clinically, with detachment, from the point of view of a natural historical approach to morals rather than from that of a naturalist's study of religion.

(f) The place of "the services of individuals" is also considered, systematically, by Hume. When he can, he names inventors, explorers, poets, soldiers, judges, scholars, criminals, and "ecclesiastics", and the odd individual, as well as kings, queens and princes. And especially in the latter cases, but occasionally for others too, he discusses individual acts for what they show of a person's moral character, as well as their harmful of beneficial public impact. He finds, as we saw, that there is no necessary connection between one's moral character and one's impact on policy. In some cases there is a tragic disparity; in some, only public folly emerges; in some, as Alfred, there is the intangible positive force of character which many emulate in their own ways. A sensitive, classical balance is achieved in this area – Hume sees the tragedy of good men, the good luck of evil men, the justice and the injustice, only rarely finding clear cases of sound intent coming to fruition. But he is neither aloof nor optimistic; he never wavers from calling for that of justice and wisdom of which one is capable, whatever else accident and fallibility may bring.

True to Bacon, and far from the drive to boil history down to an elixir of generalizations derived from mashed particulars, Hume sees that a variety of effects can flow from an individual's example or achievements, whether personal or in policy, for good and evil, and either closely related to foresight and intent, or entirely unrelated to them, unexpected and unforeseeable. This multivariant admixture of personal and public causes and effects, of intent, accident, "deep memory" and custom, in all their permutations, teaches us more eloquently than ever Bacon did, *why* Bacon's approach is superior to the one in which order and axiomaticity are imposed upon the body of evidence so as to distort and strip it of much of its utility as "active philosophy". Hume is not constrained to simplify, or clean up history by over-, or under-attributing powers to individuals. He sees the paradoxical and the ironic outcomes, as well as the good, bad, tragic, comic and mixed ones. This rich canvas is full of individuals, some typical and some unique, some with and some without effect on "the big picture". Some customs, virtually unconsciously, lend stability – while others, consciously propounded, caused disasters unbeknownst. In every case, Hume's presentation articulates Bacon's concern for rarities, for works of the arts, and for degrees of generalization as suitable.

Though they were not named in our opening epigram, we saw that Bacon continually required of a natural and experimental history that it treat of the mechanical and liberal arts. He knew this was in itself a controversial proposal, running against the grain of the more delicate sensibilities of genteel readers. But he argued for it anyway. Hume is equally aware of the social class associations of mechanical arts, as if these readers believed refinement is lacking in those who work well with their hands. But Hume, I think the first to do it in a Baconian way, consistently, systematically brings in evidence about monies, prices, weights, population, the state of agriculture, artisans, which things could then be made, and what these makings have to do with commerce and moral outcomes – connecting the invention of printing, for example, to the rise of the reformation.

Hume agrees with Bacon that what we know about how to do things, how to affect nature for her own and our benefit, or what we do not know, are directly related to the economy, to peace and war, to security and peril, and, in train, to literacy and the leisure for reflection. Hume gives us no philosophical ground for bifurcating the spiritual from the material factors in human life. To the contrary, there is argument and evidence, in abundance, for closely relating, for integrating the state of mechanical arts, trade, agriculture and weather, to the laws, politics, religion, personal and public morality, in Hume's *History*,

In brief summary of these reflections, there are fundamental features of what Bacon required for fruitful study of nature and man's work in it, which Hume emulates and even improves. Hume uses the narrative form Bacon urged, he covers the topics Bacon urged, and he seeks to do it in the way Bacon had urged, historically and with a view toward memory, imagination and practice. What Bacon barely started, Hume undertakes in a prolonged, internally-developing labor which is consistent with Bacon's program.

V. Conclusion

Logic discourses of the Understanding and Reason; Ethic of the Will, Appetite, and Affections: the one produces determinations, the other actions. It is true indeed the imagination performs the office of an agent or messenger or proctor in both provinces, both the judicial and the ministerial. For sense sends all kinds of images over to imagination for reason to judge of; and reason again when it has made its judgment and selections, sends them over to imagination before the decree be put in execution. For voluntary motion is ever preceded and incited by imagination; so that imagination is as a common instrument to both, – both reason and will; saving that this Janus of imagination has two different faces; for the face towards reason has the print of truth, and the face towards action has the print of goodness....

Bacon, *De augmentis,* V/I (IX/61)

Hume often observed that the ties of nature and morality are felt, and that they are strengthened by common experience. To conclude this study of Bacon and Hume, we need to reflect on what we have learned from our studies in the traditionally philosophical works of Hume, as to what he sees to be the outline and principles of moral philosophy, and what that has to do with his achievement in the *History*. I had hinted that there is a sense in which Section I of Hume's second *Inquiry* could be read as a program to the *History*; that hint must now be spelled out.

From the *Treatise* to his last works, Hume saw one of the hardest problems in moral philosophy to be our tendency to take the near view over the "remote" – whether remote in space, or in time. We can identify with a family member, or ponder a problem of our own for tomorrow; but to empathize with people 10,000 miles away, or our own lives ten years from now, is entirely a different issue, far harder. Passionally, we tend toward too near a view, if anything. Yet rationally, and equally dangerous, when we leap to generalizations or fall back on "abstruse" abstractions, the resulting rigidity and dogmatisms can be even more blinding than is passional narrowness – in a way, one must realize, it is a danger of *too* "remote" a view! We err if we take Hume to prefer 'the remote' over the near. We do not overcome narrowness by switching to broad dogmatism, for though one could say its view is indeed remote, it is neither philosophically well-grounded nor well-balanced.

Particularly in moral philosophy, therefore, Hume requires that reason and sentiment, each with its own merits and extremisms, somehow cooperate, as well both in our actions as in our philosophical investigations into the makings and results of those actions. Only thus can we have a strong likelihood that our moral reasonings will not stray too far from experience of persons and events, and that principles and claims will be cross-examined and balanced by reflection on the evidence as to where they do and do not apply. In moral philosophy, even more than in natural philosophy, we must spell out and resolve the difficulty of "proportioning our belief to the evidence" by philosophical art.

With reference to Bacon's "axletree of thought" and the "Idols of the Mind", Hume identifies similar dangers. Exploring the natural history of religions and the record of England from the ancient Britons to the present, he refers to the "sleep of dogma", the strength of our tendency to stay asleep, and the ways false divinity and false uses, "perversions" of philosophy can serve this sleepy, ill-tempered and barbaric mindlessness. How do we break its' grip? It is not just some theoretical sleep, like complacence about a benign belief. Rather, it is malignant for it causes a practical harm. Whether the dogma in question is selfish or tribal, abstract or entirely passional, it is unaware of itself and of what is happening in the waking world. At best, it subjects us to accident and the violent passions. Therefore we must take quite seriously Hume's claim that the only way to counteract the two grips of the too-near sentiment, and the too-remote dogmatic oblivion of the too-believing, unquestioning mind, alike, is to "enlarge the view", to "make distant comparisons", as he put it – in a word, to do the work he set himself in what I see as his two natural histories, of religion and of British morals.

Hume's natural history of British morals shows us how the one Janus face, toward truth, connects us to the other, toward good, by way of the "imaginative" connections between reason and feeling in the method as well as the execution of these works. Logic and Ethics, truth and good, are related to each other by what Bacon called "Imagination". This is the power within us to pull ourselves together, to motivate ideas and to illuminate motives, at once. And it is an *historically* activated power because without detailed and linked memory, it cannot gather the combined forces of understanding and sentiment. Bacon's natural history was to be designed to do this work of bringing reason and sentiment together. Hume often noted that sooner or later reason and sentiment concur.

But in the short run, namely just when we need to act, they may not. Therefore we must see what "helps" the philosopher's art can give us through this new way of studying thought, action and consequences. Best seen in the *History*, the reflections, principles or generalizations are few and far between. But when they appear, coming when and as they do, they carry the force of "instruction" as well as the motive force of "entertainment".

Bacon's "anticipations of mind" and his treatment of custom closely resemble Hume's "principle of belief" in explaining how we naturally form opinions and act on them, often with little immediate attention to whether 'this case' is like, or unlike, the ones from which we formed the belief. Because of this, and because our character is built from our actions, we need some philosophical way to wake ourselves, to become alert to the danger inherent in custom and belief, to halt judgment long enough to look, to do something to gain distance and enough calm to ask and listen, *before* choosing. This was the classical skepticism of Socrates. Seen this way, Hume teaches us that an informed and balanced freedom of choice *requires* a natural history approach to morals. In its largest sense, moral philosophy needs this work for substantive reasons, rather than only as the early, grubby and empirical part of an eventually pure moral theory.

It seems to me that Bacon and Hume are the first philosophers to suggest that judging is most artfully done in the course of, or after having completed some sort of historical inquiry: they continually suggest that the more knowledgeable and beneficial act, the most effective choice, is found via the questioning process made possible by this kind of memorable and imaginative history.

At the end of Section IV, I reflected on what of Bacon's 'natural history' is to be found in Hume's *History* when considering the method and movement between general or typical cases, unique cases, and works of mechanical or liberal arts. Thus far in Section VI, I have considered what of Bacon's treatment of imagination as the bond between logic and ethics, truth and good, is revealed in Hume, and why and how. Sizing up and unifying these two treatments, it seems to me that one general statement should suffice – Bacon and Hume reject the Schoolmen's model for philosophical knowing as abstruse, so abstract as to be intellectually incorrigible and practically useless. To replace that model, they strive for an understanding disciplined by experience, whose categories come only after inquiry, and whose use of evidence ranges from typical to unique to human craft, in all three of which areas they insist on considering possible significance, and seeking the working force, motive or sentiment as well as the pattern, intent or reasoning in question. They do not seek generalizations, universally and necessarily true propositions as their sole end, as might be done in a purely con-templative or "pure science" model of knowing. Rather, their end is wisdom – good human use, and that, in their view, cannot be illuminated without probing into what and how we are, in time and place, the concrete, as makers and doers under circumstances often only slightly amenable to our actions. The grand designs of later philosophies of history, of later positivism, and of earlier School metaphysics, are not on their agenda. Limited, fallible, civilizable but potentially volcanic man is on their agenda, at the top. Philosophy has the work, then, of studying man where he is, seeking the evidence where it is, in his natural moral history.

There are two insights in this new way of doing moral philosophy: (1)

The more apparent, by now, is that for Bacon and Hume, the most careful inquiry comes about when we proceed this way, and so both the leverage we need within ourselves, and that we need on the facts – on our own mental and passional sets as well as on difficult problems of evidence 'outside' us, are greater if this work is done as natural history. But (2) the less apparent insight is that both the act we plan to choose and do, and the larger problem of what we are making of ourselves, what is coming to be our life, both, require the terribly difficult achievement of integration and balance, and this way of doing moral philosophy helps us see how that achievement might be artfully counted and sustained by us, the beneficiaries. It shows how the poise of sound character is achieved. Thus both the poise of the mind, its ability to ask, and the poise of character, its wisdom in evaluating and choosing, are the same poise, the same integrated and balanced life, won by the same philosophical art.

In both Sections III and IV we have seen another discovery of Hume's that belongs in moral philosophy – that in the art of bringing about this balanced way of judging and living, the "cosmic view" or a large "order" helps us stabilize what are otherwise wild swings between opposites of belief or passion. Expectations are more controllable if we realize the larger frame in which a continuing plan will work them out, the larger view of people and events that will come to affect and be affected by our action. Whether discussing religion and the mind's innate desire to find "order" and invisible power behind the visible, or discussing King John, the barons and the gradual introduction of a sense of the public, in both sorts of places Hume is finding an orientation or set of bearings, as it were, from which to get a moral grip on ourselves by such (more "remote", less near) considerations.

An added consequence of that "enlarged view" is that it tends to convince Hume that "an universal compensation prevails", that on a par, "at the end of the day", nature and history do not wildly swing to bliss or torment, regularity or chaos, but tend on the whole to balance things out. This philosophical conservation of moral energy enables us to consider where the limits are, and consider them as added aids to help us balance ourselves and our actions. The moral life is rooted in our natures because we naturally form ties, because in our natures there are "engraven" some moral principles, and because our experience of "cosmic" and community "order" and of another's exemplary character all lead us to try to "emulate" them. That natural desire to emulate, in its turn, enables the calmer passions to thrive, and so too, it is through them that arts and sciences can flourish to produce and sustain civilization. Moral virtue,

Hume found, is nothing but "a more enlarged and cultivated reason".

Lest there be some misunderstanding, the "order" he mentions is in the universe and in nature, and not to be confused with political or social order in the sense of totalitarian or authoritarian state order. That is, security and peace having been discussed already, he later cautions us that there can be too much order, such that the arts, sciences and personal liberties all decline because dull people come to be preferred, active ones are inhibited, questioning is punished, such that submissiveness and flattery replace initiative and self-respect.

Hume is neither as optimistic as Bacon nor as despairing as Voltaire when considering human progress. Reading his *History* on this issue, it is apparent that he does see some progress in England's gradual development of institutions which provide stable government and enable some flourishing of those arts and sciences dependent on the resulting civil and personal liberty. But he sees history in nature – broadly bounded by limits such that neither bottomless pits, nor utopian peaks are included. In that way he is more modest than they, less buoyed up than Bacon and less depressed than Voltaire. Even more than they, Hume takes accident and chance into account, both in personal life and in civil history. His order is not that of a calculus. His investigations have led him, as we saw, to notice an immense variety of lives and time, exhibiting almost every sort of connection or lack of same – people with excellent character and harmful public lives, people like Henry VII with long-term good in the public life flowing from a character at least partly avaricious, people whose actions had consequences unforeseen and harmful, or unforeseen and fruitful – and so forth. Rather than feeling threatened by this sort of disorder and variety, it leads Hume to a richer, if less manageable mix.

Hume is not overcome by variety, complexity, and chance. History instructs us "in the great mixture of accident, which commonly concurs with a small ingredient of wisdom and foresight, in erecting the complicated fabric of the perfect government" (II/525). The same could be said about one's own work on the complicated fabric of personal life. In the midst of the unforeseeable, of accident and our own as well as nature's limits, there is place for a "small ingredient of wisdom" – the love of which, we see, is both aroused and instructed by Hume's *England* as a natural history of British morals.[24]

Notes

1. *The Works of Francis Bacon*, coll. and edit. by Jms. Spedding, Robt. L. Ellis, and Douglas D. Heath (Boston: Taggard and Thomason, 1864, repr. at St. Clair Shores, MI.: Scholarly Press, (n.d.). All references to the works of Bacon are to this edition.
2. David Fate Norton and Richard H. Popkin, *David Hume: Philosophical Historian* (Indianapolis: Bobbs-Merrill Liberal Arts Press, 1965).
3. David Hume, *The History of England from the Invasion of Julius Caesar to the Abdication of James the Second in 1688* [ed. Wm. B. Todd] (Indianapolis: Liberty *Classics*, 1983). All references to Hume's *England* are to this edition.
4. Peter Jones, *Hume's Sentiments. Their Ciceronian and French Context* (Edinburgh: the University Press, 1982).
5. M.M. Goldsmith, "Regulating Anew the Moral and Political Sentiments of Mankind: Bernard Mandeville and the Scottish Enlightenment", unpublished paper, read at International Project on the Scottish Enlightenment, University of Edinburgh, 25–31 August 1986.
6. Donald W. Livingston, *Hume's Philosophy of Common Life* (Chicago and London: University of Chicago Press, 1984).
7. C.N. Stockton, "Economics and the Mechanism of Historical Progress in Hume's *History*", in *Hume. A Re-evaluation*, ed. Donald W. Livingston and James T. King (New York: Fordham University Press, 1976), pp. 296–320.
8. Duncan Forbes, "Hume and the Scottish Enlightenment", in S. C. Brown, editor, *Philosophers of the Enlightenment* (Sussex: the Harvester Press, and New Jersey: Humanities Press, Inc., 1979, pp. 94–109.
9. Nicholas Phillipson, "Hume as Moralist: A Social Historian's Perspective", in S. C. Brown, *op. cit.*, pp. 140–161; and *Hume*, in the series "Historians on Historians" (London: Weidenfeld and Nicolson, 1989).
10. Craig Walton, "Hume and Jefferson on the Uses of History", in C. Walton and J. Anton, editors, *Philosophy and the Civilizing Arts* (Athens, OH: Ohio University Press, 1974), pp. 103–125; reprinted in D. W. Livingston and Jms. T. King, editors, *Hume: A Re-evaluation* (New York: Fordham University Press, 1976), pp. 389–403. Cf. also E. B. Braly, "The Reputation of David Hume in America" (University of Texas dissertation, 1955).
11. The *Oxford English Dictionary* provides a pocket natural history of that phrase, beginning in 1567 where it describes a work dealing with the properties of natural objects. In 1593, one G. Harvey discusses Aristotle's natural histories "of the Asses and Sheepe", so that, by then, it is used generically as "as scientific account of any subject on similar lines". By the time of the 1797 Third Edition of the *Encylopaedia Britannica*, "the natural history of the physical sciences" was a familiar phrase in this more modern sense. Bacon may have had one Grimstone in mind when criticizing the lack of method in these early uses, for Grimstone had described his 1604 effort as "of it self pleasing, and very profitable", as if it were a species of entertainment. Though *OED* does find it significant that in 1831 an author raised the question as to whether human feelings could admit of a natural history, it curiously omits any reference to Hume's 1757 *Natural History of Religion*. Cf. *Oxford England Dictionary* (Oxford: Oxford University Press, 1933, 1961, 1970), Vol. VII, p. 38.
12. Craig Walton, "Ramus and Bacon on Method", *Journal of the History of Philosophy*

VII/ #4 (Oct., 1972); see also "the Legacy of Francis Bacon", which is Vol, IV, No. 1 (April, 1971) of *Studies in the Literary Imagination*, especially Margaret L. Wiley, "Francis Bacon: Induction and/or Rhetoric", Maurice B. McNamee, S. J., "Bacon's Inductive Method and Humanistic Grammar", and Benjamin Farrington, "Francis Bacon after his Fall", and Paolo Rossi, *Francis Bacon, from Magic to Science*, transl. S. Rabinovitch (Bari: Editori Laterza, 1957; transl. Chicago: University of Chicago Press, 1968).

13. See, for example, ch. VI of Peter Urbach's *Francis Bacon's Philosophy of Science* (Open Court, 1987) in whcih a fresh and detailed account is given as to what the three kinds of "tables" of evidence have to do with the inductive problem of reaching middle and higher axioms. Cf. also my review of Urbach in *Journal of the History of Philosophy* (forthcoming).

14. Rossi, *ibid.*, p. 191, and Walton, "Ramus and Bacon", *op. cit.*. For Prof. L. Jonathan Cohen's treatment of these issues, see "Some Historical Remarks on the Baconian Conception of Probability", in *Jour. Hist. Ideas*, XLI/#2 (April–June, 1980), pp. 219-231, and in more detail in his *The Probable and the Provable* (Oxford: The Clarendon Press, 1977), *passim*. Hume on the two probabilities is cited on p. 42; concerning this new view of induction as it applies to history and ethics, see especially pp. 145 f.: "...so far as the logic of support-assessment is concerned – as distinct from the professional proprieties of experimental science – it does not even matter whether the events taken into account as evidence are the result of deliberately contrived test-performances or have occurred partially or wholly without human intervention. Nor does it matter whether the various trials that compose a complex test are performed at the same time or not. What is essential is just that the antecedent and consequent of the generalization at issue should be jointly satisfied at some time or set of times in such-and-such varieties of relevant circumstances, or that the antecedent should, and the consequent should not, be thus satisfied". See also his *The Dialogue of Reason. An Analysis of Analytical Philosophy* (Oxford: The Clarendon Press, 1986), *passim*, as on the sciences of ethics and jurisprudence at pp. 18f., 67 ff., and 139 ff. Though inductively-minded philosophers tend more to local and field inquiries than to global systems, and deductively minded ones the other-way-'round, in comparing them and favoring the former, Cohen explains (again with Bacon as his guide): "Indeed, while the deductivist has no inherent motive for increasing the level of generality at which his theory operates, the inductivist moves naturally, where he can, towards greater and greater generality. Only inductivism incorporates an ideal of synoptic comprehensiveness. A well-tested, yet unrefuted principle that subsumes and explains subordinate principles and also generates new knowledge, has a superior inductive claim to acceptance, as Bacon long ago recognized. But according to the inductivist such conclusions are not to be 'anticipated', as Bacon called it, in a premature straining after comprehensiveness [ref. *Nov. org.* I/aphr. 26]" (Pg. 139). None of Prof. Cohen's work on this aspect of induction bears directly on the other question discussed here, concerning what Bacon called the Janus-face of imagination as connecting sentiment to reason, ethics to logic, such that the same natural history would both aid us to know and to feel motivated to emulate those who do well what they know well, in natural and civil life; that issue is discussed chiefly in Section VI, below.

15. For a good biographical study of Bacon, including this work after his 1621 "fall", see Catherine Drinker Bowen, *Francis Bacon. The Temper of a Man* (Boston: Atlantic Monthly Press, 1963), esp. pp. 207–233.

16. Rossi, *ibid.*, pp. 218 f.

17. Cf. Rossi, *Ibid.*, p. 223. I use 'topic' and 'critic' in conformity with Max H. Fisch's explanation given in "Vico and Pragmatism", in *Giambattista Vico: An International Symposium*, ed. Tagliacozzo and White (Baltimore: John Hopkins Univ. Press, 1969), pg. 402. At that place, Prof. Fisch explains that Aristotle's *Topics* and *Posterior Analytics* "called for an art of *finding* arguments (or middle terms), called *topic*, from the *topoi* or places in which to seek them, or, in Latin, *invention*, for the skill of finding". By contrast, Aristotle's formal logic in the *Prior Analytic* and elsewhere, as developed by the Stoic and medieval logicians, "came to be viewed as an art for *judging* arguments and to be called *critic*, or, in Latin, *iudicium*. Thus the division of logic into topic and critic, invention and judgment, overshadowed, if it did not displace, the earlier division of reasoning into probable or demonstrable." Aristotle's Greek terms are in the singular. For the most careful discussion of these changes known to me, see Wilhelm Risse, *Die Logik der Neuzeit*, I.er Band: 1500–1640, and II.er Band: 1640–1780 (Stuttgart-Bad Cannstatt: Friedrich Frommann Verlag (Gunther Holzboog, 1964 [I] and 1970 [II.]). Cf. also, in this same connection, and significant between Bacon and Hume, my "Thomas Hobbes and the Reform of Logic", in *Foundations of Hobbes's Political Thought*, ed. Ross Rudolph (University of Toronto Press, forthcoming).

18. David Hume, *The Philosophical Work*, edit. Green and Grose (London, 1882; repr. Darmstadt: Scientia Verlag Aalen, 1964), Vol. 4, pp. 309–363. There are two editions more convenient to obtain – that edited by H. E. Root for Stanford University Press (Stanford, 1957), and the critical edition including also Hume's *Dialogues Concerning Natural Religion*, edited by Colver and Price (Oxford: at the Clarendon Press, 1980). Colver makes no observations on the content of the work, confining himself to the question of Hume's revisions and their significance. Root, by contrast – editing a volume in the "Library of Modern Religious Thought" – seriously explores Hume's evidence and conclusion in his introduction. Root sees Hume's explanation of religion as flawed because too clinical, but chiefly because skewed toward the history of zealotry and bigotry, so skewed away from a history of charity, compassion and mercy. It must be added here, that Root shows no sign of having considered Hume's observations on religion's value as given in the *History* – a contribution which might well have altered his own assessment of Hume on religion. Cf. Mossner, *Life*, pg. 306.

19. On "the barbarism of reflection", cf. Vico's *New Science*, section 1097 to the end.

20. *Enquiry concerning the Principles of Morals*, in Green and Grose, *op. cit.*, Vol 4, pp. 169–174.

21. Hume's "Of the Study of History", in *ibid.*, 4/390 f.

22. In *Philosophical Works*, *op. cit.*, Vol. III, pp. 1–8.

23. See Note C, Vol. III, pp. 469–472, where Hume has just found an aged "housebook" of a Tudor earl, from the prices and purchases of which book Hume pieces together a picture of home life and the economy then current. See also *New Letters of David Hume*, ed. Klibansky and Mossner, p. xvii (Bishop Percy's letter to Hume), and Hume's reply at pp. 197–199.

24. This study is a shortened version of a monograph in progress, growing out of a seminar on Liberty and Authority in Hume's *History of England*, which was sponsored by The Liberty Fund and held at the Huntington Library, San Marino, CA., in October 1985. I am indebted to the other fifteen members of that seminar, and own a particular debt of thanks to Donald W. Livingston, Nicholas Capaldi, Richard H. Popkin, Paul S. Wood, Nicholas Phillipson, Noble Stockton and Michael Barfoot since adjournment of the seminar. Their shares in its merits are great, and in its flaws, nil.

EUGENE F. MILLER

HUME ON LIBERTY IN THE
SUCCESSIVE ENGLISH CONSTITUTIONS

Of England during his own time, David Hume thought that one could affirm justly, and without any danger of exaggeration, that it enjoyed "the most entire system of liberty, that ever was known amongst mankind."[1] His *History of England* is the story of how this remarkable and unprecedented system of liberty came into being. The theme of liberty, above all other themes, gives continuity to Hume's detailed examination of English constitutional development from the Anglo-Saxon period to the Revolution in 1688. The main lessons that he wishes to draw and the major errors of interpretation that he wishes to correct have to do with liberty. In raising the question of liberty, therefore, we go directly to the heart of Hume's historical enterprise and open up the possibility of understanding English history as he meant for it to be understood.

In Hume's view, the personal and civil liberty enjoyed by a people at any given time will depend on a variety of causes. Chief among these causes are, on the one hand, laws and institutions of government and, on the other, the condition of the arts and sciences, including what Hume calls "those vulgar and more necessary arts of agriculture, manufactures, and commerce." (2.519) The first set of causes would be referred to in our day as political or constitutional, while the second set would likely be separated into the intellectual, the technological, and the economic. While Hume distinguished these two sets of causes, he believed that their interrelationship was very close. Thus he writes: "The rise, progress, perfection, and decline of art and science, are curious objects of contemplation, and intimately connected with a narration of civil transactions." (2.519) This interrelationship is suggested also by the principle, which is vital to Hume's account of English history, that "power naturally follows property." (1.203)

Since Hume's time, there has been considerable debate on the question of which of these sets of causes is fundamental or ultimate. The

N. Capaldi and D.W. Livingston (eds.), Liberty in Hume's History of England. 53–103.
© 1990 *Kluwer Academic Publishers. Printed in the Netherlands.*

tendency has been to depreciate the political in favor of the economic. While some searching might reveal where Hume would stand in this debate, the fact is that he does not address the issue thematically. He draws attention to the importance of the arts and sciences and their applications in manufacturing and commerce, but without depreciating the role of laws and institutions and the exercise of political prudence.

Political distinctions are paramount in Hume's division of English history into periods. The various chapters of the *History* are determined, of course, by the succession of monarchs, but more fundamental to his periodization of English history is the succession of constitutions. Hume began with the Stuart kings and then worked back from the seventeenth century, and it is unlikely that he had in mind at first the sequence of constitutions that he finally describes. One can be sure, however, that he opposed from the outset the prevailing view that England's history reflected the continuous development of a single constitution, which had taken shape in the centuries that preceded the Norman conquest.[2] Hume denies that English constitutional history is marked by continuity: "The English constitution, like all others, has been in a state of continual fluctuation." (4.355) To put the point another way, he denies that English history can be understood as successive confirmations of what many writers had reverently called "the ancient constitution." With Hume, the emphasis is on plurality and discontinuity. He speaks of a succession of "constitutions" and not of stages in the development of a single constitution. He thus preserves the classical view that constitutional changes of a fundamental character produce differences in kind.

This essay will trace Hume's account of the successive English constitutions and show how each one stands with respect to liberty. Since liberty is, as he often says, the "perfection" of civil society, it serves quite properly as the standard by which he measures the English constitutions. Such an endeavor should help us to understand not only how England came to enjoy the most entire system of liberty ever known to mankind, but also what liberty is and what the causes are that sustain it. We must recognize at the outset, however, that Hume's *History* is not simply an encomium to liberty. One lesson that he draws from English history, especially from the period of the Commonwealth, is that the zeal for liberty can be taken to a dangerous and destructive extreme. Hume's *History* helps us to see how liberty can be tempered or balanced so that it becomes the friend of good order.

The Sequence of English Constitutions

At the time Hume wrote his *History*, the dominant, though certainly not unchallenged, interpretation of the history of England was the one provided by various Whig historians. These writers were fond of appealing to the "ancient" or "original" constitution to support their case in constitutional disputes. The ancient constitution was said to have existed in England before the Conquest, in the time when the Anglo-Saxons flourished and perhaps even in an earlier time. Whig writers regarded the ancient constitution as the foundation of the rights and liberties of Englishmen as well as the model for judging the ongoing practices of government. In 1711, Sir Robert Molesworth had defined a *real* Whig as "one who is exactly for keeping up to the Strictness of the true old Gothic Constitution."[3] Reverence for the so-called ancient constitution persisted throughout the eighteenth century. In the 1770s, an essayist could boast: "If ever God did concern Himself about forming a government for mankind to live happily under, it was that which was established in England by our Saxon forefathers."[4] This view had important implications for the understanding of how liberty developed in England. As Herbert Butterfield has observed, most Whigs would have agreed

> that freedom had been perfect in Anglo-Saxon times. Liberty did not in fact have to be created or hatched or evolved or nursed into existence. It only needed to be restored.[5]

The Whig historians did not originate the view that England's true and ancient constitution predates Norman rule. As J. G. A. Pocock shows, it had been suggested a century earlier by writers on the common law, most notably Sir Edward Coke.[6] For Coke, the common law was the only law of consequence for England. Moreover, it was the product not of reason, but of custom. Whereas some of the Whig writers would trace the ancient laws and institutions to men's understanding of their natural rights, Coke attributed the goodness of the common law to its antiquity and durability. The common law, as customary law, had been tried and tested by Englishmen over an immense stretch of time. It embodied more wisdom than any man or any generation could hope to discover. In Coke's view, the common law had no recorded beginning in English history. It belonged to time immemorial. It could not be traced to the work of a founder or legislator. Coke maintained that the Anglo-Saxons had lived under the common law, but unlike later Whig writers, he had no particular interest in the Saxons as a people. Believing that the common law was the immemorial custom of England, he sought its beginnings in a still more distant past. Of great importance to later conceptions of the ancient constitution was Coke's insistence on the continuity of the common law. This required him to deny that the Normans had imported a new body of feudal law into England. William I had merely codified and confirmed the law of his Saxon predecessors, and John had reconfirmed the common law in assenting to the Magna Carta. Coke's teaching on the continuity of English law would be called into question later in the seventeenth century by the investigations of Sir Henry Spelman, which showed that the feudal law introduced by the Normans had departed sharply from Saxon practice. Nevertheless, Whig historians as well as common-law writers such as Blackstone would continue to hold that the Magna Carta had reconfirmed the nation's ancient laws and liberties rather than amending a new feudal arrangement.

Hume was fully aware of these claims that England's present constitution merely confirmed an ancient constitution. They were, for him, an illustration of how the history of England had been clouded and obscured by the representations of party or faction. Appeals to the ancient constitution had been employed as a political tactic throughout the seventeenth century by the "country party," whose objective had been to limit the royal prerogative, to expand the power of the House of Commons, and to protect the liberties of the people. The agreement between Whig and common-law views of the ancient constitution would likely be explained by Hume in terms of their association with the same party outlook. Coke was an early spokesman for the country party, and *Whig* was simply the appellation under which this party came to be known after about 1680.

Hume rejected from the outset this Whig or "country party" account of the ancient constitution, but there appears to have been some development in his understanding of just why it was faulty. In the volumes on the Stuarts, which were the first part of the *History* to be written, he makes a distinction between "the ancient constitution, before the seventeenth century," and "our present constitution."[7] In other words, he tends at first to treat English constitutional history from the beginnings up to the Stuarts as a single period, and he is willing to call this the "ancient constitution." Yet even here, he emphasizes the fluctuating nature of this early constitution and the presence within it of divergent and conflicting practices. The ancient constitution, thus understood, contains precedents for the crown's broad prerogative that are as strong as those for the liberties of the subject.

When Hume, in writing the later volumes of his *History*, came to examine pre-Stuart times in detail, he seems to have found that this early period could best be divided into distinct epochs; and on at least one occasion, he describes these epochs as a series of constitutions. As Hume looks back on English history, beginning from the form of government established in his own time, he uncovers these four constitutions (see 4.355):

- "Our present plan of liberty," which grew out of constitutional struggles of the seventeenth century and was confirmed by the Revolution Settlement.
- "The ancient constitution," a term that applies most properly, perhaps, to the absolute monarchy of the Tudor period, which declined under the early Stuarts.
- "A more ancient constitution," preceding the rise of Tudor monarchy, when powerful barons checked the king's authority and also tyrannized the people.
- "Still a more ancient constitution," namely, that which existed before the signing of the charters, when neither the people nor the barons had any regular privileges, and an able prince could effectively claim almost the full power of government.

As we see, Hume is willing even here to speak of an "ancient constitution," but the Tudor monarchy is scarcely a model that anyone would wish to imitate. It existed before "the settlement of our present plan of liberty," and it was preceded by at least two other constitutions – one "more ancient" and another that was more ancient still. Another striking feature of these distinctions is that England's first constitution seems to be no older than the Norman Conquest. Whereas Whig and common-law writers had located the true and ancient constitution of England in pre-Norman, times, Hume seems to deny that there was an English constitution, properly speaking, in these earlier times. This statement appears to denigrate the Anglo-Saxon period as well as that "time immemorial" in which common-law writers had located the roots of English law.

The distinctions that we have just examined come in a note to the *History*, and one would be hesitant to take them as authoritative were it not for the fact that they are repeated in the important summary statement that comes in the last part of the text to be published. It is true that this latter statement on "the constitution of the English government" begins with the Anglo-Saxon period, as if it were the first constitution, but otherwise the periods are the same. These periods are: (1) from the Norman Conquest to the establishment of the Great Charter; (2) from the accession of Edward I to the death of Richard III; (3) the "subsequent period," when the authority of the sovereigns was almost absolute; and (4) the "following age," when the people were able "to erect a regular and equitable plan of liberty." In this context, Hume explains the difficulty that the Whigs and others encounter when they make an appeal to the ancient constitution:

> [W]hatever period they pitch on for their model, they may still be carried back to a more ancient period, where they will find the measures of power entirely different, and where every circumstance, by reason of the great barbarity of the times, will appear still less worthy of imitation.[8]

These two statements on the constitutions of England, though perhaps varying a bit on details, have the same implications for our understanding of the development of liberty in England. Whereas the Whig historians had viewed the nation's liberty as an ancient heritage, Hume sees it instead as a recent acquisition. The Whig and common-law writers had thought it necessary to ground England's present liberty in the distant past in order to make it secure. The ancient institutions are good, and the present institutions are worthwhile insofar as they preserve and conform to the ancient ones. Hume rejects this implicit identification of the good with the ancestral. The beginnings, as he sees them, are barbaric and unworthy of imitation. The nation has made decisive progress since the early time in devising free institutions. It is indeed instructive to return to this early period of English history, but primarily so that readers might see how far they have come and how grateful they should be for the constitution that is presently established.

Let us now examine these constitutions in the order of their actual appearance, paying close attention to their standing with respect to liberty. We shall begin, as Hume does, with the governments that preceded the Norman conquest, the most important of which were those of the Anglo-Saxons. As we discovered, Hume may not have regarded these early governments as true English constitutions. It should be noted that Hume does not include in his enumerations the commonwealth that was established after the overthrow of Charles I. This government is perhaps excluded because it broke very sharply with its predecessors and made no fundamental contribution to the system of liberty that followed.

As we shall see, however, Hume's treatment of the Commonwealth period contains some reflections that are vital for understanding his conception of liberty.

England Before the Norman Conquest

The Whig historians, drawing heavily from Tacitus but adapting him to their own purposes, had painted an attractive picture of their Saxon forefathers in England.[9] The Saxons were said to be a rude and simple people, who subsisted mainly by agriculture, but who distinguished themselves by their fierce independence and their deep love of liberty. Though deficient in the liberal and mechanical arts, these rude farmers understood clearly the main principles of the art of government, especially the principle that monarchical power must be limited by popular consent. The Saxon kings were elected, their power was constrained by assemblies of the tribes, and they could be deposed if they became tyrannical. Security for life and property came not only from these limits to arbitrary power, but also from the ancient Saxon custom, later enacted into law, that persons accused of crimes should be tried by a jury of peers. While some of the Whig historians detected feudal elements in Saxon society, others maintained that farmers owned their land outright and could dispose of it as they pleased. This meant that all male children, and not just the firstborn, enjoyed a right of inheritance.

In looking to England's pre-Norman past for the model of true liberty, these writers had assumed that liberty can be established in rude societies, where the arts and sciences are not highly developed. This assumption implicitly takes sides on an issue of very great importance, namely, how is liberty connected to the progress of the arts and sciences. This issue was of keen interest to Hume, and it was widely debated among philosophers in the eighteenth century. All parties to this debate could agree that the arts and sciences had undergone great improvement in the modern world and that this improvement, along with the advance of commerce, had vastly increased both personal and public wealth. There was disagreement, however, as to whether or not the increase of enlightenment and "luxury" had favored the cause of human liberty. Rousseau's *First Discourse* states the case against the arts and sciences quite forcefully. If a people is to preserve its liberty and independence, it must have the desire and the ability to resist enslavement; but the public-spiritedness and martial courage on which liberty depends are undermined by the advance of luxury and knowledge. The rude, austere republic is thus the true home of liberty.[10] Hume had taken a quite different view of the matter in his *Essays*, where he observes that progress in the arts is "favourable to liberty, and has a natural tendency to preserve, if not produce a free government."[11] As we proceed in our examination of Hume's *History*, we shall wish to see if this judgment is borne out by his examination of English liberty before and after the revival of the arts and sciences.

Turning now to Hume's account of pre-Norman England, we find that it agrees in certain respects with the Whig interpretation. Thus when Hume speaks of the rude and uncultivated tribes or nations that settled in England – the Britons, the Saxons, the Danes – he draws attention to their love of liberty. The early Britons, who had descended from the nations of Gaul, were a military people whose governments, though monarchical, were free. Even the common people enjoyed a property in arms, and "it was impossible, after they had acquired a relish of liberty, for the princes or chieftains to establish any despotic authority over them." (1.5) The fate of the Britons, as Hume recounts it, seems almost to confirm Rousseau's warning that progress in learning is fatal to liberty. Once the Britons had been subdued by the Romans, their conquerors introduced laws and civility, taught the Britons to desire and raise all the conveniences of life, and instructed them in letters and science. Yet as the Britons became more civilized, they also grew accustomed to their chains. When their freedom was finally restored about the year 448 by the Roman withdrawal from England, "the abject Britons regarded this present of liberty as fatal to them." (1.13) Exposed to invasion from the north by the Picts and Scots, but unable to recover their ancient valor, the Britons sought relief by inviting the Saxons, who were one of the fiercest of the German tribes, to come to Britain to serve as their protectors. The Saxons, however, soon turned their arms against their unfortunate hosts, and after more than a century of violent struggle, succeeded in conquering the whole southern part of the island, except for Wales and Cornwal. Everything was thrown back into ancient barbarity.

The Anglo-Saxons resembled the early Britons in some important ways, but their history would take a rather different course. First, they would remain "a rude, uncultivated people," ignorant of letters and unskilled in the mechanical arts. Europe itself was now sunk in ignorance and barbarity, so that it could no longer provide a civilizing influence like that which the Romans had once introduced among the Britons. It is true that Alfred, the greatest of the Anglo-Saxon kings, improved the administration of justice and gave zealous encouragement to the arts and sciences. Nevertheless, the Anglo-Saxons would still appear as barbarians to their Norman conquerors, notwithstanding the low state of the arts among that people. (1.185) Second, perhaps because of this lack of cultivation, the Anglo-Saxons retained their martial disposition and their valor. The military courage of the Anglo-Saxons was, in Hume's judgement, "their best quality," although it was unsupported by discipline or conduct. (1.185) Finally, the Anglo-Saxons were able to preserve, and in some cases improve, the free institutions that they had brought with them from Germany. They did not accommodate themselves to tyranny until the eleventh century, when they were at last completely subjugated by the Normans.[12]

After the Anglo-Saxons had conquered Britain, they divided it into seven kingdoms, known as the Heptarchy, but by the year 827, these were united into one state under the rule of a single monarch. Hume grants that we can have but an imperfect knowledge of government and laws during this period. His own account is drawn from Tacitus's observations about the Germanic tribes, from the writings of antiquaries who had studied English history, and from conjectures about the general character of government among barbarous nations. Hume agrees with Whig historians that the authority of the Anglo-Saxon kings was very limited. These kings shared legislative power with a national council, called a Wittenagemot or assembly of the wise men. Yet Hume rejects the view that representatives of the boroughs, or what would later be called the Commons, could have had a significant place in the Wittenagemot.[13] No doubt a great number of administrative and ecclesiastical officials, who owed their appointment to the king, held membership on the national council, but these alone would not have been able to limit the royal authority. Thus the more considerable proprietors of land must also have been members, and this without any election. The key point, however, is that "the people, even if admitted to that assembly, were of little or no weight and consideration." (1.165) It is thus inaccurate to trace the authority of the house of Commons back to Anglo-Saxon times.

Although Hume believed that the general strain of Anglo-Saxon government was aristocratic, he found in its judicial system, especially as reformed by Alfred, considerable remains of the ancient democracy. In order to render the execution of justice strict and regular, Alfred "divided all England into counties; these counties he subdivided into hundreds; and the hundreds into tithings." (1.76) When minor disputes arose among the ten households that formed a tithing or decennary, the official in charge called all the families together to assist him in deciding the cause. The hundred, consisting of a hundred families of freemen, was assembled monthly to hear affairs of greater moment, appeals from the decennaries, and controversies arising between members of different decennaries. To settle a cause that was brought before the hundred, twelve freeholders were chosen, who, before examining the cause, swore together with the presiding magistrate to administer impartial justice. Hume remarks that this method of decision deserves notice

> as being the origin of juries; an institution, admirable in itself, and the best calculated for the preservation of liberty and the administration of justice, that ever was devised by the wit of man. (1.77)

The county courts, consisting of all the freeholders, were assembled twice each year to receive appeals from the inferior courts. Matters both civil and ecclesiastical were determined here by a majority of voices, and the presiding officers had no authority other than to offer their opinions and keep order among the freemen. While Hume doubts that this system of courts would have sufficed to protect the lowest of the people, without the patronage of some great lord, he does judge it to have been "well calculated to defend general liberty, and to restrain the power of the nobles." (1.172)

It is striking that Hume, in describing Anglo-Saxon jurisprudence, gives primacy to what rational design has produced and not to the products of custom. The court system that Hume applauds was the one designed by Alfred the Great, who was a legislator as well as a warrior, politician, and teacher. No one receives greater praise in Hume's *History* than Alfred. His merit in both private and public life

> may with advantage be set in opposition to that of any monarch or citizen, which the annals of any age or any nation can present to us. He seems indeed to be the model of that perfect character, which, under the denomination of a sage or wise man, philosophers have been fond of delineating, rather as a fiction of their imagination, than in hopes of ever seeing it really existing. (1.74)

Alfred designed more than a system of courts. For the guidance of magistrates in the administration of justice, he "framed a body of laws; which, though now lost, served long as the basis of English jurisprudence, and is generally deemed the origin of what is denominated the COMMON LAW."[14] Contrary to the view of Coke and his successors, the common law, properly understood, has a determinate origin in rational enactment, even though it no doubt incorporates much that is customary.

One might expect that Hume's position on the nature of English law would agree more closely with that of the common-law writers. He emphasizes the importance of accident in the formation of England's constitutions, and he also assigns a great role to custom and habit. Thus he writes at one point that each century "has its peculiar mode in conducting business; and men, guided more by custom than by reason, follow, without enquiry, the manners, which are prevalent in their own time." (2.86) Again, he observes that "habits, more than reason, we find in every thing to be the governing principle of mankind." (5.159) Nevertheless, Hume's comments here on Alfred agree with what he says later about Edward I, who ruled in the thirteenth century. Edward has justly gained "the appellation of the English Justinian" for his "correction, extension, amendment, and establishment of the laws." Hume adds: "For the acts of a wise legislator commonly remain; while the acquisitions of a conqueror often perish with him."[15] This statement echoes Hume's praise of legislators in the *Essays*:

> Of all men, that distinguish themselves by memorable atchievements, the first place of honour seems due to LEGISLATORS and founders of states, who transmit a system of laws and institutions to secure the peace, happiness, and liberty of future generations.[16]

Laws and institutions that have been carefully designed by philosophic legislators rank higher, in Hume's estimation, than those that custom and accident have produced. Thus England's established constitution, though admirable in itself, is not necessarily better for its accidental and unplanned character. Not all accident works out beneficially in political life, and even the English constitution was shaped at decisive moments by prudential actions. Hume's admiration for legislators is counterbalanced, of course, by his warnings about the damage that reckless theory can cause in the sphere of political practice. If there is a tendency in Hume's *History* to elevate the accidental and customary over the prudential, this may result from his wish to protect the English constitution by discouraging a destructive rationalism.

As we have seen, the case can be made that liberty prevailed among the early English peoples, particularly the Anglo-Saxons, and this despite, or perhaps because of, the absence of the arts and sciences, commerce, and luxury. We have seen also that Hume fully appreciates this case and, at times, seems close to endorsing some parts of it. Thus the Germanic nations, and the Saxons in particular, are praised for their love of liberty and their "noble and free genius." (1.407) The Saxons seem to have been "one of the freest nations, of which there remains any account in the records of history." (2.524) These statements, however, tell only one side of the story. In the final analysis, Hume denies that these barbaric peoples, or their descendants in England, enjoyed a genuine liberty, and he refuses to view subsequent English history as a series of efforts to restore a Gothic constitution.

The truth about Saxon or ancient English society, as Hume states it in his concluding summary, is this:

> Such a state of society was very little advanced beyond the rude state of nature: Violence universally prevailed, instead of general and equitable maxims: The pretended liberty of the times, was only an incapacity of submitting to government: And men, not protected by law in their lives and properties, sought shelter, by their personal servitude and attachments under some powerful chieftain, or by voluntary combinations.[17]

The key point here is that the liberty attributed to these barbaric peoples is "pretended," not genuine; and the chief reason for this is that men had no legal protection for life and property against the violence of other men. When liberty is carried to an excess, when it is no longer restrained by the curbs and limits of law, it then ceases to be liberty and becomes licence. Liberty, to be genuine, must be counterbalanced by authority. Thus Hume writes:

> On the whole, notwithstanding the seeming liberty or rather licentious-ness of the Anglo-Saxons, the great body even of the free citizens, in those ages, really enjoyed much less true liberty, than where the execution of the laws is the most severe, and where subjects are reduced to the strictest subordination and dependance on the civil magistrate. (1.168–69)

By denying that *even* the free citizens enjoyed true liberty, Hume points to the existence of slavery among the Anglo-Saxons. Relying on the work of Robert Brady, Hume maintains that "the most numerous rank by far" in Anglo-Saxon society "seems to have been the slaves or villains, who were the property of their lords, and were consequently incapable, themselves, of possessing any property." (1.171) This was not the case with the German nations, at least insofar as Hume can judge from Tacitus. By practicing slavery, the Anglo-Saxons proved to be less dedicated to liberty than were their ancestors. Since no genuine liberty existed among the Anglo-Saxons or other barbaric nations, it cannot be the case, as Rousseau and others maintained, that a rude and uncultivated way of life is favorable to liberty. Hume will argue, in fact, that liberty became possible again in Europe only with the revival of learning and commerce.

As we noted earlier, many historians of Hume's time had turned to the Anglo-Saxon past in order to legitimate the established constitution, which they described as a restoration or confirmation of England's ancient constitution. This use of history presupposed that the good is identical with the ancestral and customary or else that the Anglo-Saxons had discerned clearly what man's natural rights are and how these are best protected. One might say that Hume also discusses Anglo-Saxon government and manners with a view to legitimating the established constitution, but clearly he does not presuppose the goodness of this early time. The present constitution of England is a good one not because it restores Anglo-Saxon practices, but because it avoids them. Hume's discussion of the Anglo-Saxons thus has the character of a warning:

[A] civilized nation, like the English, who have happily established the most perfect and most accurate system of liberty that was ever found compatible with government, ought to be cautious in appealing to the practice of their ancestors, or regarding the maxims of uncultivated ages as certain rules for their present conduct. An acquaintance with the ancient periods of their government is chiefly *useful* by instructing them to cherish their present constitution, from a comparison or contrast with the condition of those distant times. (2.525)

England's Constitution from the Conquest to the Magna Carta

We have seen that the English constitution was commonly viewed in Hume's time as one thing, one durable system of laws and liberties, with a continuous history. Its main principles were said to have originated

with the Saxons, if not in time immemorial, and to have been reconfirmed at decisive points in English history. Hume, by contrast, depicts a
series of distinct and very different constitutions. Anglo-Saxon government, as Hume describes it, is hardly worthy of imitation; and he even
omits it from at least one of his listings of the historic English constitutions. Hume may have believed that the first constitution of England,
strictly speaking, was the one established by William I soon after the
Norman invasion. This constitution was, in any event, a very early one,
and by Hume's reckoning, it lasted until the time of the Magna Carta. Its
demise was signaled not so much by King John's signing of the Magna
Carta, which occurred some 150 years after the Conquest, as by the
"establishment" of the Magna Carta, which by Hume's reckoning came
during the reign of Edward I, almost 100 years after the charter was first
signed. Three issues regarding this first Anglo-Norman constitution
deserve our attention: William's title to rule; the character of the laws
and government; and the relevance of the Magna Carta.

Whig and common-law writers took pains to deny that William's title
to rule could have proceeded from the right of conquest. In their eyes, a
true conquest would have ruptured the continuity of the English constitution. It would have placed on the throne an absolute sovereign, whose
laws owed their authority to that sovereign's will and not to their
antiquity or their foundation in consent. To admit a conquest would
establish a precedent for unlimited powers and obscure the real basis of
political authority. Accordingly, these writers argued that William's
"conquest" was nothing more than a victory over a rival claimant to the
Anglo-Saxon crown, that this victory gave him no right to change the
laws of England, and that he had in fact confirmed the laws of Edward
the Confessor.[18]

To this view of William's rule, Hume has a twofold reply: William
was, by any reasonable measure, the conqueror of England; but the fact
of his conquest is quite irrelevant to constitutional disputes in the
eighteenth century. Hume grants that William took steps at first to give
his rule the semblance of legality and to make it appear that there had
been a change only in the succession of monarchs, not in the form of
government. Yet when the opportunity arose, most probably from
William's own design, to crush resistance and to establish his unlimited
authority, he seized on it and reduced the nation to complete servitude.
William thus ruled England by the right of conquest. Nonetheless, to
those who are not blinded by the controversies of faction, it is evident
"that the present rights and privileges of the people, who are a mixture of

English and Normans, can never be affected by a transaction, which passed seven hundred years ago." (1.227) William's rule is no more a binding precedent for Hume's time than is the rule of Anglo-Saxon kings.

Hume opposes Whig and common-law interpretations by holding not only that William conquered England, but also that he broke sharply with the Anglo-Saxon past. William's great innovation was to establish the feudal law as the chief foundation for English government and jurisprudence. Hume explains that the feudal law developed in Europe, following the collapse of the Roman empire, as the means by which the northern nations could secure their new conquests. Under this law, the various kingdoms of Europe were divided into baronies, and these into inferior fiefs. Although some land was held at first by an allodial or free title, the king eventually came to be the supreme lord of all the landed property. The land, with a few exceptions, was granted conditionally by the king to the barons and by the barons, in turn, to their knights or vassals, for stated services and payments. The vassal was obliged to defend his baron in war; and the baron, at the head of his vassals, was bound to fight in defense of the king and kingdom. Civil services were required in addition to those of a military nature. The barons assembled to give their consent when the king found it necessary to demand any service of them beyond what was due by their tenures, and they gave their advice on the resolution of controversies involving the barons themselves. In the baronies, the vassals assembled to vote on general matters and to assist in trials.

Drawing on the work of Spelman and Brady, Hume shows that William established a feudal kingdom of this sort in England. He specifically denies the claim of Whig and common-law writers that much of the land, under Norman rule, continued to be held by free title and by the Anglo-Saxon population. William's policy "produced almost a total revolution in the landed peoperty of the kingdom." (1.203) William seized the land, retained some of it as royal demsesnes, and conferred most of what remained, subject to stated services and payments, on his foreign adventurers. A few of the English kept their landed property, but only in return for service to some Norman chief. By and large, the ancient and noble families were reduced to beggary and excluded from every road that led either to riches or to preferment. A great part of the inhabitants of the country lived as serfs in a condition of absolute slavery or villainage, while the townspeople were subjected to the will of the king or some great baron, depending on whose land they were situated.

Of great importance to Hume's interpretation of English history is the principle that "power naturally follows property." (1.203) The feudal law led, by that principle, to the concentration of political power in the king and in his barons. In England, the supreme legislative power was lodged in the king and great council, or what later was called the parliament. The great council consisted of the barons, the prelates of the church, who were also the king's vassals, and, most likely, the intermediate military tenants who held knights' fees. Hume rejects the view that the commons, or the representatives of the counties and boroughs, were constituent parts of parliament at this time. The land within a barony was represented in parliament by the baron himself, and "it would have been deemed incongruous to give it any other representation." (1.468) The Anglo-Norman kings enjoyed, in addition to their share of the legislative power, the executive power of government; and they were able to dominate the administration of justice by virtue of the wide jurisdiction of the king's court and its authority to hear appeals both from the courts of barony and the county courts.

Hume argues that early feudal government took a somewhat different form in England than in Europe, and this argument is vital to his interpretation of the Magna Carta. In Europe, the feudal governments followed their natural tendency to exalt the aristocracy and depress the monarchy, especially where the monarch was elective rather than hereditary. Yet in England, where a strong prince was needed to maintain military domination over the native population, the Norman barons were forced "to submit to a more severe and absolute prerogative than that to which men of their rank, in other feudal governments, were commonly subjected." (1.437) The early Anglo-Norman kings could crush any obnoxious baron by their arbitrary power to levy exactions and impose judicial sentences on their subjects. Only a great combination of barons could hope to succeed in opposing the royal authority. It was just such a combination, in the year 1215, that forced King John to sign the Magna Carta.

By Hume's account, the barons acted chiefly with a view to their own benefit in drawing up the Magna Carta and imposing it on the king. The principal articles of this charter define the barons' privileges under feudal law and restrain the king's arbitrary power. The Magna Carta thus marks the end of one feudal constitution, in which the power of the monarch was raised to an uncommonly high pitch, and the beginning of another, in which the barons would emerge as the dominant power. If this charter had contained no other provisions, it would have made very little contribution to the nation's liberty and happiness, for the barons' yoke "might have become more heavy on the people than even that of an absolute monarch." (1.444) Yet the barons were forced to insert clauses favorable to the inferior ranks of men in order to win their concurrence. These clauses offered specific guarantees to the inferior vassals, to merchants, to the cities and boroughs, to owners of goods, to those accused and tried for crimes, and even to the villains. Hume concludes that these latter provisions of the Magna Carta "involve all the chief outlines of a legal government, and provide for the equal distribution of justice, and free enjoyment of property," which are the great objects for which political society was first founded by men. (1.445) He even conjectures, in a rather Whiggish vein, that these provisions were drawn from the laws of Edward, the last Anglo-Saxon king. These were laws whose reestablishment the English people had long desired.

Hume is very careful to specify what the Magna Carta did and did not accomplish. It did not introduce specific changes in the political or public law of the kingdom or in the existing institutions of government. Though it guarded against those tyrannical practices that are incompatible with civilized government, it did so only by verbal clauses. Almost a century would pass between the concession of the charter and its full establishment during the reign of Edward I. Nevertheless, the charter did, in some degree, restrain the barbarous licence of the kings and perhaps of the nobles, bring men more security for their properties and liberties, and contribute to justice and the equal protection of citizens. Acts of violence and iniquity by the crown would come to be seen as public injuries, or as infringements of a charter designed for general security, and not simply as injuries to individuals. (1.442–46) The Magna Carta was followed by another charter, granted by John's weak successor, Henry III, that established the people's right to use the forests. These charters would be important not only for what they accomplished directly, but also for what they came to mean to the English nation. They were, during many generations,

> esteemed as the most sacred rampart to national liberty and indepen-
> dance. As they secured the rights of all orders of men, they were
> anxiously defended by all, and became the basis, in a manner, of the
> English monarchy, and a kind of original contract, which both limited
> the authority of the king, and ensured the conditional allegiance of his
> subjects. (2.6)

England's Second Feudal Constitution:
"A Turbulent and Barbarous Aristocracy"

Hume explains that great changes took place in the English government after the signing of the charters. These changes resulted partly from the charters themselves and partly from the general loosening of feudal ties that accompanied improvements in commerce and the arts. These changes in the English government were of such a fundamental and far-reaching character as to produce what Hume describes as a new constitution. This late-feudal constitution would last some 250 years, from the signing of the charters to the accession of the first Tudor monarch, Henry VII.

As we have seen, England's first feudal constitution was an uneasy mixture of monarchy and aristocracy, in which the king enjoyed somewhat greater powers than did the feudal monarchs of Europe. The constitution that followed the charters was also a mixed government, but with some important differences both in the elements of the mixture and in the authority of these elements relative to each other. One major difference between this late-feudal constitution and its predecessor lies in the relation of its monarchical and its aristocratical parts. The king and the barons continued to be the major centers of political authority, but a variety of causes had tended to weaken the king and increase the power and independence of the barons. A coalition of barons could now control the government, or at least prevent the king from doing so, unless the king were an exceptionally able person. Hume calls this constitution an "aristocracy," since it was favorable to rule by a few, but he is careful to point out that the barons were not men of genuine merit and that their rule was arbitrary and turbulent. A second difference of great consequence between this constitution and its predecessor lay in the opportunity it gave the lower orders of the state to take part in the public councils. This period of English history marks the epoch or beginning of the house of Commons. The king and the barons would increasingly find it necessary to take the opinions of the Commons into account, even though its role throughout the period would remain a subordinate one.

The monarch's position in this late-feudal constitution depended very much on the personal character of the prince who succeeded to the throne; and several of the kings who ruled in this period were able, by their prudence and vigor, to keep the turbulent barons under control. Nevertheless, the power of the monarch had been greatly reduced, since the time of the Conquest, by alterations both in the public laws and in the feudal relationships. Royal power was limited, first of all, by the provisions of the Magna Carta, which the kings were forced to confirm regularly throughout this period. It is true that the crown, despite these concessions, still enjoyed large discretionary prerogatives. Hume judges, in fact, that it would have been dangerous, under the conditions of the time, to limit them too greatly: "If the king had possessed no arbitrary powers, while all the nobles assumed and exercised them, there must have ensued an absolute anarchy in the state." (2.331) Even so, the precedent of the Magna Carta "rendered it more difficult and dangerous for the prince to exert any extraordinary act of arbitrary authority." (2.103–104) John's successor, Henry III, "was the first king of England since the conquest, that could fairly be said to lie under the restraint of law." (2.21) Henry was a particularly weak ruler, however, and his compliance with the charter did not insure that it could also bind a strong and ambitious monarch. Edward I, Henry's successor, proved to be such a monarch, but like Henry, he found it necessary to give the charter his grudging confirmation. With Edward's confirmation, "the Great Charter was finally established," It would thenceforth be regarded as "the basis of English government, and the sure rule by which the authority of every custom was to be tried and canvassed." (2.122–23)

The royal power came to be limited also by alterations that took place gradually in the feudal relationships. Under the feudal system as originally established, the barons had been obliged, along with their vassals, to render military service to the king in return for land. This feudal militia proved to be a disorderly and feeble army, which was often more formidable to the king who summoned it than to foreign powers. Monarchs thus adopted the practice of exchanging the military service for pecuniary supplies, and forces were then enlisted by means of a contract with capable officers. This disuse of the feudal militia had the consequence, however, of making the barons "almost entirely forget their dependence on the crown." (2.103) Monarchs would later find that feudal tenures could not be counted on even as a source of supplies. The barons' obligation to render service or supplies depended on the land that they held of the king by military tenure, which was divided into knights' fees. The number of knights' fees was steadily reduced by various artifices and by a failure to keep accurate rolls, so that at last the king found them to be unreliable as a source either of military services or of pecuniary scutages in lieu of service. The king's expense in levying and maintaining a military force now greatly exceeded the revenues he received from the scutages of his military tenants, and he was forced to turn for assistance to the representatives of the boroughs, upon whom he became increasingly dependent. These representatives formed the basis for what came to be known as the house of Commons.

In order to understand why the commons emerged as an important force in the constitution, we must note that the decline of the feudal system was accompanied by a great improvement in the condition of the lower orders of the state. Hume traces this improvement to a variety of causes, including a general progress in the arts, the independence of the boroughs, and a change in the distribution of property. Following the age of Augustus, Europe witnessed a decline of art and science that reached its low point in the eleventh century, about the age of William the Conqueror; but from that point, they began to revive. Improvements in the law, resulting from a rediscovery of Roman jurisprudence, gave security to the vulgar but necessary arts of agriculture, manufactures, and commerce; and letters were finally revived in the fifteenth century. (See 2.518–22) These improvements would serve to increase the wealth and the freedom of the lower orders, as we see from the example of the Flemings:

> As the Flemings were the first people in the northern parts of Europe, that cultivated arts and manufactures, the lower ranks of men among them had risen to a degree of opulence unknown elsewhere to those of their station in that barbarous age; had acquired privileges and independance; and began to emerge from that state of vassalage, or rather of slavery, into which the common people had been universally thrown by the feudal institutions. (2.201)

By the late-thirteenth century, the kings of England had begun to encourage and protect the lower and more industrious orders of the state. Boroughs were erected on the king's domains, and liberty of trade was conferred upon them. The inhabitants of the boroughs were permitted to farm their own tolls and customs and to elect their own magistrates, who could administer justice independently of the sheriff or county court. These measures increased the liberty and security of citizens and permitted them to enjoy unmolested the fruits of their labor, but they also benefitted the monarch. The inhabitants of the boroughs, by their ingenuity and labor, "furnished commodities, requisite for the ornament of peace and support of war," (2.105) and the kings retained the power to levy talliages or taxes upon them at pleasure. The peasants remained for a longer time under domination of the barons, but the progress of agriculture and the arts, along with the relaxation of feudal tenures and a stricter enforcement of the public law, would liberate them entirely from villenage or slavery before the end of Elizabeth's reign. (See 2.523–24)

With the rise of the boroughs, we find another illustration of Hume's principle that "power naturally follows property." As the boroughs grew in freedom and opulence, they came to enjoy constitutional power in a house of Commons. The beginnings of this institution can be traced to the reign of Henry III. In the year 1265, the Earl of Leicester, who had usurped the powers of government from Henry, summoned a new parliament in London. Included in the parliament, for the first time, were representatives from the boroughs. (See 2.56–57) Quite apart from Leicester's doubtful precedent, legal princes were soon pressed by their financial needs to summon deputies from the boroughs. The first prince to do so was Edward I, in the year 1295. When Edward, for reasons discussed earlier, found that the feudal tenures could no longer supply his expenses, he employed his power to levy talliages or taxes upon the boroughs. Kings had learned that in order to enforce such edicts, it was necessary to obtain the previous consent of the boroughs. Recognizing the inconvenience of obtaining consent in each particular borough, Edward assembled the deputies of all the boroughs "to lay before them the necessities of the state, to discuss the matter in their presence, and to require their consent to the demands of the sovereign." (2.106) Hume emphasizes that these early deputies did not compose an essential part of the parliament. They sat apart from the barons and knights; and they departed after giving their consent to the taxes required of them. In the course of time, however, it became customary for the deputies, "in return for the supplies which they granted, to prefer petitions to the crown for the redress of any particular grievance, of which they found reason to complain." (2.107) These petitions later served as the basis for statutes, which became law after passing Commons in the form of a bill and receiving the assent of the house of peers. The composition of the house of Commons also changed in time. A distinction had once been drawn between the representatives of the counties, who belonged by tenure to the order of peers and were thus entitled to sit in parliament when summoned by the king, and the representatives of the boroughs, who were excluded from the parliament. These county representatives were drawn from the knights and lesser barons, whose numbers had increased steadily with the partition of landed property into moderate estates. The distinction between these two sets of representatives was eventually lost. They were united into the same house, and the country gentlemen came to be selected as deputies from the boroughs along with men whose wealth was derived from commerce and manufacturing. This addition of the gentry to the membership of the Commons enhanced greatly its weight and importance. (See 2.101–104; 2.108–109)

England's late-feudal constitution was, like those that followed, a mixed government, consisting of the monarch, the aristocracy, and the commons. Hume emphasizes, however, that the government was not yet

> regulated by any fixed maxims, or bounded by any certain undisputed rights, which in practice were regularly observed. The king conducted himself by one set of principles; the barons by another; the commons by a third; the clergy by a fourth. All these systems of government were opposite and incompatible. Each of them prevailed in its turn, as incidents were favourable to it. (2.284)

Even though the emergence of Commons gave evidence of the growth of personal freedom, this constitution did not have those inner regulations or balances that are necessary to a regular plan of civil liberty.

Hume thought that a mixed constitution, if it is well-regulated, will protect against "the turbulence of the great" and the "madness of the people" as well as against "the tyranny of princes." (2.174) Depending on their relative strength, any one of these elements can overawe the others and use its powers abusively if constitutional checks and controls are missing. Under the late-feudal constitution, the king exercised arbitrary powers that are inconsistent with a free government; and there were occasional insurrections by the populace. Nevertheless, the main threat to peace and security in those times came from the turbulent barons, who were able on more than one occasion to establish their unlimited authority in the state. The Magna Carta, by imposing regular limits on the royal power, had exalted the aristocracy still higher. Even though the newly-formed Commons supported the king against the power of the aristocracy, these great nobles remained "a kind of independant potentates, who, if they submitted to any regulations at all, were less governed by the municipal law, than by a rude species of the law of nations." (2.179) These "seditious grandees" were often at war with the king or with each other, and their power was the chief obstacle to the execution of justice.

> The barons, by their confederacies with those of their own order, and by supporting and defending their retainers in every iniquity, were the

chief abettors of robbers, murderers, and ruffians of all kinds; and no law could be executed against those criminals.(2.279)

Retainers looked upon their patrons as "more their sovereign than the king himself; and their own band was more connected with them than their country." (2.331) Under these circumstances, Hume concludes, it would have been dangerous to limit the crown's large discretionary prerogatives.

Hume's account of England's feudal constitutions serves to establish that there can be no true liberty without laws to protect individuals from the arbitrary will of others. The chief defect of the feudal law was that it promoted arbitrariness rather than curbing it by general restrictions. Under this law, "the far greater part of the society were everywhere bereaved of their *personal* liberty, and lived entirely at the will of their masters. Every one, that was not noble, was a slave." (2.522) Even the barons, who seemed to enjoy great independence, possessed no true liberty, for "the security of each individual among them, was not so much derived from the general protection of law, as from his own private power and that of his confederates." (2.179) Since there was no law either to limit or to protect the barons, Hume prefers to speak of their "licentiousness" and not their liberty.

In comparing England's two feudal constitutions – the one established by the Normans when the feudal law was in full flower and the one that came later with feudalism's decay – it is clear that the latter provided somewhat more security and personal freedom for the people at large. The increasing prosperity of the Commons allowed them to claim at least a small share of the constitutional power, and their efforts to curb the arbitrary power of the king and the barons proved their attachment to liberty. Yet even this late-feudal constitution lacked those effective legal restraints that are essential to personal security and freedom.

Although these feudal constitutions were greatly defective, Hume nonetheless seems to prefer them to the governments that they replaced. Speaking generally of feudal government in Europe, Hume observes that while this

strange species of civil polity was ill fitted to ensure either liberty or tranquillity, it was preferable to the universal licence and disorder, which had every where preceded it. (2.520)

This judgment agrees with Hume's general view that improvements in the arts and sciences will favor improvements in government and liberty. The feudal period was a rude and barbaric age, but less so than the preceding one, when the conquering peoples from the north still knew little of agriculture, manufacturing, commerce, and law. Applying this judgment to English history, we have another indication that Hume wished to depreciate Anglo-Saxon government, which many had lauded as the nation's true and ancient constitution. The feudal constitutions established after the Norman conquest were not only different in principle from Anglo-Saxon government, but also an improvement on that ancient government.

The Tudor Monarchy: An "Authority Almost Absolute"

The Tudor monarchs ruled England for just over a century, from the accession of Henry VII in 1485 to the death of Elizabeth in 1603; but they were able during this time to establish a constitution that departed sharply from the one that had prevailed in the late-feudal period. The distinguishing feature of this new constitution was its elevation of the monarch's power to the point where it was virtually unlimited or absolute. Kings had been restrained earlier by the barons, as they would be later by the house of Commons, but in the meantime, the Tudor princes "introduced that administration, which had the appearance of absolute government." (5.550)

The Tudor monarchs increased their power chiefly at the expense of the great barons, who under the previous constitution had often overawed the king and disregarded the laws. As Hume explains, it required "the authority almost absolute" of the sovereigns "to pull down those disorderly and licentious tyrants" and to establish "the regular execution of the laws." (2.525) The Tudor kings owed their success partly to their own ability and enterprise, but it was due also to other causes. First of all, most of the great barons had been destroyed in the long and bloody civil wars between the House of Lancaster and the House of York. Hume reports that these wars are "computed to have cost the lives of eighty princes of the blood, and almost entirely annihilated the ancient nobility of England." (2.443) By the time Henry VII came to the throne, therefore, the power of the nobility had been fatally weakened, and the people were willing to submit to the king's usurpations in order to escape from the turmoil and devastation of war.

The expansion of royal power was favored also by more general causes, which undermined the feudal system on which the power of the barons had depended. Hume gives some credit to the laws of the Tudor monarchs, especially those of Henry VII, for discouraging the nobility from engaging retainers and for permitting them to break the ancient entails and to alienate their estates. Yet continuing improvements in the arts and commerce were more important than the severities of law in disrupting feudal ties and changing what Hume calls the "manners" of the age. As these improvements made new luxuries and refinements available,

> [t]he nobility, instead of vying with each other, in the number and boldness of their retainers, acquired by degrees a more civilized species of emulation, and endeavoured to excel in the splendour and elegance of their equipage, houses, and tables. (3.76)

These new expenditures by the nobles had the effect both of dissipating their own great fortunes and of encouraging industry among the common people. The mechanics and merchants who subsisted from these expenditures "lived in an independant manner on the fruits of their own industry," and the nobles were unable to exercise over them the unlimited authority that they had once held over their servants and retainers. (4.384) The landed proprietors, having now a greater demand for money than for men, sought to turn their land to the most profitable use. Enclosing their fields or joining small farms into larger ones, they dismissed those useless hands who formerly had been available for military purposes. These changes in the "manners" of the age would, by Hume's reckoning, have far-reaching consequences:

> By all these means the cities encreased; the middle rank of men began to be rich and powerful; the prince, who, in effect, was the same with the law, was implicitly obeyed; and though the farther progress of the same causes begat a new plan of liberty, founded on the privileges of the commons, yet in the interval between the fall of the nobles and the rise of this order, the sovereign took advantage of the present situation, and assumed an authority almost absolute. (4.384)

The power of the king had scarcely ever been so absolute, since the establishment of the Magna Carta, as it became during the reign of Henry VII. The weakness of the barons and the submissiveness of the people enabled Henry to exalt "his prerogative above law." (3.74) His successor,

Henry VIII, exercised an "absolute, uncontrouled authority" over his subjects. (3.321) From the fact that the subjects of this prince continued to feel some measure of love and affection for him, Hume concludes that the English, in that age, "were so thoroughly subdued, that, like eastern slaves, they were inclined to admire those acts of violence and tyranny, which were exercised over themselves, and at their own expence." (3.322–23)

Nonetheless, Hume in large measure approves, or at least excuses, these extensions of the royal prerogative on the ground that they were necessary at the time, even though they would not be conducive to liberty under better circumstances. For example, in discussing the reign of Elizabeth, Hume says of the Court of Star Chamber that this court alone in any government would "put an end to all regular, legal, and exact plans of liberty." (4.356) The reason for this judgment is not hard to see. The Star Chamber possessed an unlimited discretionary authority to impose penalties for a variety of offences not reached by the common law; and its members consisted of men who enjoyed their offices during the king's pleasure. The king himself was, in fact, the sole judge when he was present. Early in the reign of Henry VII, parliament confirmed in some cases the authority of the Star Chamber. In a note concerning this action, Hume observes:

> It must indeed be confessed, that such a state of the country required great discretionary power in the sovereign; nor will the same maxims of government suit such a rude people, that may be proper in a more advanced stage of society. The establishment of the Star-chamber or the enlargement of its power in the reign of Henry VII. might have been as wise as the abolition of it in that of Charles I. (3.469)

Later, in discussing the prospect of violence from opposing religious sects during the reign of Henry VIII, Hume affirms that "in this dangerous conjuncture, nothing ensured public tranquillity so much as the decisive authority acquired by the king, and his great ascendant over all his subjects." (3.227)

The broad implications of Hume's volumes on the Tudor constitution come to light most fully in his treatment of Elizabeth. In his initial volumes on the Stuarts, Hume had challenged the prevailing Whig view that James I and Charles I tried to extend royal power and that parliament opposed them out of a desire to preserve limits set by the ancient constitution. By Hume's account, James and Charles were seeking only to maintain the crown's established prerogatives, so that parliament, and not these two monarchs, was the real aggressor and innovator. Hume is able to support this argument in his volumes on the Tudors by demonstrating that royal power had become virtually absolute before the accession of James I. Elizabeth's reign is crucial, because the Whigs had bestowed "unbounded panegyrics" on her virtue and wisdom as a way of casting blame on the Stuarts. (4.354) In fact, as Hume shows, Elizabeth supported the enormous prerogatives that had been transmitted to her by previous kings; and she exercised the royal authority in a manner "contrary to all the ideas, which we at present entertain of a legal constitution." (4.354) Elizabeth was no less arbitrary than her predecessors. Her immense popularity with her subjects is a sign not that she protected their liberties, but that the "inclination towards liberty" ran very low at that time. (5.558) Hume's Whig readers must have found particularly galling his suggestion that we must study this government – the one that Elizabeth inherited and jealously maintained – if we want to understand England's "ancient constitution."

Hume illustrates the broad scope of royal power at this time by recounting some of the prerogatives that Elizabeth enjoyed. In addition to her Court of Star Chamber, which rendered arbitrary judgment on civil offenses, the Court of High Commission exercised jurisdiction over the crime of heresy. Martial law powers could be used to inflict swift punishments on the pretext of insurrection or public disorder. On warrant of a secretary of state or the privy council, any person could be imprisoned during any time that the ministers thought proper, and torture could be used to obtain confessions. Jurors could be punished, at the discretion of the court, for rendering a verdict contrary to the judges' direction. Any person could be pressed into sea or land service or obliged to accept any office, however mean or unfit for him. Although the sovereign could not impose taxes without parliament's consent, she had many other ways to extort money arbitrarily from her subjects. She could, for example, exact interest-free loans, which often were not repaid, demand benevolences, or seize goods by perveyance and preemption. Monopolies could be erected and patents granted for exclusive trade. When estates were inherited by minors, wardships were established; and the whole profit of the estate during the minority went to the crown. Merchandise could be embargoed until the needs of the court were supplied. Although the legislative power supposedly rested in parliament, the sovereign could, by the dispensing power, invalidate all the laws and render them of no effect. Moreover, she could issue proclamations on any matter, and the Star Chamber saw to it that they were executed more rigorously than the laws themselves. Without the sovereign's consent, no member of the nobility could marry; no person could enter or leave the kingdom; and no commodity could be imported or exported. Particular persons could be exempted from all lawsuits and prosecutions by warrant of the queen. These prerogatives, all later abolished, were at that time the foundation of the sovereign's "most absolute authority." In Hume's judgment, each and every one of them was "totally incompatible with the liberty of the subject." (4.367; see 4.355–67)

In order to round out the picture of the Tudor constitution, we must give some attention to the position of the parliament and the situation of the people. The parliament, which had come to enjoy considerable independence and power during late-feudal times, was now, in a great degree, "the organ of royal will and pleasure." (5.557) Monarchs now possessed revenues sufficient for their ordinary expenses, and they were no longer required to meet parliamentary requests in order to obtain supplies. The parliament complied blindly with the monarch's caprices, for "opposition would have been regarded as a species of rebellion." (5.557) Its statutes paid no regard to the safety or liberty of subjects. Thus under Elizabeth, the parliament provided for the persecution of papists and Puritans, and it acknowledged the Queen's inherent right to an unlimited supremacy. (See 4.366) Among the people themselves, the spirit of liberty was almost extinguished. In keeping with his principle that government rests only on opinion, Hume declares that the established principles of the times, which attributed an unlimited and indefeasible power to the prince, were more effectual than even the royal prerogative in insuring the slavery of the people. The clergy were required to read each Sunday, in all the churches, homilies that inculcated a blind and unswerving obedience to the prince; and this principle was imbibed so thoroughly that the people came to regard any opposition to it as the most flagrant sedition. (See 4.367–68)

Hume does find one notable and, in the long run, crucially important exception to this general servility of the populace in the Tudor age. In writing of Elizabeth's reign, he observes:

So absolute, indeed, was the authority of the crown, that the precious spark of liberty had been kindled, and was preserved, by the puritans alone; and it was to this sect, whose principles appear so frivolous and habits so ridiculous, that the English owe the whole freedom of their constitution. (4.145–46)

This statement reminds us that religious belief is, for Hume, a very powerful force in human affairs. Hume divides such belief into two basic types, which he calls "superstition" and "enthusiasm." Whereas superstition encourages deference to both civil and ecclesiastical authority, enthusiasm naturally resists established ceremonies, rites, and forms, for these constrain its rapturous flights and ecstasies. In Hume's view, Christian beliefs, up to the time of the Reformation, were very largely of the superstitious variety, and they tended to support the authority of the crown as well as that of the prelates of the church. The Protestant sects, however, were mostly enthusiastic in their discipline and mode of worship, and their adherents were inspired to question established authority. The Puritans were one of these enthusiastic sects. Having come under Calvinist influence, they insisted on carrying the reformation of the Church of England even further than it had been taken under Henry VIII and Elizabeth. Much to Elizabeth's displeasure, the principles of civil liberty were strongly embraced by the Puritans. Hume gives as an example the speech delivered to the parliament in 1576 by Peter Wentworth, which contained "a rude sketch of those principles of liberty, which happily gained afterwards the ascendant in England." (4.178) Wentworth objected to the Queen's practice of forbidding the parliament to discuss or treat such matters as she wished to withdraw from their consideration, and he defended the right of members of parliament to speak freely and even to criticize the policies of the crown. For his speech, which displeased the Commons as well as the crown, Wentworth was imprisoned for a month, until released with a stern warning by the Queen. (See 4.178–81) The Puritans nevertheless continued on a course that would eventually bring them great power in the nation:

> actuated by that zeal which belongs to innovators, and by the courage which enthusiasm inspires, they hazarded the utmost indignation of their sovereign; and employing all their industry to be elected into parliament; a matter not difficult, while a seat was rather regarded as a burthen than an advantage; they first acquired a majority in that assembly, and then obtained an ascendant over the church and monarchy. (4.146)

In the next generation, "the noble principles of liberty" would take root and spread themselves "under the shelter of puritanical absurdities," until they "became fashionable among the people." (4.368)

The Establishment of England's "Present Plan of Liberty"

With Elizabeth's death in 1603, her kinsman James, king of Scots, succeeded to the English throne; and the crown passed peacefully from the family of Tudor to that of Stuart. To all appearances, and certainly by his own reckoning, James I inherited as well the vast prerogative that Elizabeth had exercised over her obedient subjects. James's power seemed, at the beginning of his reign, to be almost unlimited or absolute. Yet within the span of less than fifty years, the house of Commons would force James's successor, Charles I, to surrender most of these prerogatives. After defeating his forces in a long and bloody civil war, it would bring Charles to trial and execute him on a charge of treason. It would abolish the monarchy, the house of peers, and the ecclesiastical hierarchy and transform the constitution into a popular government or commonwealth. The next forty years, from 1749 to 1789, would bring constitutional changes no less drastic. The Stuart monarchy would be restored, following Cromwell's rise and fall as military dictator. Charles II and his successor, James II, would try to reassert the old prerogatives; but the parliament, apprehensive of James's use of his powers and his encouragement of Roman Catholicism, would depose him and bestow the English crown on William and Mary, the prince and princess of Orange.

In Hume's view, the great force behind these constitutional struggles was the nation's newly-awakened desire for liberty. The great problem was to accommodate this desire while at the same time preserving a due regard for authority. The conflict over the proper boundaries of liberty and authority would rage in England throughout the seventeenth century. Hume's account of this conflict can be divided conveniently into three main periods. In the first period, which concludes about 1641, the crown's vast prerogatives are curtailed and the monarch is brought under the limitations of the law. In the second, which lasts from 1641 to 1660, the zeal for liberty is carried to a destructive extreme, with the result that the nation is subjected to a tyranny far more oppressive than anything it complained of under the Stuart kings. In the third period, which culminates with the Revolution Settlement of 1689, liberty and authority are at last combined in a just and stable balance. Let us examine each of these periods in turn.

1. *1603 to 1641*. Hume's account of the early Stuart monarchs, aside from being the part of the *History* that he wrote first, was surely also the most controversial part of that work. These monarchs had long been portrayed in Whig writings as tyrants, who had tried to extend the royal power and make it absolute, in violation of the ancient constitution. The house of Commons was applauded for its decisiveness in opposing them, and Charles's fate was said to be appropriate for one who had violated the established liberties of his people. Hume replies that it is unjust to decry these monarchs so violently and throw all of the blame on their side. Their administration was not, as Whig writers have claimed, "one continued encroachment on the *incontestable* rights of the people." (6.531) Hume defends the first two Stuarts as largely well-intentioned and virtuous rulers, who had the misfortune of coming to power when "the conjunctures of the times" were unfavorable to pretensions of absolute power.

Hume denies that James and Charles tried to extend their powers in an unconstitutional way. The truth of the matter, he argues, is that they sought only to exercise prerogatives that they had inherited from Elizabeth. The people had been entirely satisfied with her government and had applauded it. It was natural, therefore, for the Stuarts to take the government as they found it and to try to rule in the same way that Elizabeth had done. (See 5.558; 5.572) Hume likewise rejects Whig claims that James I and Charles I violated the nation's "ancient constitution." He shows that the Whigs here were only echoing a claim made earlier by "the country party," which had first emerged in the house of Commons during the reign of James I. The leaders of the country party had justified their opposition to the king on the ground that they were attempting to restore ancient rights or liberties of the people and the Commons. Hume points out that the ancient constitution – by which, at this early point in the writing of the *History*, he means the constitution as it existed before the Stuart accession – is quite ambiguous, so that the Stuart monarchs could find ample support in it for their lofty ideas of monarchical power. In fact, the leaders of the Commons "less aspired at maintaining the ancient constitution, than at establishing a new one, and a freer, and a better." (5.42) There is no doubt in Hume's mind as to who the aggressor was in the great constitutional struggle between the first two Stuarts and the people: "[I]t was the people who encroached upon the sovereign; not the sovereign, who attempted, as is pretended, to usurp upon the people."[19] Hume concludes that James I was in practice a weak and inoffensive ruler, despite his attachment to "a speculative system of absolute government." (See 5.19; 5.121–22) Charles I was a man of considerable virtues, and his reign would have been a happy one if he had been born either as an absolute prince or as one whose prerogatives were fixed and certain. Unhappily, his fate "threw him into a period when the precedents of many former reigns favoured strongly of arbitrary power, and the genius of the people ran violently towards liberty." (5.543) As for the allegation that Charles governed by arbitrary principles, Hume ventures to say that

> the greatest enemies of this prince will not find, in the long line of his predecessors, from the conquest to his time, any one king, except perhaps his father, whose administration was not more arbitrary and less legal, or whose conduct could have been recommended to him by the popular party themselves, as a model, in this particular, for his government. (5.583)

As we see, the rapid decline of royal power after Elizabeth's death could have been arrested, if at all, only by monarchs of exceptional ability; and the first two Stuarts were not of this type. The question remains, however, as to why the times were so unfavorable to the maintenance of the crown's old prerogatives. One reason for the Stuarts' difficulties was the continuing shift in the balance of property toward the Commons. As Hume remarks, "[n]o one was at that time sufficiently sensible of the great weight which the commons bore in the balance of the constitution." (5.170) Whereas Elizabeth had been able to avoid a dependence on the Commons by using her resources frugally, the Stuarts had greater needs, especially during times of war, and they were often extravagant in their expenditures. Lacking sufficient revenues and having no standing army to impose their will, the Stuarts were forced to turn to the Commons for supplies. The leaders of the newly-formed "country party" shrewdly exploited the crown's necessities, and also exacerbated them, in order to make it surrender its prerogative powers. Hume describes the motives of these men as follows:

> Animated with a warm regard to liberty, these generous patriots saw with regret an unbounded power exercised by the crown, and were resolved to seize the opportunity which the king's necessities offered them, of reducing the prerogative within more reasonable compass. Though their ancestors had blindly given way to practices and precedents favourable to kingly power, and had been able, not-

withstanding, to preserve some small remains of liberty; it would be impossible, they thought, when all these pretensions were methodized and prosecuted by the encreasing knowledge of the age, to maintain any shadow of popular government, in opposition to such unlimited authority in the sovereign. It was necessary to fix a choice: Either to abandon entirely the privileges of the people, or to secure them by firmer and more precise barriers than the constitution had hitherto provided for them. In this dilemma, men of such aspiring geniuses and such independent fortunes could not long deliberate: They boldly embraced the side of freedom, and resolved to grant no supplies to their necessitous prince without extorting concessions in favour of civil liberty. (5.160)

The increasing property of the Commons and the high capacity of its leaders were necessary conditions, but by no means sufficient ones, for its ascending power. We must remember that for Hume, the authority of government rests chiefly on opinion. The rise of the Commons was possible only because the opinions that had favored Elizabeth's broad prerogatives were somehow radically altered in the four decades that followed her death. One way to describe this alteration is to say, as Hume does, that opinions came increasingly to be shaped by the spirit of liberty. At the time of James I's accession, the principles of liberty had been adopted by "men of genius and enlarged minds," such as Sir Francis Bacon and Sir Edwin Sandys, but as yet they were "pretty much unknown to the generality of the people." (5.550) A jealousy of liberty grew quickly in the Commons, however, and by the time that Charles I succeeded to the throne, "the spirit of liberty was universally diffused." (5.179) Charles had the misfortune to govern in "a period when the precedents of many former reigns favoured strongly of arbitrary power, and the genius of the people ran violently towards liberty." (5.543) Even the bulk of the nobility and gentry who sided with Charles

> breathed the spirit of liberty, as well as of loyalty: And in the hopes alone of his submitting to a legal and limited government, were they willing, in his defence, to sacrifice their lives and fortunes. (5.394)

Yet to say that opinion shifted in favor of liberty is not to identify the teachings and practices that brought this change about. Hume attributes this shift in opinion to several sources. The revival of classical literature was one important source of the new regard for liberty, especially among men of learning: "A familiar acquaintance with the precious remains of antiquity excited, in every generous breast, a passion for a limited constitution..." (5.18–19) For the commercial part of the nation, "the new splendour and glory of the Dutch commonwealth, where liberty so happily supported industry," was an attractive example; and they hoped to see "a like form of government established in England." (5.387) Certainly the most important source of the new spirit of liberty, however, was theological doctrine. As we have seen, Hume gives great credit to the Puritans for nurturing civil liberty. In Stuart as well as Elizabethan times, *puritanical* principles were understood to favor both political and ecclesiastical liberty. The Puritans' opposition to the hierarchy of the established church and the persecutions under which they labored were sufficient to throw them

> into the country party, and to beget political principles little favourable to the high pretensions of the sovereign. The spirit too of enthusiasm; bold, daring, and uncontrouled; strongly disposed their minds to adopt republican tenets; and inclined them to arrogate, in their actions and conduct, the same liberty, which they assumed in their rapturous flight and ecstasies. (5.558–59)

The Presbyterians and Independents were also led, by their opposition to the governance of the established church, to oppose the monarch and embrace republican principles. Hume thus concludes that "theological zeal," rather than political motives, was mainly responsible for the great change in opinion that elevated the Commons, destroyed absolute monarchy, and plunged the nation into civil war. As he points out, all authors of the time "represent the civil disorders and convulsions as proceeding from religious controversy, and consider the political disputes about power and liberty as entirely subordinate to the other." (5.303; see 5.380, 5.572)

What judgment does Hume finally render on the great conflict between the first Stuart kings and the Commons? We must notice, first of all, that he takes great pains to present this conflict as it was viewed by the contending sides and to bring out the principles by which each side justified its cause. Both sides in this conflict turned for justification to the same sources, to ancient constitutional practice and to divine revelation. From Hume's standpoint, of course, the arguments from revelation were completely without merit; and the arguments from "the ancient constitution" were inconclusive, since at least as strong a case could be made, on constitutional grounds, for the prerogatives of the crown as for the rights of the people and the Commons. Hume's critics charged that he supported the Stuart cause, but in fact what he did was to show that the case made by the crown was as strong, or at least no weaker, than the case made by the other side.

In order to reach a final judgment on the conflict between king and Commons, Hume, as a philosophical historian, was forced to transcend the ground on which the contending parties had struggled, since neither ancient practices nor principles of revelation could settle the matter. Hume's judgment was guided, finally, by philosophical reflections on the nature of good government. Good government requires the proper balance between liberty and authority, and just where this balance lies will depend on the circumstances of the time.

At the conclusion of his treatment of the four Stuart reigns, Hume charges that the Whig ascendancy in government, for a period of nearly seventy years, has "proved destructive to the truth of history, and has established many gross falsehoods, which it is unacountable how any civilized nation could have embraced with regard to its domestic occurrences." (6.533) He then goes on to make this interesting observation, which indicates how he approached the writing of his own history of the Stuarts:

> And forgetting that a regard to liberty, though a laudable passion, ought commonly to be subordinate to a reverence for established government, the prevailing faction has celebrated only the partizans of the former, who pursued as their object the perfection of civil society, and has extolled them at the expence of their antagonists, who maintained those maxims that are essential to its very existence. (6.533)

The Whigs, in their immoderate attacks on the Stuarts, had brought all authority into question. Hume thus gives the Stuarts their due, not because he values liberty any less than the Whigs did, but because he thinks it important to uphold authority in government.

Even though Hume might seem in large measure to vindicate the first Stuarts, the weight of his approval comes down finally on the side of the Commons, certainly up to 1628, when the Petition of Right was enacted, and even up to 1641. Hume judged that by the time the Stuarts came to power, conditions in England no longer required such a broad prerogative as the Stuarts had inherited. In the Tudor period, an "authority almost absolute of the sovereigns" had been required to pull down the turbulent aristocracy and establish the "regular execution of the laws," but once this was accomplished, the people could proceed "to erect a regular and equitable plan of liberty." (2.525) In reflecting on what "the wise and moderate in the nation" might have thought of the breach between James I and the country party in the parliament, Hume writes:

> From long practice, the crown was now possessed of so exorbitant a prerogative, that it was not sufficient for liberty to remain on the defensive, or endeavour to secure the little ground, which was left her: It was become necessary to carry on an offensive war, and to circumscribe, within more narrow, as well as more exact bounds, the authority of the sovereign.[20]

The house of Commons was quite justified, therefore, in circumscribing the royal prerogative so as to protect the liberties of the subject. In Hume's view, the assent of Charles I to the Petition of Right "produced such a change in the government, as was almost equivalent to a revolution." (5.200) This was "the epoch of true liberty, confirmed by the Restoration, and enlarged and secured by the Revolution." (2.536) What is striking, however, is that Hume is willing to approve even the harsher steps that the Commons took, as late as 1640–41, to limit the king's prerogative, such as: requiring triennial parliaments; forbidding the king to adjourn, prorogue, or dissolve parliament, after it was assembled, during a period of fifty days; and abolishing the Courts of High Commission and Star Chamber.

Hume's observations on this period of English history are of utmost importance in understanding his conception of liberty. Nowhere in Hume's *History* or in his other writings do we find a thematic discussion of what civil liberty is. In fact, his general view of philosophy discourages speculation about the essences or "whats" of things and directs inquiry instead to their genesis and their associations. Nevertheless, the *History* clearly presupposes a conception of liberty, and we must try to understand what it is. Although Hume often uses the term *liberty* in a way synonymous with *licentiousness*, as when he speaks of the way of life of the ancient Britons and Saxons or of the Norman barons, he does not approve liberty of this type. It leaves individuals largely unregulated by laws and government, so that while they might enjoy wide freedom to do as they please, they are exposed to harm from others who possess an equal freedom. True liberty, as Hume understands it, incorporates the restraints of law. It requires such limitations as are necessary to make the individual secure from harm, whether from other individuals or from government. It is liberty, in this sense, that Hume has in mind when he uses such phrases as "a regular plan of law and liberty" or "the plan ... of regular and rigid liberty." (See 5.308 and 5.281)

Perhaps the closest that Hume comes anywhere to an implicit definition of liberty is this comment on a bill passed under James I against monopolies:

> It was there supposed, that every subject of England had entire power to dispose of his own actions, provided he did no injury to any of his fellow-subjects; and that no prerogative of the king, no power of any magistrate, nothing but the authority alone of laws, could restrain that unlimited freedom. The full prosecution of this noble principle into all its natural consequences, has at last, through many contests, produced that singular and happy government, which we enjoy at present. (5.114)

Liberty, in the strict sense of the term, seems to require an adherence to law so rigid as to exclude executive prerogative entirely. This helps to explain why Hume ultimately takes the side of the Commons against the early Stuarts, even though he can blame the Commons for some of its extreme actions, such as the attainder of the Earl of Strafford, and can appreciate the constitutional ground on which the Stuarts based their claim to absolute power. In the final analysis, however, Hume does not exclude prerogative as completely as the above statement might lead one to think, for to do so would cripple that authority on which the very existence of liberty depends.

In both the *Essays* and the *History*, Hume indicates the relationship of liberty and authority by this formula: liberty is "the perfection of civil society," while authority is "essential to its very existence."[21] The first part of this formula suggests that liberty is not merely an instrumental good, but is somehow the crowning good of society. In keeping with this suggestion, Hume observes that England, under Charles I, enjoyed peace, industry, commerce, opulence and, in large measure, justice and lenity of administration: "All these were enjoyed by the people; and every other blessing of government, except liberty, or rather the present exercise of liberty, and its proper security." (5.250) The point is that civil society remains incomplete without liberty, even though it can enjoy the other goods in a considerable degree. The second part of Hume's formula makes it clear, however, that liberty must be counterbalanced by authority and a respect for established government. In Hume's view, the Whigs had forgotten this requirement; and his own *History*, especially in its treatment of the Stuarts and the Commonwealth, seeks to reaffirm it.

Hume appears to set very strict limits to authority when he insists that the freedom of individuals can be limited only by the laws, and not by a prerogative or discretionary power in the executive. He surely regarded this as a salutary teaching, but it is doubtful that he thought it to be strictly true. Thus he writes: "In every government, necessity, when real, supersedes all laws, and levels all limitations." (5.128) Prerogative becomes objectionable when it can be exercised merely at the executive's convenience. In commending the parliament for abolishing the Court of Star Chamber, which had punished infractions of the king's edicts, Hume goes on to reflect that there has never yet been a government

> which subsisted without the mixture of some arbitrary authority, committed to some magistrate; and it might reasonably, beforehand, appear doubtful, whether human society could ever reach that state of perfection, as to support itself with no other controul than the general and rigid maxims of law and equity. But the parliament justly thought, that the king was too eminent a magistrate to be trusted with discretionary power, which he might so easily turn to the destruction of liberty. And in the event it has hitherto been found, that, though some sensible inconveniences arise from the maxim of adhering strictly to law, yet the advantages over-balance them, and should render the English grateful to the memory of their ancestors, who, after repeated contests, at last established that noble, though dangerous, principle. (5.329–30)

We note here that a strict adherence to law by the executive is called a "noble" principle. Hume does not speak of it as true, and he says quite clearly that it is "dangerous."

2. *1641 to 1660.* Although Hume gives at least a qualified approval to the steps taken by the Commons, as late as 1640–41, to curb the king's prerogative, he judges the subsequent actions of the popular leaders very harshly. In particular, he criticizes those leaders, such as John Hambden, who sought the total annihilation of monarchical power, even after it was clear that the king no longer posed a danger to the people. By undertaking measures that would lead to a civil war and the numberless ills inseparable from it, these men "exposed liberty to much greater perils

than it could have incurred under the now limited authority of the king." (5.574) Moreover, these measures, so perilous to liberty, were pursued in the name of liberty itself. The fate of liberty continued to be Hume's principal concern as he turned to the Civil War and to the regime that followed it. Just as he had used the reigns of the early Stuarts to bring out the true character of liberty, he uses these later developments to show where an immoderate zeal for liberty can lead. Liberty is a great good for human beings and, indeed, is the perfection of society, but it becomes very dangerous when it throws off all established authority. Hume's *History* is intended, therefore, both to commend liberty and to warn against its abuses.

Hume makes it quite clear that the spirit of liberty must itself share in the blame for the Civil War and its aftermath. Thus he speaks of "that slavery, into which the nation, from the too eager pursuit of liberty, had fallen." (5.502) The Long Parliament, after making a violent attack on kingly power and involving the nation in war, "had finally lost that liberty, for which they had so imprudently contended." (6.174) England had never known a more severe and arbitrary government "than was generally exercised, by the patrons of liberty." (5.528) Nevertheless, Hume did not think that the spirit of liberty produced these evils by itself; for as he shows, it was powerfully augmented by religious zeal and by the desire for equality and republican government.

In explaining the rising tide of opposition to James I and Charles I, Hume had emphasized that the demand for civil liberty was linked very closely to religious enthusiasm and the distaste for ecclesiastical hierarchy. He continues to make this point in his account of the Civil War and the Commonwealth. Thus he suggests that for the people, the controversy with the king was "entirely theological." (5.572) He says of the soldiers in the parliamentary army that "[r]eligion and liberty were the motives, which had excited them to arms." (5.494) Of the Commonwealth period, he writes: "Religion can never be deemed a point of small consequence in civil government: But during this period, it may be regarded as the great spring of men's actions and determinations." (6.86) Hume undoubtedly believed that the wild fury and fanaticism which the partisans of liberty exhibited was due in large measure to their religion. It is unlikely that the generality of the nation could ever "have flown out into such fury, in order to obtain new privileges and acquire greater liberty than they and their ancestors had ever been acquainted with." (5.572)

The interesting question is whether or not Hume would grant that the zeal for personal and civil liberty can burn this fiercely by itself, without the fuel of religion. Since Hume's time, revolutions undertaken in the name of liberty have often exhibited this same fury and fanaticism, even though they have had a secular and even anti-religious character. Hume does acknowledge that there were, during the Commonwealth period, republican writers, such as James Harrington and Algernon Sidney, who "had no other object than political liberty" and who "denied entirely the truth of revelation." (6.59) Nevertheless, it is clear from his account that the most important leaders of the time were strongly under the influence of religious enthusiasm. Hume may have anticipated the secular or political enthusiasm that would erupt later in France and elsewhere, but in speaking of seventeenth-century England, he emphasizes that the spirit of liberty became destructive because of its unfortunate association with religious zealotry.

The spirit of liberty was also reinforced in England at this time by a keen desire for popular government and political equality. According to Hume, the current for popular government was so strong "that the most established maxims of policy were every where abandoned, in order to gratify this ruling passion." (5.337) A "total confusion of all rank and order was justly to be apprehended" from the "democratical, enthusiastic spirit." (5.361) In fact, the Independents, who were "more ardent in the pursuit of liberty" than even the Presbyterians, advanced just such a program. This party sought to abolish the aristocracy as well as the monarchy, and it "projected an entire equality of rank and order, in a republic, quite free and independent." (5.443) Within the army, the Levellers supported the demand for equal power and called in addition for "an universal equality of property." (5.513) Perhaps Hume would have granted that in the absence of religious motives, the passion for equality and popular government can blend with the spirit of liberty and drive it to dangerous extremes. We cannot infer this from the present discussion, however, because this passion, in seventeenth-century England, took an overtly religious form.

The relationship of liberty to equality and popular government is for Hume a complex one. It is obvious that he did not follow radical opinion of the seventeenth century in simply equating them; for if he had done so, he could not have argued, as he does in the *History*, that England's mixed constitution provides more liberty than any government ever known to man. The fact is, however, that Hume himself, in his *Essays*, describes the "perfect commonwealth" as a republic, in which all officials must be elected annually.[22] Hume thus agrees, in principle, with the most radical opponents of the Stuart monarchy that a republic is the simply best form of government. He disagrees, of course, with their claim that republics are the only legitimate forms of government. The principle that "the people are the origin of all just power" is noble in itself and seems plausible, but it is "belied by all history and experience." (5.533) He disagrees also with the radical republicans on the feasibility of ever establishing a perfect commonwealth, especially in England. In the *History*, Hume brings out the differences between his own view of government and that of the radical republicans, but needless to say, he is silent about his very striking agreement with them in regard to the simply best constitution. Thus while he grants that Harrington's *Oceana* is "a work of genius and invention," he cautions that the idea "of a perfect and immortal commonwealth will always be found as chimerical as that of a perfect and immortal man." (6.153)

Hume's *History* treats republicanism not as a theoretical issue, but as a problem to be understood within the framework of England's mixed constitution. As we have seen, the English constitution, at least since late-feudal times, had been an uneasy mixture of monarchy, aristocracy, and democracy. The problem in maintaining such a constitution is to prevent any one of these elements from gaining a dominant position and using its power abusively. Thus "every well regulated constitution" will guard equally against "the tyranny of princes," "the turbulence of the great," and the "madness of the people." (2.174) In former periods, a preponderance of power had been enjoyed first by the great barons and then by the monarchs, but each of these elements of the constitution had been brought under control. What happened in the mid-seventeenth century is that the popular element, after imposing strict limits on the prerogative of the crown, went on to usurp total power and thus to change a mixed government into a republic. The events of this period serve, in fact, to instruct us concerning "the madness of the people, the furies of fanaticism, and the danger of mercenary armies." (5.546) Yet Hume places the blame for this not so much on the people as on their leaders. Later, in writing of medieval England, he would observe:

But of all the evils incident to human society, the insurrections of the populace, when not raised and supported by persons of higher quality, are the least to be dreaded: The mischiefs, consequent to an abolition of all rank and distinction, become so great, that they are immediately felt, and soon bring affairs back to their former order and arrangement. (2.293)

In a similar vein, he notes that while the fury of the populace is "the most dangerous of all instruments," the people are "the least answerable for their excesses." (2.170) What Hume fears is not so much the tyranny of the people as the tyranny of popular assemblies, dominated by leaders who claim to speak for the people. Popular assemblies are, by their size, exempt in great measure from the restraint of shame; and when they "overleap the bounds of law," they "naturally break out into acts of the greatest tyranny and injustice." (5.457) The people of England, during the reigns of the first Stuarts, can be excused for not recognizing this danger:

> The veneration for parliaments was at this time extreme throughout the nation. The custom of reviling those assemblies for corruption, as it had no pretence, so was it unknown, during all former ages. Few or no instances of their encroaching ambition or selfish claims had hitherto been observed. Men considered the house of commons, in no other light than as the representatives of the nation, whose interest was the same with that of the public, who were the eternal guardians of law and liberty, and whom no motive, but the necessary defence of the people, could ever engage in an opposition to the crown. The torrent, therefore, of general affection, ran to the parliament. (5.388–89)

The experience of the Civil War and the Commonwealth instructed the people on the dangers of popular assemblies and showed them that their liberties could best be safeguarded by restoring a mixed constitution.

There are several other points about Hume's account of events in England between 1641 and 1660 that deserve our attention. First, what happened was a constitutional change of the most fundamental character, involving the way of life of the people as well as their political institutions: "No people could undergo a change more sudden and entire in their manners, than did the English nation during this period." They passed in an instant "to a state of faction, fanaticism, rebellion, and almost frenzy," and social relationships were torn asunder by the violence of the parties. (6.141)

Second, this fanatical spirit seized the republican leaders in particular and shaped their thought and actions. Hume declares that "[n]o character in human society is more dangerous than that of the fanatic." (6.113) This section of the *History* provides us with valuable insights into this character. One quality of fanatics or enthusiasts is that they are likely to be the dupes of their own zeal and not cynical hypocrites. They disguise even to themselves the extent to which their actions are governed by interest and ambition. (See 5.572) Moreover, they invoke high moral purposes in order to excuse the most despicable acts of immorality. Hume says of Ireton, Cromwell's son-in-law and lieutenant, that "in prosecution of his imagined religious purposes, he thought himself dispensed from all the ordinary rules of morality, by which inferior mortals must allow themselves to be governed." (5.514) Because of the predominancy of enthusiasm among the parliamentary forces, moral principles lost their credit and came to be regarded as mere human inventions, fitter for heathens than for Christians:

> The saint, resigned over to superior guidance, was at full liberty to gratify all his appetites, disguised under the appearance of pious zeal. And, besides the strange corruptions engendered by this spirit, it eluded and loosened all the ties of morality, and gave entire scope, and even sanction, to the selfishness and ambition which naturally adhere to the human mind. (5.493–94)

Third, the republican leaders deprived the people of their liberties in the very name of liberty itself. The people of England and Scotland had never known "a more severe and arbitrary government, than was generally exercised by the patrons of liberty." (5.528) The parliamentary leaders pretended to bestow new liberties on the nation, but "they found themselves obliged to infringe even the most valuable of those which, through time immemorial, had been transmitted from their ancestors." (6.39) The law of high treason was extended to comprehend "verbal offences, nay intentions, though they had never appeared in any overt-act against the state." (6.13) Nevertheless, these leaders, "who possessed little of the true spirit of liberty, knew how to maintain the appearance of it." (6.44) The "masque of liberty" was not thrown aside until Cromwell dissolved the parliament and established a military government for the entire nation. (6.74) The fanatical republicans probably acted more from self-deception, however, than from hypocrisy. They actually believed that a more perfect system of liberty could be imposed on the nation "by the terror of the sword" or by "arbitrary power." (5.509; 5.514)

Fourth, the furious animosities of the several factions brought affairs to such a pass that "the extensive authority and even arbitrary power of some first magistrate was become a necessary evil, in order to keep the people from relapsing into blood and confusion." (6.65) When the right moment came, Cromwell, who had secretly paved the way to his own unlimited authority, seized control.

Interestingly enough, Hume finds some merit in Cromwell's plea that his usurpation was required by necessity and the public good, although he refuses to excuse Cromwell's earlier actions, especially his complicity in the murder of the king. (See 6.65; 6.110) Cromwell's rise to power is for Hume another example to confirm the principle that "illegal violence, with whatever pretences it may be covered, and whatever object it may pursue, must inevitably end at last in the arbitrary and despotic government of a single person." (6.54)

Finally, Hume concludes that the people seldom gain anything by revolutions in government, since "the new settlement, jealous and insecure, must commonly be supported with more expence and severity than the old." (5.520) In reflecting on the consequences that followed from the murder of Charles I, Hume suggests that while it might be true that the people are entitled to judge and punish their sovereign, it is best for speculative reasoners to conceal this truth from the populace. They should "observe, with regard to this principle, the same cautious silence, which the laws, in every species of government, have ever prescribed to themselves." (5.544) In Hume's view,

> the doctrine of obedience ought alone to be *inculcated*, and ... the exceptions, which are rare, ought seldom or never to be mentioned in popular reasonings and discourses. Nor is there any danger, that mankind, by this prudent reserve, should universally degenerate into a state of abject servitude. When the exception really occurs, even though it be not previously expected and descanted on, it must, from its very nature, be so obvious and undisputed, as to remove all doubt, and overpower the restraint, however great, imposed by teaching the general doctrine of obedience. (5.544)

It would be interesting, in an appropriate context, to consider the parallels between these events in mid-seventeenth century England, as Hume describes them, and the pattern of later revolutions that were conducted in the name of liberty or freedom. In fact, Hume's history of the Stuarts was read avidly in France, both before and after the Revolution, with a view to finding or else denying such parallels. Whereas Hume had been applauded earlier by the *philosophes* for his enlightened and sceptical views, French liberal idealists had, by the 1770's and 1780's, become quite wary of the political views expressed in Hume's *History* and had, in many cases, criticized them sharply. Yet French thinkers of the Right, who were appalled by Hume's religious scepticism, nonetheless treated his history of the Stuarts as a prophetic work and drew important counter-revolutionary lessons from it. Laurence L. Bongie, who discusses these French reactions to Hume's *History* in detail, estimates that Hume's influence on rightist literature was "greater before the turn of the century than even the sensational but somewhat speculative impact of Burke."[23] One important French writer who turned to Hume for illumination was Joseph de Maistre, whose *Considerations sur la France* was published in 1797. The final chapter of this book consists entirely of excerpts from the portion of Hume's *History* that we have just considered. It carries the motto: *Eadem Mutata Resurgo* [I rise again, transformed, but the same].[24]

3. *1660 to 1689*. Hume credits the restoration of the Stuart monarchy with ending the sectarian violence and political oppression that had afflicted England since the outbreak of the Civil War. No figure in the entire *History* is praised more highly than General George Monk, who engineered this event. Monk,

> by restoring the ancient and legal and free government to three kingdoms, plunged in the most destructive anarchy, may safely be said to be the subject, in these islands, who, since the beginning of time, rendered the most durable and most essential services to his native country. (6.247)

The restoration of the Stuart line was possible because the parliamentary leaders and the people had been largely cured of their excessive zeal for liberty. The new parliament, recognizing that the Long Parliament, by its violent attack upon kingly power, "had finally lost that liberty, for which they had so imprudently contended," (6.174) went so far as to renounce all right even of defensive arms against the king. Nevertheless, it had no desire to remove the major limitations that earlier parliaments had placed on the royal prerogative. It sought to repair only those breaches "which had been made, not by the love of liberty, but by the fury of faction and civil war." (6.173) The king's restoration received a torrent of support from the people, who dreaded "lest the zeal for liberty should engraft itself on fanaticism, and should once more kindle a civil war in the kingdom." (6.377) Their passion for liberty, "having been carried to such violent extremes, and having produced such bloody commotions, began, by a natural movement, to give place to a spirit of loyalty and obedience." (6.136) In Hume's estimation, this deference to the established government continued to be so great, even after the accession of James II, that this monarch might have succeeded in his designs against the religion and constitution of the country, had not an attack been made from abroad. (See 6.497)

It was in this period that the house of Commons came to be regularly and openly divided into two parties, the court and the country, or, to use the terms that originated around 1680, the Tories and the Whigs. The Tories were generally supportive of the king's policies and opposed to alterations in either civil or ecclesiastical government, while the Whigs, "if they did not still retain some propensity towards a republic, were at least affected with a violent jealousy of regal power." (6.223) Although Hume found much to criticize about these parties and their influence on public affairs, he believed that each of them represents something vital to England's free and mixed constitution:

> In every mixed government, such as that of England, the bulk of the nation will always incline to preserve the entire frame of the constitution; but according to the various prejudices, interests, and dispositions of men, some will ever attach themselves with more passion to the regal, others to the popular, part of the government. (6.375–76)

The country party safeguards the liberties of the people, while the court party gives the crown some measure of control over the actions of the house of Commons. The Commons had been greatly alarmed upon first discovering, during the reign of James I, that the king had undertaken to secure a majority for the court by influencing elections throughout the country. Yet as Hume points out, it was the increasing power of Commons, as evidenced by their refusal to grant supplies, that led the king to take an interest in their elections: "So ignorant were the commons, that they knew not this incident to be the first infallible symptom of any regular or established liberty." (5.58) Each party evokes the other in a free and mixed constitution, just as each keeps the other within its proper boundaries.

In reading Hume's *History*, is essential to keep in mind that he wrote it with a view to preserving a proper balance between the English parties. This practical aim, along with his concern for the truth of history, led him to direct the main force of his criticism against the Whigs. Hume could agree with the Whigs in admiring liberty and republican government, but he resisted their inclination to push these principles to their limit, lest England's mixed constitution be undermined.

Hume is more critical of the later Stuart kings than of the earlier ones, but even so, he is far from agreeing with the Whig opinion that they were great tyrants. Of course, he strongly disapproves of their attempts to reestablish absolute monarchy and to change the established religion; but he excuses, to some extent, Charles II's effort to gain ascendancy over the parliament through his alliance with France. He finds much to admire in the private virtues of both Charles II and James II, even though, to the nation's good fortune, their public conduct was deficient in energy and prudence.

Just as Hume depicts the later Stuarts somewhat more favorably than the Whigs had done, he paints a rather unfavorable picture of some Whig heroes of this period. For example, he is highly critical of Algernon Sidney, "whom the blind prejudices of party had exalted into a hero." (6.317) Even more blameable than Sidney's intrigues with France was his "ingratitude and breach of faith, in applying for the king's pardon, and immediately on his return entering into cabals for rebellion."(6.317) It is true that Sidney's execution, partly on the basis of unpublished discourses whose authorship was uncertain, was a great blemish on the reign of Charles II. The principles of liberty contained in these discourses are "such as the best and most dutiful subjects in all ages have been known to embrace." (6.436) Nevertheless, Sidney's zeal for liberty led him to support extreme measures on behalf of popular government during the Commonwealth period; and when the opportunity arose under Charles II, he "was even willing to seek a second time, through all the horrors of civil war, for his adored republic." (6.435) Since Sidney was a deist, who imbibed his principles of liberty from the great examples of antiquity, Hume may have called attention to his imprudence in order to show that the zeal for liberty and popular government can lead to dangerous extremes, even apart from the influence of religious fanaticism.

We come, finally, to the point at which Hume's own *History* terminates, the Revolution in 1688 and the settlement that it produced. The great achievement of this Revolution was to establish what Hume, on various occasions, refers to as a "regular" plan of liberty. Hume wrote his account of the Revolution in 1688 at a fairly early point in his composition of the *History*, and he had not yet made the distinctions regarding England's earlier constitutional development that he would subsequently employ. Thus when he speaks in this context of "the old English government," he means the constitution that came down from ancient times and was was inherited by the Stuarts in 1603. This old English government had an "irregular nature," in that the unlimited prerogative of the crown subsisted with some degree of liberty in the subject. With "the acquisition of real liberty" during the course of the seventeenth century, men began to see the danger of a such a prerogative. (6.476) Speaking of the events of 1688–89, he writes:

> The revolution alone, which soon succeeded, happily put an end to all these disputes; By means of it, a more uniform edifice was at last erected: The monstrous inconsistence, so visible between the ancient Gothic parts of the fabric and the recent plans of liberty, was fully corrected: And to their mutual felicity, king and people were finally taught to know their proper boundaries. (6.475–76)

A bit later, Hume makes this observation:

> The revolution forms a new epoch in the constitution; and was probably attended with consequences more advantageous to the people, than barely freeing them from an exceptionable administration. By deciding many important questions in favour of liberty, and still more, by that great precedent of deposing one king, and establishing a new family, it gave such an ascendant to popular principles, as has put the nature of the English constitution beyond all controversy. And it may justly be affirmed, without any danger of exaggeration, that we, in this island, have ever since enjoyed, if not the best system of government, at least the most entire system of liberty, that ever was known amongst mankind. (6.531)

These statements suggest that the character of the English constitution was settled by the Revolution in a definitive and final way. One must wonder, however, if Hume does not deliberately overstate his point. As we have seen, the English constitution changed constantly before the Revolution, and Hume gives us some reason to think that these changes will continue. In discussing the reign of Charles I, he writes that "all human governments, particularly those of a mixed frame, are in continual fluctuation." (5.160) Even in the *History*, Hume takes notice of some important constitutional changes that took place after the Revolution. The Revolution Settlement had not resolved the problem of how the king, whose prerogative had been severely curtailed, could establish his authority in the house of Commons. Yet "many accidents" would subsequently throw into the hands of the crown the disposal of a large revenue, which the king's ministers would use to gain control of the Commons. (See 5.569) Moreover, a great increase would occur in religious toleration and in the liberty of the press. These changes are favorable to liberty, and they fit in with the general picture of progress or improvement that Hume's *History* conveys. Yet if Hume had thought that the general direction of change is always beneficial to the cause of liberty and good government, he would have had little reason to praise the Revolution Settlement so highly and to give such strong encouragement to the maintenance of the established order.

If the Revolution Settlement is less stable than Hume might wish his readers to believe, what pressures could change it in an unfavorable way? We note that Hume credits this settlement with establishing "the most entire system of liberty" that mankind has ever known. He does not claim, however, that it produced "the best system of government." As we have noted, Hume says in the *Essays* that the best form of government, in principle, is not a mixed monarchy, but a republic. Even if this had not been Hume's view, it was surely one that enjoyed broad, and growing, support in his time. Yet unlike the doctrinaire republicans, Hume recognized "that, in public deliberations, we seek not the expedient, which is best in itself, but the best of such as are practicable."[25] Hume doubted that a republic was practicable in England, and he did not believe that efforts to establish one would be favorable to liberty. In fact, he asserts in the *Essays* that if and when England's limited monarchy decays, he would wish to see it replaced by an absolute monarchy rather than a republic.[26]

Hume claims that the Revolution "gave such an ascendant to popular principles, as has put the nature of the English constitution beyond all controversy," but surely he knew that this limited monarchy was vulnerable to the charge that it is insufficiently republican. This must be one reason why he directed the weight of his criticism against the Whigs, who were the party of "liberty and a popular government,"(4.354; see 6.531) rather than against the Tories. Hume knew that England's limited monarchy could not be defended effectively unless the cause of liberty were divorced from the cause of popular government.

Notes

1. David Hume, *The History of England from the Invasion of Julius Caesar to the Revolution in 1688*, edited by William B. Todd (Indianapolis: Liberty Classics, 1983–85),

vol. 6, p. 531. Subsequent citations to this edition of the *History* will appear in the text of this essay.

2. Paul Rapin, whose *History of England* was read widely in the eighteenth century, wrote that "whatever changes have occurred in other European nations, the English constitution has remained the same." Quoted in Victor G. Wexler, *David Hume and the History of England* (Philadelphia: The American Philosophical Society, 1979), p. 73. Wexler adds: "… this insistence on the fundamental continuity of English institutions and customs, from Saxon times to the Glorious Revolution, was indeed the hallmark of Whiggery."

3. Quoted as the epigraph to H. Trevor Colbourn, *The Lamp of Experience* (New York: W. W. Norton & Co., 1974).

4. Quoted in Wexler, *David Hume and the History of England*, p. 72.

5. Quoted in Wexler, *David Hume*, pp. 71–72.

6. See J. G. A. Pocock, *The Ancient Constitution and the Feudal Law: A Study of English Historical Thought in the Seventeenth Century* (Cambridge: Cambridge University Press, 1957).

7. (5.569). It should be noted that Hume sometimes speaks of an ancient constitution in something like the Whig sense, even in the volumes of the *History* that were written last. See 2.38 and 2.346.

8. (2.524–25). This may be taken as Hume's mature historical judgment, for it falls in the very last section of the *History* to be published – a retrospective statement that follows the reign of Richard III.

9. Accounts of the Whig view of the Saxon period can be found in Colbourn, *The Lamp of Experience*, pp. 25–32; Wexler, *David Hume and the History of England*, pp. 70–74; and Duncan Forbes, *Hume's Philosophical Politics* (Cambridge: Cambridge University Press, 1975), pp. 233–260. It should be noted that not every Whig between 1680 and the mid-eighteenth century subscribed to this view of England's Saxon past. The most notable exceptions were the writers who, in the 1730's, defended Walpole's ministry against the attacks of Bolingbroke.

10. See Jean-Jacques Rousseau, *The First and Second Discourses*, edited by Roger D. Masters and translated by Roger D. and Judith R. Masters (New York: St. Martin's Press, 1964). The Introduction and Editor's Notes to this edition bring out the ironic character of Rousseau's praise of rude and unenlightened societies.

11. David Hume, *Essays, Moral, Political, and Literary*, edited by Eugene F. Miller (rev. ed.; Indianapolis: Liberty Classics, 1987), p. 277.

12. Early in the reign of William Rufus, the native English people were so thoroughly subjugated by the Normans that "they no longer aspired to the recovery of their ancient liberties, and were content with the prospect of some mitigation in the tyranny of the Norman princes." (1.230)

13. One statement of this view is that by William Petyt, in 1680: "… in the British, Saxon, and Norman Governments, the Commons (as we now phrase them) had Votes, and a share in the making and enacting of Laws for the Government of the Kingdom … before and after the supposed Conquest by King William the First." Quoted in Wexler, *David Hume and the History of England*, p. 77.

14. (1.78). Although Hume praises Anglo-Saxon law here, he depreciates it later in comparison to Roman law. He observes that there was perhaps no event more important to Europe's emergence from barbarism than the accidental discovery of a copy of

Justinian's *Pandects*, about the year 1130, in a town in Italy. What bestowed additional merit on the civil law of Rome was "the extreme imperfection of that jusrisprudence, which preceded it among all the European nations, especially among the Saxons or ancient English." (2.521) Anglo-Saxon law was filled with absurdities, as might be expected at a time when "the judges were rustic freeholders, assembled of a sudden, and deciding a cause from one debate or altercation of the parties." (2.521)

15. (2.141). Hume does go on to acknowledge that Edward's achievements were recognized also by Sir Edward Coke.

16. *Essays, Moral, Political, and Literary*, p. 54.

17. (2.521–22). See also 1.174: "We must conceive, that the ancient Germans were little removed from the original state of nature…"

18. See Pocock, *The Ancient Constitution and the Feudal Law*, pp. 42–45; 53–55; 192–93; Wexler, *David Hume and the History of England*, pp. 72–78.

19. (4.403). This quotation, in the text, is a rhetorical question rather than a statement.

20. (5.95–96). In speaking later of parliamentary opposition to Charles II, Hume writes that public liberty was so precarious, under the "exorbitant prerogative" claimed by the king, "as to render an opposition not only excuseable, but laudable, in the people." (5.236)

21. *Essays, Moral, Political, and Literary*, p. 4l; *History*, 6.533.

22. See "Idea of a Perfect Commonwealth," in *Essays, Moral, Political, and Literary*, pp. 512–529.

23. Laurence L. Bongie, *David Hume: Prophet of the Counter-revolution* (Oxford: Clarendon Press, 1965), p. 78.

24. Joseph de Maistre, *Considerations on France*, translated by Richard A. Lebrun (Montreal: McGill-Queen's University Press, 1974).

25. (5.391). Hume does not say this in his own name, but puts it forth as one of the arguments that the Court Party might have made, in 1679, in opposing the bill to exclude the Duke of York's succession to the English crown. In any event, the distinction between what is best in itself and what is the best of the practicable alternatives is vital to Hume's political thought.

26. See "Whether the British Government inclines more to Absolute Monarchy, or to a Republic," in *Essays,* pp. 47–53.

DONALD W. LIVINGSTON

HUME'S HISTORICAL CONCEPTION OF LIBERTY

Hume's concept of liberty is not framed in a speculative theory of
liberty. There is, for instance, nothing in Hume comparable to Mill's
discussion in *Of Liberty* of a "simple" theoretical principle which can
distinguish the liberty of the individual from the liberty of the state.
Liberty is mentioned often in Hume's philosophical and historical
writings but the remarks are usually brief and in the context of discussing
something else such as the nature of government or the process of
civilization. When Hume does discuss liberty directly, it is not to define
and fix its limits but to make historical, causal observations about the
conditions that produce, sustain, and threaten the existence of liberty and
the values it makes possible. Hume always supposes liberty to be
something about which his readers are familiar and which needs no
definition or explication. Accordingly, Hume's writing on liberty is more
rhetorical than speculative, and to many this will mean that Hume can
have nothing of philosophical interest to say about liberty. Mill, for
instance, seems to have regarded all of Hume's work as merely
"rhetorical." He wrote: "Hume possessed powers of a very high order;
but regard for truth formed no part of his character ... His mind, too, was
completely enslaved by a taste for literature ... that literature which
without regard for truth or utility, seeks only to excite emotion."[1] But
this is profoundly mistaken. Hume conceives of rhetoric as a bearer of
truth, not a barrier to it. And there is no speculative theory of liberty in
Hume's writings, not because he failed to present one but because his
conception of critical philosophical reflection rules such theories out of
order. I shall explore Hume's reasons for doing so in this essay. In the
meantime, a few observations need to be made by way of introduction.

Philosophical theories of liberty are typically framed in an ahistorical
framework and purport to be timeless and universal. Mill's "simple"
theoretical principle, for instance, specifies timeless conditions of liberty
for an abstract entity called the individual and one called the state.

N. Capaldi and D.W. Livingston (eds.), Liberty in Hume's History of England. 105–153.
© 1990 *Kluwer Academic Publishers. Printed in the Netherlands.*

Likewise, in all contract theories principles of liberty are constructed in a timeless order in abstraction from the established norms of any actual social and political order. These abstract principles are then applied as stern measuring rods to any actual society. This way of thinking is so well established in both political philosophy and political science that we are apt to demand such theories from Hume and be disappointed. One commentator found their absence, for "admirers of Hume," to be "downright depressing."[2]

But if we are to reject a priori philosophical theories of political conceptions such as liberty, how is critical reflection to proceed? The traditional model of critical reflection for philosophy and political science is a spectator model. This is as true of empirical as of rationalistic theories. On this model, the thinker must, at some methodological point, step out of all existing political order for the purpose of critically surveying it. In this moment, the existing regimes of the world are viewed as alien objects having no normative authority for the spectator. The critical spectator conceptually ceases to be a *participant* in any regime whatsoever.

By contrast, Hume proposed a participation model of critical reflection. The thinker originally finds himself to be a participant in some practice of which he may have no concept. Hume observes: "we can give no reason for our most general and most refined principles, beside our experience of their reality; which is the reason of the mere vulgar, and what it required no study at first to have discovered..." (T, xxii). The principles of a practice are preconceptually internal to the practice. Practices may and often do conflict. The task of critical reflection is to conceptualize the principles internal to a practice, systematize them with principles of other practices, and critically adjust principles to each other to avoid conflicts. The Humean critical thinker begins in the established practices of common life, and, although practices may be modified by reflection, he ends there too. At no time does he become an outside spectator of the practices, and at no time do these become alien objects of theoretical reflection.

Such a model of critical thinking requires a historical investigation into the evolution and rationale of original practices. But such a historical inquiry is not "theoretical" in the sense in which Marxist and liberal historical inquiry is, that would be to make the practice an alien object. Humean historical inquiry into practice is by and for participants who, whatever the critical results of inquiry might be, must be able to recognize themselves in it. The practice must be illuminated from within. For this project the art of rhetoric is essential. The reason is that original participation in a practice is preconceptual. The process of conceptualizing the principles immanent in the practice (that is, of bringing them to consciousness) requires a critical act of thought which can test the purported conceptualization against the primordial, preconceptual practice. This critical act is in fact a rhetorical speech in which we are called upon to recognize who we are as participants in the practice and so are able to recognize ourselves in the conceptualization. The arts of rhetoric and history are essential to the participation model of critical inquiry; they are irrelevant to the spectator model. The spectator model has proved successful in the natural sciences; it has been a disaster in the human sciences.

In what follows, I shall piece together Hume's concept of liberty from the philosophical, rhetorical, and historical structures in which it is embedded. In the first section, Hume's theory of concept formation is briefly examined. I show that all Humean concepts have a historical content. The concept of liberty is a reflection of historically evolving customs, conventions, and traditions. In the second section, I discuss three senses of 'liberty' in Hume's works and determine the primary meaning the term has for him. In the third section, Hume's views on the value of liberty and its relation to tradition and civilization are examined. Liberty makes possible and is the perfection of the process of civilization.

In the fourth section, I discuss further the distinction between the spectator and participation models of philosophical reflection. These models enable us to appreciate Hume's own distinction between true and false philosophical reflection. In the light of this discussion, I explore Hume's prophetic but undeveloped insights into a peculiarly modern form of barbarism: the conceptual destruction of liberty by false philosophy.

I. The Historicity of Concept Formation

We cannot fully appreciate Hume's conception of liberty without some understanding of the theory of concept formation by which any Humean concept is shaped. What Hume calls the "first principle" of his philosophy is the principle that simple ideas follow simple impressions which they exactly resemble and that complex ideas follow complex impressions which they may or may not resemble. I have argued elsewhere that this theory of concept formation is profoundly historical and must be quarantined as far as possible from the ahistorical theories that inform most of the empirical tradition: phenomenalism, pragmatism, and logical empiricism.[3]

The governing principle of the theory is that the experiences (impressions) rendered intelligible by ideas are not constituted by those ideas. That is not to say, though, that no ideas at all figure into their constitution. It is true that no idea is part of the constitution of a simple impression of, say, red. But, as Hume himself observes, it is not these simple ideas that he is concerned to examine (though they are usually taken to be the paradigms of Humean ideas), but complex ideas of the passions (impressions of reflection), and these presuppose ideas of the self and of the object of the passion. But though impressions of reflection "arise mostly from ideas" (T, 8), the ideas that enter into the impression are not identical to the idea of the impression itself. Thus the experience that Hume is concerned to illuminate is not the timeless experience of classical empiricism of which sense perceptions are the paradigms but the historical experience of a self seeking order in a historical world constituted by the passions. In this, Hume belongs more to the Latin rhetorical tradition of philosophy that runs through the Roman jurists, Cicero, the Italian humanists, the English common lawyers to Shaftesbury than to the Greek speculative tradition which includes such thinkers as Plato, Descartes, Hegel, and, I would say, modern and contemporary empiricists. If we are forced to it, the model for understanding Hume is not so much empiricists such as Mill, Carnap, or Ayer as Cicero, Richard Hooker, and Shaftesbury.

The distinction between the Greek speculative tradition and the Latin rhetorical tradition in philosophy is roughly parallel to the distinction between the spectator model and the participation model of philosophy. The Latin rhetorical tradition is humanistic and teaches that custom and tradition are better guides to life than reflection methodologically purged of the authority of *all* custom. Peter Jones has shown the all pervasive influence that Cicero's thought had on Hume.[4] For Cicero and Hume, custom and established practice are the great guides of life. The propositional content of Hume's famous maxim that "Reason is, and ought only to be the slave of the passions, and can never pretend to any other office than to serve and obey them" (T, 415) is reflected in Cicero's challenge to all speculative political philosophers: "For what speech of theirs is excellent enough to be preferred to a state well provided with law and custom?"

In what I have called the Greek speculative tradition, ideas are thought of as timeless and as, in someway, constituting reality. The real is the rational as Hegel was to say. Likewise, moral reality is determined by ideas. To be alienated from these ideas is to be morally unreal. Knowledge is virtue as Plato was to say. But for Hume the matter is entirely different. Ideas are not timeless (except as abstractions) and do not constitute reality. They function more as historical mirrors which reflect and make us self-conscious of experiences that were lived through in ignorance of the ideas that now render them intelligible.

Something of this historical notion of intelligibility is framed even in Hume's account of simple ideas. An impression of red, on its *first* appearance, is unintelligible. It is only after it is over with and securely in the past that we can have its idea. And so it is with more complicated experiences (complex impressions). The English language occurs and evolves spontaneously without any self-conscious understanding of the rules and principles of grammar that later render it intelligible. Once English, as a practice, is established, it is possible to have its idea. But the practice itself can and is lived out in radical ignorance of its idea.

Ideas as historical mirrors of experience function as instruments of self-consciousness and of self-criticism. As such, they make possible a wider and more controlled scope of experience. Having seen oneself in the mirror or on a video tape, one may or may not like what is seen and alter behavior accordingly. Having become aware of various ways of speaking English, I may decide to alter my manner of speech. Complex ideas of established practices are necessarily normative. The idea of English is necessarily both a passive reflection and a set of norms to guide practice. Through comparison with other norms and by abstraction, the norms of a practice may be brought to the conscious level and shaped up into critical models, ideals, standards, rules, and principles which may be used to alter experience by expanding it or restricting it. The fundamental error of the Greek speculative tradition is to read these ideals, rules, and principles back into the experiences they reflect as constituting their reality in much the way Michelangelo imagined himself, in neo-Platonic fashion, to be liberating the sculpture from the rock of marble.

Hume entirely reverses this way of thinking. For him the heart of every idea is the living experience of which it is a reflection. The *formal* analysis of an idea, from Plato to Descartes, is the most important form of self-knowledge. For Hume, it is of minor importance. Having uncovered eight rules for judging causes and effects, he cautions: "Here is all the Logic I think proper to employ in my reasoning; and perhaps even this was not very necessary ... Our scholastic headpieces and logicians shew no such superiority above the mere vulgar in their reason and ability, as to give us any inclination to imitate them in delivering a long system of rules and precepts to direct our judgment, in philosophy" (T, 175). Ideas do not structure or constitute a practice; they are mirrors of something lived through in ignorance. The important thing for self-knowledge is grasping the experience, and this is accomplished through the arts of history and rhetoric by telling a story to participants of what they have lived through and such that they can recognize themselves in the story. In recalling their own experience, they necessarily gain its idea. Nor is one's historical experience limited to what one can remember. One can identify with a larger community such as a religious community or a nation in which case one's experience extends to the historical life of the community. And one can, through sympathy, participate in the experiences of alien communities.

Whatever value a formal analysis of ideas may have, everything, for Hume depends on grasping the living practice of which they are reflections. The danger of formal analysis is that one might come to think that the practice is merely a matter of following the "rules" or "principles" which are in fact mere abstractions from the practice. Such intellectualism may hinder or even destroy the practice. Hume observes: "there is no virtue or moral duty but what may, with facility, be refined away, if we indulge a false philosophy in sifting and scrutinizing it, by every captious rule of logic, in every light or position in which it may be placed" (E, 482).

In some cases, where the practice is evolving and variable, the belief that formal analysis uncovers the constitution or reality of a practice can obscure it. Thus Hume complains that Royalist historians treated the British constitution at the time of Charles I as an unchanging substance: "as something real and durable; like those eternal essences of the schools, which no time or force could alter" (H, V, app. 127). They failed to understand the historical and necessarily ambiguous reality of British constitutional experience. The error of intellectualism made the constitution appear more clear than it was. Some practices can perhaps never be made clear such as the nature of the Whig and Tory parties: "To determine the nature of these parties is perhaps one of the most difficult problems that can be met with, and is a proof that history may contain questions as uncertain as any to be found in the most abstract sciences" (E, 69). Many of our fundamental beliefs are radically incoherent such as the belief that we perceive material objects and causal connections. The most we can do is work through our experience, register this fact about it, and adjust our critical norms accordingly.

The most important concept in Hume's philosophy is that of *convention*. A Humean convention is not the result of conscious agreement but evolves over time as the unintended result of man's successful involvement with the world and with his fellows. Hume's paradigm of a convention is language. Language is an instrument insensibly contrived by men to satisfy human needs: the need to communicate and the need to create an artificial and symbolic world of social order, rank, and distinction. The social world is constituted by "performative" utterances, that is, ritualistic uses of words which, for participants in the ritual, are taken to constitute social realities such as contracts, marriage, property, and political authority.[5] The convention of language is highly ordered, but the order is not the result of conscious planning. Language developed spontaneously, and although it has served to bring order to men's lives, and although it may be said to be the work of men, it is not an order for which any person or group (or God for that matter) is responsible.

When Hume talks about "experiences" he has in mind not the private experience of traditional sense-datum empiricism but a public, historical experience shaped by spontaneously evolving conventions. Hume makes this methodological point clear at the very beginning of the *Treatise*: "We must ... glean up our experiments in this science from a cautious observation of human life, and take them as they appear in the common course of the world, by men's behaviour in company, in affairs, and in their pleasures" (T, xxiii). Man's experience of language, morals, justice, government, God, causal relations, and even his perception of the external and internal world is structured by these insensibly contrived conventions. The positive task of Hume's philosophy is to bring these conventions in which we preconceptually participate to the light of self-conscious reflection, to uncover their rationale, their causal tendencies, and to render them mutually coherent: "philosophical decisions are nothing but the reflections of common life, methodized and corrected" (EU, 162).

II. What Liberty Is

Given Hume's theory of concept formation, we can understand why he shows no interest at all in working out a speculative theory of the nature of liberty or of specifying the necessary and sufficient conditions for applying the predicate 'is free'. There is no timeless object called liberty or freedom about which a philosophical spectator can devise a theory. Liberty is a Humean convention that has evolved over time. In its most differentiated form, it is a British experience, though less differentiated forms of it can be found throughout Europe. This primarily British experience that has evolved is modern; and although analogues may be found in the past, they must not be confused with it. Consequently, Hume's understanding of liberty is not presented through a speculative *theory* but through *stories* of the evolution of the experience of liberty as shaped by the conventions of common life. The stories are presented with rhetorical force to those who are participants in the conventions. Nearly everything Hume wrote on liberty can be viewed as a speech addressed to the dominant whig literary and political establishment of his time. It was this powerful group that claimed to be the spokesmen for and guardians of British liberty. Although the whig establishment participated in the experience of liberty, it seemed to Hume that its thought about that experience was confused. Distorted thinking about an experience, if extreme, can so alienate one from it that one loses one's grip on the experience itself and ceases to participate in it. As Hume's career developed, he became increasingly alarmed that the distorted thinking about liberty of the dominant whig literary and political establishment threatened to destroy the newly emerged experience of liberty.

Liberty appeared to Hume and his contemporaries as opposed to slavery. The feudal distinction between the free man and the serf was still a vivid part of 18th century cultural memory. The slave is one who cannot determine his life by his own plans and decisions but is coerced to act by the arbitrary will of another. The stress is on "arbitrary" since the free man may be under many restraints from government, custom, and morals which are not arbitrary. Constraints are not arbitrary if they are publically known and equally applicable to all who are supposed to be free. It was liberty in this sense of the equal rule of law that the Glorious Revolution of 1688 had secured and which made British political order the wonder and envy of 18th century Europe. Throughout most of the 17th century, Britain was a weak, politically chaotic country with less than half the population of France. But by the first quarter of the 18th century, Britain appeared as a rich, powerful, and populous nation. It was generally agreed that this success was due entirely to her constitution of liberty which had unleased the productive powers and ambitions of the populace.

Bernard Bailyn observes that "It would be difficult to exaggerate the keenness of eighteenth-century Britons' sense of their multifarious accomplishments and world eminence and their distinctiveness in the achievement of liberty. From the end of the war in 1713 until the crisis over America a half-century later the triumph of Britain in warfare, in commerce, and in statecraft was the constant theme not only of formal state pronouncements and of political essays, tracts, and orations but of belles-lettres as well. There was a general paean of praise to the steady increase in wealth, refinement, and security, and to the apparent perfection of government."[6] Hume complained bitterly about the whig panegyric literature that had dominated British letters from the late 17th century throughout his lifetime. In 1769, he confessed that "It has been my Misfortune to write in the Language of the most stupid and factious Barbarians in the world" (L, II, 209). The charge of whig barbarism occurs often in letters written during the last decade of Hume's life. In section IV, I examine the sense in which the Whig establishment is barbarous. In the meantime, it is important to observe that Hume's attack on the whig *interpretation* of the British experience of liberty is not an attack on the experience itself. No whig panegyrist ever surpassed Hume (except in excess) in praise either of liberty or of the British constitution. The following passages exhibit the depth of Hume's commitment to a free political order.

Liberty is an original demand of human nature: "The heart of man delights in liberty: the very image of constraint is grievous to it" (E, 187). Hume roundly condemned the "remains … of domestic slavery in the American colonies, and among some European nations" not only because slavery is intrinsically odious but because it corrupts the humanity of the slave holder. "The little humanity commonly observed in persons accustomed, from their infancy, to exercise so great authority over their fellow-creatures, and to trample upon human nature, were sufficient alone to disgust us with that unbounded dominion" (E, 383-84). As he rejected the institution of domestic slavery as incompatible with human nature, so he recognized the rational autonomy of the mass of mankind: "It has been found as the experience of mankind increases, that the *people* are no such dangerous monsters as they have been represented, and it is in every respect better to guide them like rational creatures than to lead or drive them like brute beasts" (E, 604-605). It was this recognition of the rationality of human nature that led Hume to present the freedom of the press as a demand of human nature: "But I would fain go a step further, and assert, that such a liberty is attended with so few inconveniences, that it may be claimed as the common right of mankind, and ought to be indulged them almost in every government except the ecclesiastical, to which, indeed, it would be fatal" (E, 604n). More generally, Hume could say: "For my part, I esteem liberty so invaluable a blessing in society, that whatever favours its progress and security, can scarce be too fondly cherished by every one who is a lover of human kind" (E, 646n).

Hume agreed with the whig panegyrists about the intrinsic worth and valuable consequences of the British constitution of liberty: "during these last sixty years" Hume could write at the middle of the 18th century, "Public liberty, with internal peace and order, has flourished ... trade and manufactures, and agriculture, have increased: the arts, and sciences, and philosophy, have been cultivated. Even religious parties have been necessitated to lay aside their mutual rancour; and the glory of the nation has spread itself all over Europe; derived equally from our progress in the arts of peace, and from valour and success in war. So long and so glorious a period no nation almost can boast of: nor is there another instance in the whole history of mankind, that so many millions of people have, during such a space of time, been held together, in a manner so free, so rational, and so suitable to the dignity of human nature" (E, 508). Hume recognized and affirmed the great variety of customs, manners, and characters that a constitution of liberty necessarily produces, and he observed that British society had developed a pluralistic tone which distinguished it from the more uniform national characteristics of other nations. "The great liberty and independency which every man enjoys, allows him to display the manners peculiar to him. Hence the English, of any people in the universe, have the least of a national character, unless this very singularity may pass for such" (E, 207). The increase in manufacturing that liberty makes possible has resulted in wealth being "dispersed among multitudes," satisfying another demand of human nature: "every person, if possible, ought to enjoy the fruits of his labour, in a full possession of all the necessaries, and many of the conveniences of life. No one can doubt but such an equality is most suitable to human nature and diminishes much less from the *happiness* of the rich, than it adds to that of the poor" (E, 265).

Like his whig contemporaries, Hume was "alarmed by the danger of universal monarchy" from the authoritarian regimes of the Continent. The Emperor Charles had tried and failed to establish Europe under one monarch. the new and more formidable threat is the absolute monarchy of France: "Europe has now, for above a century, remained on the defensive against the greatest force that ever perhaps was formed by the civil or political combination of mankind" (E, 634n). In the struggle to achieve a balance of power against "this ambitious power," Hume saw Britain as playing a world historical role. British liberty serves as a model to Europe and British power serves to protect the liberties of Europe. And so Hume could describe Britain's role as "the guardian of the general liberties of Europe, and patron of mankind." (E, 635n).

Hume is often thought of as a Tory and (given the violent reaction as expressed in the letters of the last decade of his life to an extension of republican institutions in Britain) as a reactionary. Caroline Robbins, in her magisterial study of the whig tradition makes no mention of Hume on the grounds that he was a Tory and so not part of that tradition.[7] Yet the above passages and many similar ones that could be cited present a different picture. They suggest that Hume viewed liberty as a demand of human nature which, ideally, should be extended as much as possible to all men. They suggest also a view of society as an order of self-directing individuals and imply that the task of society is not to constrain personality but to allow it expression so that, as in the liberal order of 18th century Britain, each may "display the manners peculiar to him" (E, 207). Yet these passages do not tell us exactly what Hume meant by 'liberty,' and it is to this question that I now turn.

Hume uses the term 'liberty' in three main senses. The first and by far the most important is the one we have already mentioned. The free man is not a slave. He can determine his life by his own thought and decisions uncoerced by the arbitrary will of another. The institution which men have contrived to secure liberty in this sense is government. The coercion of government is not arbitrary if it is in accord with law. Hume adopts here the classical expression: "a government of Laws, not of Men" (E, 94). In such a government, whatever its form, law is conceived to pre-exist the statutes enacted by the sovereign power. Hume affirms the classical checks to arbitrary power embodied in the traditional notion of "the rule of law." Law must be known, regular, and predictable; the rules of justice must be applied equally to all; imprisonment or confiscation of property cannot occur without due process of law; and there must be an independent judiciary capable of reviewing the statutes of the sovereign and their administration by magistrates.

The primary sense of liberty in Hume's thought is unoriginal. It is simply the familiar whig notion of liberty as the rule of law. What is original with Hume is the historical, dialectical, and evolutionary context in which he places the concept. We shall discuss this context later; in the meantime we turn to Hume's second sense of liberty. In the primary conception of liberty, coercion, by virtue of the concept of law, is not only compatible with liberty, it is internal to it. The presence of "coercion" in the concept of liberty logically implies a weaker sense of the term according to which liberty is the absence of any constraint. Hume uses the term in this way when discussing the traditional problem of free will in the *Treatise* and the *Enquiry* on understanding. There a person is said to have "liberty" of the will when his actions flow from his character and are independent of any external constraint. Liberty, so conceived, is morally neutral. Whether it is good that anyone possess liberty in this second sense is a contingent question. Liberty in the first sense (as the rule of law) is presumed good. I say "presumed" because Hume thinks reasons of public interest may arise for suspending the rule of law.

Although liberty in the second sense is morally neutral, Hume often uses it in political contexts where it can be confused with the morally favorable connotations of liberty in the first sense. For example, religious liberty and liberty of the press are ornaments of political society that may be "indulged" under certain conditions.

Liberty in the second sense is also used to describe the liberty of the state of nature and conditions of society approximating it. Liberty in such contexts is usually a bad thing. For instance "The abject Britons" upon being free from the coercion of Roman rule "regarded this present liberty as fatal to them ..." (H, I, 13). In opposition to the popular whig belief that the British constitution can be traced back to the Saxon forests Hume sarcastically remarks: "the same picture of a fierce and bold liberty, which is drawn by the masterly pencil of Tacitus, will suit these founders of the English government." And of the liberty of the feudal order, Hume writes: "the pretended liberty of the times was only an incapacity of submitting to government ..." (H, II, 521).

Hume's third use of the term is for that form of government which he calls "free" and which he defines as follows: "That government, which, in common appellation, receives the appellation of free, is that which admits of a partition of power among several members, whose united authority is no less, or is commonly greater, than that of any monarch; but who, in the usual course of administration, must act by general and equal laws, that are previously known to all the members, and to all their subjects" (E, 40-41). Free governments contain a division of powers and are either republics or limited monarchies such as Britain. Liberty as the rule of law usually attends free government but is not confined to it since

Hume thinks that civilized absolute monarchies can embody the rule of law to a degree equal to or even higher than republics and limited monarchies. Hume uses the term 'liberty' in this third sense when attacking the demand for greater representation in government which found expression in the Wilkes and Liberty affair. In October, 1769, he wrote: "So much Liberty is incompatible with human Society: And it will be happy, if we can escape from it, without falling into a military Government, such as Algiers or Tunis," (L, II, 210). Hume does not mean here too much liberty in the sense of the rule of law. He means rather that the "free government" of Britain is "too free," that is, the monarchical part of the government is too weak to punish displays of disrespect. Free governments are not presumed by Hume to be good. Indeed, the freest are the worst. The freest government would be a democratic republic where the majority rules directly as in the "Athenian Democracy" where the "whole collective body of the people voted in every law, without any limitation of property, without any distinction of rank, without control from any magistracy or senate; and consequently without regard to order, justice, or prudence" (E, 368-69).

Hume rejected the main thesis of the individualistic whig tradition as taught by such thinkers as Sidney and Locke, and followers such as Price and Macaulay which forged a conceptual connection between representative government and liberty as the rule of law. For Hume, it is a contingent question as to whether free governments embody liberty to a greater degree than absolute monarchies. Locke had argued that absolute monarchy is "*inconsistent with Civil society*, and so can be no Form of Government at all."[8] Likewise, Sidney held that "Whatever ... proceeds not from the consent of the people, must be 'de facto' only, that is, void of all right."[9] In contrast, Hume taught that "human nature, in general, really enjoys more liberty at present, in the most arbitrary government of Europe, than it ever did during the most flourishing period of ancient times" (E, 383). Hume includes here the Roman and Spartan republics, so much admired by popular whig ideology. And he argued that the free government of Britain (the limited monarchy), given its peculiar historical conditions, most likely would and should develop into a civilized absolute monarchy: "Absolute monarchy, therefore, is the easiest death, the true *Euthanasia* of the British constitution" (E, 53).

To sum up. The primary sense of liberty for Hume is action uncoerced by the arbitrary will of the sovereign power. The other two senses of liberty (freedom from external constraint and free government) are subordinate to liberty as the rule of law. Having examined the substance of liberty, we may ask about its relation to governmental authority. It might appear that liberty as the rule of law is essential to legitimate government. But this does not appear to be Hume's view. Sometimes he writes as if liberty were a perfection of government and detachable from it. For instance, the monarch in a free government must abide by the rule of law, that is, he "must act by general and equal laws, that are previously known to all ... In this sense, it must be owned, that liberty is the perfection of civil society ..." (E, 41). This passage suggests that liberty is a perfection of government but not essential to it. Consider also the following passage where Hume distinguishes his own reading of the political conflict during the reign of the Stuarts with the dominant Whig interpretation: "Forgetting that a regard to liberty, though a laudable passion, ought commonly to be subordinate to a reverence for established government, the prevailing faction has celebrated only the partisans of the former, who pursued as their object the perfection of civil society, and has extolled them at the expense of their antagonists, who maintained those maxims that are essential to its very existence" (H, VI, 533). The liberty here that is a non-essential perfection of society is not merely the liberty from constraint or free government but liberty as the rule of law. For one charge against the Stuarts was that they had violated some of those checks traditionally thought to be essential to the rule of law.

No check to arbitrary power is more important than habeas corpus, a rule which Hume fully celebrates, but he does not construe it as an absolute limit to governmental authority: "It must, however, be confessed, that there is some difficulty to reconcile with such extreme liberty the full security and the regular police of a state, especially the police of great cities" (H, VI, 367). Hume mentions other checks essential to the rule of law which have been secured in the limited monarchy of Britain. These checks are designed: "to remove all discretionary powers, and to secure every one's life and fortune by general and inflexible laws. No action must be deemed a crime but what the law has plainly determined to be such: no crime must be imputed to a man but from a legal proof before his judges; and even these judges must be his fellow-subjects, who are obliged, by their own interest, to have a watchful eye over the encroachments and violence of the ministers" (E, 12). But Hume's praise of these checks against arbitrary power is qualified: "From these causes it proceeds, that there is as much liberty, and even perhaps licentiousness, in Great Britain, as there were formerly slavery and tyranny in Rome" (E, 12). Habeas corpus is described as "extreme liberty," the checks just mentioned yield "licentiousness" as well as liberty.

Clearly Hume does not conceive of the traditional checks internal to the rule of law as absolute limits to government authority. His own view of the relation between liberty and authority seems to be a dialectical one with an ambiguity at the core that can never be eliminated: "In all governments, there is a perpetual intestine struggle, open or secret, between Authority and Liberty; and neither of them can ever absolutely prevail in the contest" (E, 40). By authority Hume means the commands of the sovereign independent of the rule of law. And since authority is essential to government, it takes precedence over liberty. But it can never be detached from it: "A great sacrifice of liberty must necessarily be made in every government; yet even the authority, which confines liberty, can never, and perhaps ought never, in any constitution, to become quite entire and uncontrollable" (E, 40).

But what form will this control take? And, if not identical to, how close is it to that control known as the rule of law? To answer these questions, we must look briefly at Hume's conception of the rationale of government. Government exists to interpret and to enforce the rules of justice: the stability of possession, its transference by consent and the performance of promises. Government that violates the reason for its existence loses its authority and may be overthrown by violence. There is, then, a minimum "rule of law" that government must satisfy, namely the laws of justice. No rule can be given as to when revolution is justified except to say that the circumstances must be extraordinary and desperate and must be so recognized by the public. "I must confess," Hume writes, "that I shall always incline to their side, who draw the bond of allegiance very close, and consider an infringement of it as the last refuge in desperate cases, when the public is in the highest danger from violence and tyranny" (E, 490).

This, of course, is vague. The contract theory, in contrast, appears to provide a clear rule for deciding when revolution is justified: whenever the terms of the contract have been broken by government. From Hume's point of view the apparent rational superiority of the contract theory is illusory. The theory assumes that since government is constituted by self-consciously imposed rules, there must be such rules for dissolving it. But Hume holds that government is established not by the imposition of rules but spontaneously; its dissolution likewise must be spontaneous. There is a Humean metaphorical notion of consent involved in the formation of government, but it is not the consent of a self-reflective, self-assertive individual. Rather, it is the sort of consent implied in Humean social conventions. The "consent" is of the sort, for example, without which

120 *Donald W. Livingston*

language would be impossible. It is deeply social and not self-assertive. Nor is the Humean consent that founds and dissolves government the numerical majority of individual wills as in contemporary democratic theory. For Hume, the political individual is always the individual rooted in an actual historical community whose will cannot be detached from the prejudices, traditions, and bonds of affection that hold the community together.

One reason, then, why no rule can be given a priori as to how the laws of justice are to be interpreted or when revolution is justified is that the content of the laws is historically relative to the customs and prejudices of the people. Since, for Hume, the authority of government is based not on contract but on opinion, authoritarian regimes that would appear arbitrary and oppressive to those accustomed to the rule of law would appear just to those who share the prejudices of the order. For example, the reign of Elizabeth I was considered, at the time, a regime in which the laws of justice were instantiated. Yet Hume observes that there were many institutions which violated the rule of law as understood in 18th century Britain, the most notorious being the Star chamber "which possessed an unlimited discretionary authority of fining, imprisoning, and inflicting corporal punishment." The members were not subject to judicial review and held office at the Queen's pleasure. Hume adds that such an institution was needed as much then as it would be oppressive now. Generally the prejudices which support an authoritarian regime contain checks to that authority which are peculiar to the order and which are considered satisfactory. "The sultan is master of the life and fortune of any individual; but will not be permitted to impose new taxes on his subjects: a French monarch can impose taxes at pleasure; but would find it dangerous to attempt the lives and fortunes of individuals. Religion also ... is commonly found to be a very intractable principle; and other principles or prejudices frequently resist all the authority of the civil magistrate; whose power, being founded on opinion, can never subvert other opinions equally rooted with that of his title to dominion" (E, 40).

So in the usual course of affairs, authority and liberty (liberty conceived now as the "irregular" checks necessary to secure the laws of justice) will be established spontaneously. Since it is the habits, customs, and traditions of the people that ultimately constitute authority and, at the same time, are the basic rules for interpreting the laws of justice, these same prejudices (and not the empty and arbitrary reasonings of contract philosophers) will dictate when authority has failed to establish the laws of justice. The reasonings of contract philosophers are empty because the contract is framed in a hypothetical state uncontaminated by any prejudice or custom of an actual social and political order. It is also arbitrary because, being purely formal, any arrangement in the world may appear to satisfy the contract or no arrangement may appear to satisfy it. The contract can serve as a guide for political action only if given some content by the very prejudices that were methodologically eliminated in the first place. And there can be no non-arbitrary way to choose which prejudices should fill the contract with content. For the choice must be made either by another prejudice or by a principle free of all prejudice. If the latter, we are back to another formal principle which is empty; if the former, we have abandoned the whole point of contract theory. The apparent superiority of the contractarian criterion for when revolution is justified as opposed to Hume's criterion of public prejudice is an illusion.

A final point should be observed on the question of when revolution is justified. Hume thinks of government authority as something we are born into, roughly in the way we are born into parental authority. In both cases, we enter in a vulnerable state and feel the effects of both power and benevolence. Over time these feelings generate a sense of loyalty as one identifies with the authority. In the way in which children are loath to leave their natural parents, even when abusive, for artificial and morally improved substitutes, so citizens and subjects of long established authority are loath to overthrow the constitution of that authority for an improved instrument.

And this brings up another way in which government, for Hume, is like a family. A family does not think of itself as an instrument designed to serve some goal other than the natural associations provided by the family itself. A family like a friendship is an end in itself. Families and friendships may serve temporary goals. But the bonds that constitute them do not dissolve upon achieving the goals or upon failure to achieve them. Likewise, Hume does not think of government as an instrument for achieving some end other than the natural associations out of which government was spontaneously generated in the first place. The utility of government is a value internal to established practice. Government, therefore, is not an instrument for bringing into being the rights of man, or human equality, or the classless society, or freedom, as liberal and marxist political theory in various ways have supposed.

In these theories, revolution is a forward looking idea: if a better instrument can be devised for accomplishing the ends of government, there is no reason, in principle, why the new instrument should not replace the old. For Hume, the idea of a just revolution is an essentially present and backward looking notion: rebellion appears reasonable in the face of a present and serious usurpation of established entitlements.

By "the rule of law," we have meant those traditional checks to arbitrary power, equal laws known to all, habeas corpus, judicial review, etc., usually associated with the expression. But there is a wider and weaker sense that can be given to the expression, for we may include the establishment of the laws of justice done in the "irregular" way (whether or not they conform to the traditional checks to arbitrary power) as a minimum condition of lawlikeness in government. The rule of law in this weak sense is internal to authority and cannot be separated from it. What we have called "the rule of law" is not a feature of government as such but of what Hume calls *civilized* government as opposed to barbarous government. It is internal to the concept of governmental authority, whether civilized or barbarous, that it be limited by the laws of justice, but these limits can take many forms depending on the established prejudices and opinions of the people. In barbarous ages, the checks to encroachment are "irregular," eclectic, and short lived. Hume, for instance, describes the government of pre-Tudor England as "limited," but it is limited only in that the prince was, at point of sword, "restrained by the barons" (H, V, 550). More generally, Hume says that throughout the barbarous ages of English history the monarch was never absolute. But again the "limit" was barbarous, being dependent not on the "legal and determinate liberty" of the rule of law but on the personalities and power of individuals.

The story of civilization is largely the story of how the checks to arbitrary power framed in the modern notion of the rule of law have gradually become established. Of Elizabeth's reign, which was emerging out of barbarism, Hume observes that "the jealousy of liberty, though roused, was not yet thoroughly enlightened" (H, V, 550). What does it mean to be enlightened here? It is to understand the rationale of government in human nature and to bring to conscious awareness and to make regular those checks to arbitrary authority of which even barbarians, being "novices ... in the principles of liberty," have some dim understanding. The rule of law occurs to some degree in all the countries of civilized Europe. It is better established in limited monarchies than in republics such as Holland or in absolute monarchies such as France. But the rule of law has reached its highest development in the limited monarchy of Britain: "we in this island have ever since [the Revolution of 1688] enjoyed, if not the best system of government, at least the most entire system of liberty, that ever was known amongst mankind" (H, VI, 531).

As men become more self-conscious about the advantages of the rule of law and as they evolve into "free governments" with publically acknowledged constitutions, their rights become more explicit and are more jealously guarded. Particular violations of the constitution then become publically obvious as when one branch of the government usurps the rights of another. Paradoxically, the conditions for rebellion are clearer and easier to justify the more civilized and constitutional a regime becomes. Of a prince who would encroach on "other parts of the constitution" in a civilized regime, Hume says "it is allowable to resist and dethrone him; tho' such resistance and violence may, in the general tenor of the laws, be deem'd unlawful and rebellious" (T, 564). It was in this way that Hume justified the dethroning of James II even though, unlike Nero, he was not guilty of "enormous tyranny and oppression." Such resistance is justified because it can be viewed as an act of conservative reform motivated by respect for the constitution rather than by a desire to innovate. In this Hume affirmed the classical republican wisdom of "Machiavel" that the founding of a state is good and that "A government … must often be brought back to its original principles" (E, 516).

III. Liberty, Tradition, and Civilization

Hume's conception of convention exposes a peculiar sort of order which cannot be thought of as the product of human design and need not be thought of as the product of Divine design but is the unintended result of man's attempt to satisfy human needs. The total set of these historically evolving conventions (language, law, art, religion, etc.), Hume calls the moral world. To the degree that men become *aware* of the evolutionary process of the moral world and gain some measure of control over it, they become to that degree *civilized*. Civilization, then, is not merely a matter of acting according to certain principles, it is a form of the most important self-knowledge and so, philosophy being the most developed form of self-knowledge, there is a close connection between Hume's conception of civilization and philosophy. Although Hume does not make the point himself, it is not an extravagance to say that the civilized man plays the role in Hume's philosophy that the sage or wise man plays in the eudaemonistic philosophies of the ancients. For Hume, the true philosopher and the truly civilized man are the same. We shall discuss

Hume's conception of true and false philosophy and its relation to civilization in section IV of this essay. In the meantime, I want to explore Hume's conception of civilization further and show how two conceptions are essential to it: tradition and liberty.

The story of civilization is the story of the improvements of the human mind. This seems to imply a standard of goodness which is the aim of civilization. But Hume rejected the Aristotelian *telos* luring men on to self-realization. Hume's conception of good can be inferred from his conception of moral virtue. Personal virtue consists in qualities of character useful or agreeable to ourselves and others. Social virtue consists in qualities of institutions that are useful or agreeable to ourselves and others. The good is not conceived as an a priori form, as in Plato and Aristotle, to which men are driven by eros; nor is it the forward looking species being of Marx from which man is alienated by class struggle. For Hume, the good is, as it were, present and backward looking; it is what has been hammered out over time through a largely unreflective process of trial and error. These goods are housed in the prejudices, customs, and traditions that make up the substance of the moral world.

These prejudices constitute the moral world not because they are known to be good by some theoretical grasp of the good independent of the prejudices; rather they are known to be good because they are the deeply established prejudices that constitute the moral world. It is because they have been lived through and found useful and agreeable to ourselves and others that they are considered good. Custom and tradition, then, are the great guides of life in the radical sense that there is no standard of goodness independent of tradition that can either certify them or criticize it. Of course, one custom may be used as a standard to criticize another custom, and abstract standards, ideals, and models can be constructed to criticize or affirm particular customs, but such standards are reflections of existing customs and cannot be applied in a non-arbitrary way to the world without the mediation and interpretation of existing custom.

Two features of Hume's conception of tradition must be mentioned. First, tradition is *dynamic* and *open ended*. Tradition originates in ignorance and issues in ignorance. No one knows the ultimate ground of the qualities of virtue framed in traditions. One just finds oneself approving these values as internal to one's existence. Some values are common to all traditions; some vary with the "manners" of the age. But all are, as it were, accidents coughed up by the interplay of human propensities, needs, and historical events. What qualities will be established as virtues cannot be known before hand, nor can any established set of qualities preclude the emergence of new qualities unthought of by participants in the tradition. Hume stresses that human nature, as manifest in the world of custom and tradition, is in constant change: to be "inconstant and irregular ... is, in a manner, the constant character of human nature" (EU, 88). Just as no one could have known what modifications would be made in virtue today, so no one can know what changes in virtue may appear in the future: "It is not fully known what degree of refinement, either in virtue or vice, human nature is susceptible of, nor what may be expected of mankind from any great revolution in their education, customs or principles" (E, 87-88).

The second feature of tradition is that it is *dialectical* and *ingenious*. Tradition is not only in constant change; it is in conflict with itself. The new values that emerge in a tradition will typically be in conflict with the old and a painful process of adjustment will ensue in which new and old values are mutually selected, modified, and rejected. The process of grafting new, conflicting values onto established values follows no rational process. It is carried out largely in ignorance and can be understood only after the values are settled into common life. A tradition such as Christianity, for instance, is able to bring into some sort of unity the conflicting Hebrew, Greek, and Roman traditions. Hume, in the *History*, sought to forge a new national unity out of the warring Puritan and Royalist traditions and the present Hanoverian regime.

Tradition as a form of thought which brings opposites into unity is simply an expression of the workings of the imagination in the moral world. In the *Treatise*, Hume had shown how rational analysis of our experience of physical objects, causal connections, ourselves and others renders these experiences incoherent. All are viewed by reason as structured by inconsistent elements which can be neither logically denied nor reconciled. The mind must somehow come to terms with "principles, which are contrary to each other, which are both at once embrac'd by the mind, and which are mutually unable to destroy each other" (T, 215). Reason dissolves. The imagination unifies, reconciles, and constructs even with elements that are logical contraries. Reason reveals that man "is ... but a heap of contradictions" (E, 188). But "the heart of man is made to reconcile contradictions" (E, 71). On Hume's famous account of causation, the orderly perceptible world of causally connected objects is the expression of the reconciling "fictions" of the imagination. Hume calls these fictions "the cement of the universe," where the universe is conceptually dissolved by rational reflection. The contrarieties reconciled in the conventions and traditions of common life which constitute the moral world are expressions of the same imagination at work.

Hume often makes a special point of showing how apparently rationally ordered structures such as the British constitution are, in fact, fragile instruments containing the most jarring and discordant elements. One example is Hume's analysis of what the opposition called "court corruption," that is, the patronage system following upon the crown's right to appoint magistrates and to grant titles. The charge was that the crown had used this power to corrupt the integrity of Parliament and so to undermine the constitution. Hume granted that such power could be abused, but observed that the famous "balance" of the constitution which all affirmed was not possible without the patronage system. The crown had been so reduced in formal powers and revenue that Parliament was virtually supreme. Cry as moralists might against corruption, court patronage was the only means left to insure some independence to the crown and so the only way of securing an independent executive and judiciary, so important to the traditional concept of the rule of law.

Hume devoted an entire essay "Of Some Remarkable Customs" to this subject. One of these customs is the arbitrary pressing of seamen in violation of the rights of "English subjects." Hume shows the bizarre way this violation of the rule of law serves the interests of liberty and for that reason is tolerated: "Authority, in times of full internal peace and concord, is armed against law ... Liberty, in a country of the highest liberty, is left entirely to its own defense, without any countenance or protection. The wild state of nature is renewed in one of the most civilized societies of mankind ..." (E, 375–76). What is true here of the British Constitution, that its unity is an uneasy tension of contrary elements, is true of all the Humean conventions and traditions that make up the moral world.

Hume often describes the process of civilization as one of experimentation where men, through trial and error, discover new and successful ways of living. There are three models of "experimentation" that can be confused with the process Hume picks out. One is the Darwinian model of natural selection where, out of a life and death struggle, successful traits are genetically communicated to succeeding generations. The other is the abstract model of classical economics, where an unintended order, e.g., the market price and wage arises spontaneously in a condition of free competition. Finally, there is the model of scientific or technological experimentation which has been applied to social reality by utilitarians such as Bentham and pragmatists such as Dewey.

Hume's model differs from the Darwinian in that the new traits are transmitted not genetically but by sympathetic communication and emulation. And they are established not by their survival value but by opinion in being qualities useful and agreeable to ourselves and others. Nor is the model of unrestrained competition in a free market helpful. The market, on this model, is conceived as a timeless order of rational individuals, free of traditional constraints, seeking to maximize their gains and minimize their losses. By contrast, the Humean model of "experimentation" requires agents that are fully social but not fully rational in the sense of self interested prudence. Their very thoughts and motives are clothed with the restraints woven historically into the prejudices, customs, and traditions of their order. Finally, the Humean model has little affinity with the model of technological experimentation. This model too conceives of individuals and groups in a timeless manner; whereas Humean individuals and groups are conceived internal to a unique historical order. But most importantly, the technological model implies a degree of self-conscious control which is entirely absent from the Humean model. The conventions of the moral world, though the result of trial-and-error-experience over many generations were not intended by any individual or group. "It is not with forms of government, as with other artificial contrivances, where an old engine may be rejected, if we can discover another more accurate and commodious, or where trials may safely be made, even though the success be doubtful" (E, 512). Technological experiments can be called off. A historically developed "experiment" such as the British Constitution cannot be called off.

Hume stresses so strongly the authority of custom and tradition that one is apt to overlook the remarks he makes on behalf of novelty and invention: "I have sometimes been inclined to think, that interruptions in the periods of learning, were they not attended with such a destruction of ancient books, and the records of history, would be rather favourable to the arts and sciences, by breaking the progress of authority, and dethroning the tyrannical usurpers over human reason" (E, 123). In the *History*, he considers that "Governments too steady and uniform, as they are seldom free, so are they, in the judgment of some attended with another sensible inconvenience: they abate the active powers of man; depress courage, invention, and genius; and produce a universal lethargy in the people" (H, VI, 531). Hume grants that "this opinion may be just." His only dissent is that the value of novelty cannot be used to justify the radical changes that were attempted during the reigns of James I and Charles I. That "spirit of innovation with which the age was generally seized" was too radical and violent for safety.

One value of liberty, as the rule of law, is that it provides an orderly and secure framework in which emerging novelties may be tested, modified and incorporated into the fabric of tradition. In this way, institutions of liberty bring to conscious awareness and make rational the process of "experimentation" that had more or less blindly characterized the historical process.

Civilization, then, is a process whereby the conventions of common life are raised to the level of critical self-consciousness. The difference between the barbarous man and the civilized man is not marked by a difference in political regimes, for any regime may be barbarous. The difference is a *cognitive* one. The barbarous man is lost in the conventions of common life; the civilized man has some critical understanding of them. The self-knowledge of the civilized man is identical to that of the philosopher since Hume holds that: "philosophical decisions are nothing but the reflections of common life, methodized and corrected" (EU, 162). Philosophical understanding, for Hume, is a social act. The more civilized a people become, the more philosophical they become.

Not only is philosophy a social act, it is internally connected to all the other conventions that make up the moral world: "industry, knowledge, and humanity, are linked together, by an indissolvable chain" (E, 272). "We cannot reasonably expect, that a piece of woollen cloth will be wrought to perfection in a nation which is ignorant of astronomy, or where ethics are neglected" (E, 270–71). Nor "Can we expect that a government will be well modelled by a people, who know not how to make a spinning wheel, or to employ a loom to advantage" (E, 273). It is for this reason that Hume could say, in the first *Enquiry*, that the cultivation of philosophy in modern times had led to the stability of government (the rule of law) and hope that the cultivation of philosophy would lead to further political improvements (EU, 10). In the last section, we shall see how Hume's hope turned to despair. In the meantime, we observe that, ideally, the perfection of civilization is philosophy, that is, a finely cultivated science of man which can provide causal understanding of, and norms for, the evolving and insensibly contrived conventions of the arts, sciences, morals, and government.

Liberty is essential to the process of civilization viewed as a social, philosophical act. Just as liberty of thought and expression are necessary for the perfection of philosophy and science, so liberty of *action*, under the rule of law, is necessary for the perfection of civilization generally. For, as we have seen, the rule of law provides a secure and orderly framework through which novelties may emerge and be tested for inclusion in the conventions of common life. If the perfection of civilization is the achievement of philosophical self-knowledge, as expressed in the arts and sciences, then the original instrument of this perfection is republican government: "it is impossible for the arts and sciences to arise, at first, among any people, unless that people enjoy the blessing of a free government" (E, 115). By a "free" government, Hume means a republic. Liberty as the rule of law may flourish in a *civilized* monarchy but not in a barbarous one. Before "science were known in the world," it is impossible to suppose a barbarous monarch to be a "legislator, and govern his people by law, not by the arbitrary will of their fellow-subjects" (E, 117). But a republic, though barbarous, "necessarily, by an infallible operation, gives rise to law, even before mankind have made any considerable advances in the other sciences. From law arises security; from security curiosity; and curiosity knowledge. The latter steps of this progress may be more accidental; but the former are altogether necessary. A republic without laws can never have any duration" (E, 118).

Hume links liberty, as the rule of law, to free government by a historical causal bond, not, as Locke does, by a logical one. For Locke, government that is not free cannot contain the rule of law. For Hume, such governments can and do operate by law. The primacy of republican government for Hume is its *causal* power to generate some idea of the rule of law, even under barbarous conditions before men have come to self-consciously understand the nature of law. But republican forms, especially when barbarous, are not sufficient to secure liberty in the full sense. The rule of law must be settled deeply in the habits, prejudices, and traditions of men, and this process takes time and is the work of countless generations: "no human genius, however comprehensive, is able, by the mere dint of reason and reflection, to effect it. The judgments of many must unite in this work: experience must guide their labour: time must bring it to perfection: and the feeling of inconveniences must correct the mistakes, which they inevitably fall into, in their first trials and experiments" (E, 124).

In this way, law, like language or any other profound Humean convention, evolves spontaneously, guided by custom and tradition. It is not due to insights of speculative philosophers and the craft of constitution makers. Hume does celebrate the founders of states and considers them among the greatest of men: "Of all men that distinguish themselves by memorable achievements, the first place of honour seems due to Legislators and founders of states, who transmit a system of laws and institutions to secure the peace, happiness, and liberty of future generations" (E, 54). But what the founders establish is what many generations have prepared men to approve of: "In vain are we asked in what records this charter of our liberties is registered. It was not written on parchment, nor yet on leaves or barks of trees. It preceded the use of writing, and all the other civilized arts of life" (E, 468). But most important, *who* the founders are is not a decision that can be made by the founders themselves nor by their contemporaries but must be left to *future* generations (T, 566).

The rule of law is the source of "all security and happiness" that civilization can afford, and although it is the spontaneous, "slow product of order and liberty, it is not preserved with the same difficulty with which it is produced; but when it has once taken root, is a hardy plant, which will scarcely ever perish through the ill culture of men, or the rigour of the seasons" (E, 124). Through sympathy and emulation, the rule of law is, to some degree, communicated from republics to monarchies, bringing the latter into the process of civilization: "From these causes proceed civilized monarchies, where the arts of government, first invented in free states, are preserved to the mutual advantage and security of sovereign and subject" (E, 125). Once civilized by the rule of law, monarchies may even surpass republics in the perfection of art, science, and government; but this is only because of the "republican" elements contained within the larger sphere of prejudice and tradition of which the monarchy is a part. Civilized monarchy "owes all its perfection to the republican" (E, 125). The rule of law and hence the process of civilization originates in barbarous republics. Hume salutes these in the *History* when discussing the evolution of the British constitution from the Saxon forests. The British owe the advantages of liberty "chiefly to the seeds implanted by those generous barbarians" (H, I, app. i, 161).

If barbarous republics are the original and "proper *nursery* for the arts and sciences," an order of neighboring civilized states (whether republican or monarchical) tied together by commerce and policy is the *laboratory* (E, 119). Hume observes that the competition for the glory of scientific and artistic approval enabled the free Greek city states "to make such considerable shoots as are even at this time the objects of our admiration" (E, 121). Christian hegemony put an end to cultural competition, but this yoke has at length been thrown off, and the civilized monarchies and republics of Europe present an order which "is at present a copy, at large, of what Greece was formerly a pattern in miniature" (E, 121). Hume observes that it was British criticism that "checked the progress of the Cartesian philosophy, to which the French showed such a strong propensity." Likewise, "The severest scrutiny which Newton's theory has undergone proceeded not from his own countrymen, but from foreigners" (E, 121).

Hume held not only that civilization originates in republics but that the most perfect form of civilized government would be a republic; albeit a republic of a special kind. In "Idea of a Perfect Commonwealth" (1752), he argued for "the falsehood of the common opinion, that no large state, such as France or Great Britain, could ever be modelled into a common-wealth, but that such a form of government can only take place in a city or small territory" (E, 527). Indeed, Hume went so far as to argue that "The contrary seems probable. Though it is more difficult to form a republican government in an extensive country than in a city, there is more facility when once it is formed, of preserving it steady and uniform, without tumult and faction" (E, 527). Hume then laid out a federal hierarchy of electoral bodies ordered from the local to the national level where each local unit is "a kind of republic within itself" having a certain degree of autonomy and the power to elect representatives to the higher levels (E, 520). At the top would be a chamber of magistrates who would have the legislative power and a chamber of senators who would, among themselves, constitute an executive branch with a presiding chief executive. The higher magistrates would be indirectly elected by the people through their elected representatives. Such a government could claim consent of the people and so could command popular loyalty and authority.

Hume went out of his way to stress that the very size of the republic which at first had seemed the greatest barrier was, given the carefully graded hierarchy of magistrates and the fragmentizing of electoral districts, its best guarantee of stability: "In a large government, which is modelled with masterly skill, there is compass and room enough to refine the democracy, from the lower people who may be admitted into the first elections, or concoction of the commonwealth, to the higher magistrates who direct all the movements. At the same time, the parts are so distant and remote, that it is very difficult, either by intrigue, or prejudice, or passion, to hurry them into any measures against the public interest" (E, 528–29).

Douglas Adair has shown how James Madison, the architect of the U.

S. Constitution, used Hume's political essays but particularly "Idea of a Perfect Commonwealth" to argue in the *Tenth Federalist* that a federal constitution could be constructed in the large territory of America which could reconcile factions and conflicting interests without sacrificing liberty and justice.[10] The situation was similar to that in science where mathematicians idly construct formal systems which a generation or so later are used by physicists as conceptual frameworks for interpreting the world. Yet there is a difference. Hume was not constructing the idea of a commonwealth for its own sake. Hume's perfect commonwealth was a theoretical abstraction from his historical and philosophical study of ancient and modern political order. It is not a utopia, but takes men as they are: "All plans of government, which suppose great reformations in the manners of mankind, are plainly imaginary" (E, 514). But most important, as we have seen, Humean abstractions, models, and ideals must both transcend and bear the imprint of some actual order. Hume's ideal of a perfect commonwealth was a self-conscious solution to political problems of the modern age. Hume compared his model of government to Huygen's model of the form of a ship which is the most commodious for sailing. Hume's model republic is the ship of state best able to sail through modern waters.

Why did he choose the counter-intuitive model of a large republic for the ideal constitution for the modern age in the face of the dominant view of his contemporaries that republics must be small? The answer is that Hume believed the civilizing social, economic, and political forces at work in Europe ("modern manners") held open unlimited possibilities for the development of liberty, commerce, and culture. This trend had introduced "irregular" republican elements into the prejudices and customs of most European monarchies. But though Hume embraced the republican ideal, he resisted republicanism in Britain, as we shall see in the next section, because of historical circumstances just as he pointed out the growth of republican values in the absolute monarchies of France. The modern trend was toward large nation states, commercial empires, and republican prejudices, and so the question must eventually arise of how to reconcile liberty and authority in a commercial republican empire. Hume's "Idea of a Perfect Commonwealth" is an answer, indeed the first answer, to this question.

Hume's model republic, then, is a concrete idealization of the civilizing forces he had identified at work in Europe. But no large country in Europe comes close to approximating it, nor were there any prospects in the near future. It is as if Huygen's model of the most efficient sailing vessel were available but the technology and materials were not at hand for building a ship in close approximation to it. Hume's hope was that by articulating the concept of a commercial republican empire, already immanent in the conversation of the learned world, discussion could ensue and perhaps a consensus reached on a model of government that could guide political activity. But the hope lay not in Europe but in a "distant" land, and not in the present but "in some future age [where] an opportunity might be afforded of reducing the theory to practice, either by a dissolution of some old government, or by the combination of men to form a new one, in some distant part of the world" (E, 513).

Hume's attempt to quarantine the instantiation of his model republic as far away in space and time from contemporary Europe as possible is no doubt due, in part, to the desire not to arouse revolutionary passions. But one wonders if Hume did not have in mind, at least dimly, the application of the model to the new world. Very early in his career he had thought that "The Charter Governments in America" are "almost entirely independent of England" and that the American colonies were already an order of virtually self-governing republics.[11] In any case, as Douglas Adair has shown, Madison wrote the *Tenth Federalist* under the guidance of Hume's "Idea of a Perfect Commonwealth." Looking upon the disordered political scene that had prompted the constitutional convention through the lens of Hume's essay, Madison was able to see what many of his republican loving contemporaries could not. Hume had turned the republican theory inside out. Though more difficult to establish, yet once established, a republic would work best in a large territory. A monarchy, then, was not necessary after all, and what had appeared as the main obstacle to a republican America could now be seen as its chief support. Moreover, the jealousy of the states and local unities which seemed to require either control by oppressive monarchy or a system of totally independent republics could be a positive asset if ordered through a carefully graded hierarchy of liberty, authority, and indirect elections. Madison did not use Hume's theory of an ideal republic as a utopian scheme to be imposed upon practice but, as Hume intended it, as a guide to correct and render more coherent an already established practice. Hume's theory enabled Madison to see that America had already developed a quasi-federal order in which each local political body was, to use Hume's expression, "a kind of republic within itself."

Gerald Stourzh has discussed the decisive influence Hume had on Alexander Hamilton's political thought.[12] Here we need mention only that Hamilton learned from Hume not only that a republic need not be confined to a small country but also that it need not have a frugal, agrarian economy as taught by the ancients and early moderns. If properly ordered, a republic could flourish best in a large territory and under conditions of great commercial wealth. Henceforth modern republican *virtue* could be thought of as an appendage of expanding commercial wealth and not of rustic frugality.

Hume's argument that the ideal model of government for the modern age is a large commercial republic and that such a republic would be more durable than any alternative was prophetic. The political world today is, for the most part, an order of large nation states with commercial economies that claim to be republics. Something like the model Hume discerned implicit in the conversation of the 18th century learned world has become the explicit ideal of public discourse.

IV. The New Barbarism: The Conceptual Destruction of Liberty

The rationale of much of Hume's writing on liberty is to explain that modern liberty is something new and valuable that has unexpectedly appeared in the world, the nature and value of which is still not understood. Hume stresses the accidental and fragile character of liberty. He speaks, for instance, of the "wisdom of the [British] constitution or rather the concurrence of accidents" (H, V, note e, p. 569). And he considers many threats to liberty such as economic (the national debt), political (the expanding British empire – Hume believed republican empires tend to be oppressive and to degenerate into tyranny), and moral (the personal ambitions of demagogues such as Pitt, and Wilkes at the expense of the constitution and which threaten a replay of the oppressive Cromwellian republic). But since our concern in this essay is with Hume's *concept* of liberty, we shall discuss only one of these threats and one which has not, I think, received adequate attention, namely the threat to liberty posed not by wrong economic, social, or political policies but by false ways of *thinking* about liberty. The discovery of this threat is, as far as I can see, original with Hume in the 18th century and is peculiar to the sort of philosophy he worked out.

Hume taught that most values in the moral world and all political values depend on opinion. An entire political order may dissolve due to a disorder in *opinion*. He also taught that ideas follow impressions. The idea of liberty grows out of the experience of liberty. But ideas are not confined to the experiences which generate them. The imagination is capable of constructing the most bizarre ideas. A disordered conception of liberty can alienate one from the experience of liberty, so that one may come to deny the reality of the liberty he actually enjoys. Madness and superstition are forms of thinking which obscure reality. One caught in the grip of such alienation is in the unhappy state of disowning the experience of reality he actually lives out.

But madness and superstition are not the only ways in which thought can obscure reality. Critical reflection can yield a similar error, and one all the more difficult to detect and to cure because the error is covered with the mantle of something called *reason*. Indeed critical reflection poses a special problem. Critical reflection is a process in which a practice is raised to the level of self-consciousness. But this process presupposes that the practice was carried out successfully prior to reflection, e.g., that the practice of speaking English was successfully carried out prior to a reflective understanding of the rules which, looking back, we may read into the practice. The act of critical reflection opens up a distance between thought and the pre-reflectively lived out practice. In this distance thought can get lost. True critical reflection will both mirror and transcend the practice which it brings to awareness. But false critical reflection may imagine itself to be the absolute legislator of the practice with the authority to declare the practice real or unreal: "Reason first appears in possession of the throne, prescribing laws, and imposing maxims, with an absolute sway and authority" (T, 186). Thus one may participate in a practice, say, of knowledge or justice but be in the grip of a false philosophical theory of knowledge and justice whereby one disowns the experience of knowledge and justice that one has.

Since the act of critical reflection presupposes an ability to recognize the difference between participation in the practice and a theory of the practice, it is always possible to be emancipated from philosophical illusions. But it is difficult. The reason is that the critical thinker imagines himself rationally superior to those who merely live through a practice unreflectively. One who acts in the name of custom is conceptually capable of seeing that his act may not be rational. But one who acts in the name of reason has a conceptual problem in recognizing that his act may not be rational. Likewise, one who acts in the name of liberty by that very fact erects a conceptual barrier to seeing that his action may be illiberal. Hume saw that there is a special bigotry that attaches not to custom and prejudice but to the reflective intellect itself.

Hume thought there were two forms of critical reflection that threatened to alienate Britons from the liberty they actually enjoyed: one was philosophical, the other historical. Both, he thought, informed the thinking of the whig literary and political establishment which had dominated British letters and policy from the end of the 17th century throughout his life. For over two generations this philosophically and historically disordered whig view of political experience had been hammered into the national consciousness. The disorder was more or less safely contained, Hume thought, until the late 1760's with the ascendancy of the demagogue Pitt, the Wilkes and Liberty riots, the inchoate demand for more democratic representation, and the American crisis. Prior to the late 60's Hume's letters are relatively silent on political matters. But from then on until his death in August, 1776, the letters contain a voice of prophetic alarm. Looking back, Hume's attack on the whig partizans of liberty has seemed reactionary. But it is possible to view it as a *defense* of liberty and as a response consistent with his conception of the proper philosophical and historical framework through which liberty must be understood. I shall take up first Hume's conception of how false philosophical thinking may conceptually destroy liberty and then turn briefly to the corresponding error in historical thought.

I have discussed elsewhere Hume's distinction between true and false philosophy.[13] Here only its main features can be touched. As traditionally conceived, philosophy is an attempt to gain an understanding of ultimate reality. In doing this it is radically autonomous, that is, philosophy cannot accept as a starting point any custom, prejudice, or tradition of common life, otherwise it would become the mere handmaiden of these prejudices. Philosophy is radically free and self-justifying inquiry. No prejudice of common life can be accepted that is not philosophically certified, and any criticism of philosophy must be a case of it.

Hume sought to show, through skeptical arguments, that this traditional picture of philosophical inquiry is incoherent. Philosophy, independent of the prejudices of common life, ends in total skepticism, and is not self-justifying but self-destructive. Philosophers, in fact, never end in total skepticism because they unknowingly smuggle in some favorite prejudice of common life to give content and decision to what is otherwise an entirely vacuous form of thought. But just as philosophers do not consistently push through the autonomy principle, so men cannot consistently refuse to philosophize (T, 268–269). Hume's solution to this conflict is to abandon the pure form of the autonomy principle for a modified version: philosophical inquiry into the real must accept the prejudices of common life as a whole as a necessary condition for inquiry. Any prejudice *within* the order may be questioned in the light of abstract rules, ideals, models, and other prejudices. What cannot be done is to suppose that one is free from the prejudices of common life as a whole. True philosophy instantiates this modified form of the autonomy principle; false philosophy is sunk in the illusions of the pure form.

In the last section of Book I of the *Treatise*, Hume dramatizes the state of mind of the false philosopher. By virtue of the autonomy principle, the false philosopher pompously imagines himself free from the prejudices of common life. In their place, he constructs an *alternative world* which alone has the title of reality. But he is inescapably part of the world of common life. This tension sets up a profound alienation in the philosopher's soul. Due to the autonomy principle, he cannot *participate* in the prejudices of common life on pain of losing his integrity as a thinker. The authority of the whole order of prejudice has been *conceptually* eliminated. Yet, logically and psychologically, he is part of the very order he disdains. This leads to feelings which move from arrogant self-sufficiency ("forlorn solitude") to resentment ("cannot prevail with myself to mix with such deformity") to self-disgust ("fancy myself some strange uncouth monster").

Much has been made of Hume's remark that it is "nature" which frees him from this "philosophical melancholy and delirium," and Hume is usually pictured as a cheerful philistine. But that is not the whole story. Nature and "back-gammon" prevents one, momentarily, from being condemned to the radical freedom of autonomous philosophy. But nature cannot reconcile the conflicting demands of *philosophy* and nature, and Hume is clear that both demands are legitimate (T, 214–15; 268). The reconciliation is not the work of nature but of critical *reflection*. Superstition is cured not by nature but by philosophy (T, 271, EU, 12). Likewise, *philosophical* melancholy can be cured only by a deeper sort of philosophical reflection. Hume distinguishes three stages in the natural history of philosophical consciousness: "according as the persons, who form them, acquire new degrees of reason and knowledge. These opinions are that of the vulgar, that of a false philosophy, and that of the true; where we shall find upon enquiry, that the true philosophy approaches nearer to the sentiments of the vulgar, than to those of a mistaken knowledge" (T, 222–223). The true philosopher is one who recognizes this dialectical movement in his own thinking. He realizes that if philosophical inquiry is to continue at all, it must reform itself by abandoning the autonomy principle in its pure form and by recognizing unreflective common life not as an object of critical reflection but as a category internal to its own critical activity. He ceases to see himself as the spectator of the prejudices of common life and instead views himself as a critical participant in them.

The true philosopher, then, has both an immanent and a transcendent existence relative to the world of common life. He exists within insofar as his thought presupposes the order. He exists without insofar as his thought is aimed at understanding ultimate reality. No prejudice of common life can fully satisfy the demand of philosophical thought to know the real. Yet it is only through these prejudices that we can think about the real. Skepticism, then, is not the enemy of true philosophy; rather, it makes true philosophy possible: the true philosopher recognizes his cognitive alienation from ultimate reality but continues to inquire, though he has nothing but the "leaky weather-beaten vessel" of the prejudices of common life through which to think (T, 263).

It is common to view Hume as an empiricist who set out to attack rationalism. There is some truth in this, but it obscures Hume's main philosophical achievement. Hume set out to reform the traditional practice of *philosophy* as such. Rationalism is simply one form of philosophy. Hume's criticism applies equally to most forms of empiricism: phenomenalism, logical empiricism, pragmatism, and utilitarianism. In all of these, the autonomy principle runs free and is undisciplined by common life. Berkeley taught, for instance, that one must think with the learned and speak with the vulgar. Hume teaches that one must not only speak with the vulgar, but also that there is no escaping thinking with them (although, of course, one can do so in a critical way).

What bearing does this discussion of Hume's distinction between true and false philosophy have on our discussion of his conception of liberty? Simply this. All philosophical concepts, whether of liberty, truth, knowledge or whatever, that are structured by the autonomy principle of false philosophy are illegitimate. The mark of such concepts is that they entail the conceptual destruction of the domain of common life that they purport to illuminate. Proudhon's dictum that "property is theft" is a paradigm case of such concepts. Here the authority of the entire order of property relations in common life is conceptually destroyed. Thought, though a reflection of fundamental practices of common life, has so far lost its way as to turn in impious destruction upon those very practices. All property is theft. The true order of property is a *totally* different system discovered by the Archimedian principle of autonomous philosophy. Proudhon's dictum provokes the feeling of philosophical alienation which Hume explored in the conclusion of Book I: *resentment* that one's own has been taken away and *self-disgust* that one continues to participate in the order of theft.

All contract theories of government from Hobbes, Locke, Rousseau, Kant to Rawls are the work of false philosophy. All entail, methodologically, the conceptual destruction of the prejudices that constitute the political order of common life. For the rationale of the contract theory is that no authority is legitimate unless it is, in some way, chosen by those subject to it. All contract theories require that the choice of legitimate authority be made in a vacuum (the state of nature of Hobbes, the veil of ignorance of Rawls, etc.) methodologically sealed off from the influence of existing custom. Thus the *entire* order of custom is rejected as having no original authority to determine judgment. But principles of legitimacy framed in a vacuum have no content. As we have seen, anything may appear to satisfy them or nothing may appear to satisfy them. Only custom can give them the content necessary for a non-arbitrary application to the world. But the original authority of custom having been rejected, the principles themselves cannot determine which customs are to fill and guide the principles in critical thinking. The customs that are in fact used cannot be justified by the vacuous contract principles. And so the contract theory is arbitrary, being nothing more than a rationalization of a favorite set of customs which it would have been best to have openly affirmed as a participant of common life in the first place and to have argued for in a different way.

Although different in many respects, Marxism is like liberalism in methodologically eliminating the original authority of established custom. For Marx, the existing political world has no authority of its own to command judgment. The true political reality is locked into the future classless society immanent in history. And Marx's utopian vision of a classless society in which the free development of one is a condition for the free development of all is not unlike the vacuum of liberal contract theory in which, unspotted by existing custom, all choose the same principles of legitimacy.

It is common to think of Marxism as revolutionary and of contract-theory liberalism as not. But this is a profound mistake. Liberalism and Marxism are revolutionary in the same way. Both are instantiations of false philosophy and both entail the conceptual destruction of the prejudices of common life as a whole. Total conceptual destruction must issue in either a bad faith accommodation with the world of illusion and illegitimacy or an attempt at total revolution, that is, the total destruction of these prejudices in favor of the alternative world contrived by autonomous philosophical reflection. The natural progress of revolution, then, is first total conceptual destruction, total revolution, and finally totalitarian power. The first step in this process is entailed in *any* criticism of autonomous philosophy. The next steps are contingent. Liberalism has its Robespierre as Marxism has its Stalin. And Marxism need not lead to revolutionary action. A Marxist may ride the fateful tide of history with the equanimity of Seneca.

If liberalism has been less violent and destructive in history than Marxism, it has also issued in greater guilt and self-disgust as it has had to morally compromise with the world of illusion and illegitimacy. The vulgar journalistic notion of the guilty liberal has its philosophical explication. What has kept liberalism from being less revolutionary is the unrecognized prejudices of the historical traditions out of which it grew and to which it has remained, on the whole, *loyal*. It is these beneficent prejudices alone and not any strength of the theories themselves that keep the liberal moderate and humane.

This interpretation of Marxism and liberalism may seem extreme. Is there not some truth in these philosophical theories? If Hume's criticism of philosophy is basically correct, and I think it is, the answer must be no. The *theories* themselves, as shaped by the autonomy principle are and must be entirely vacuous. Whatever truth may appear in them is due entirely to the unacknowledged prejudices which are naturally absorbed from the tradition out of which they grew and in which they may still more or less participate. If these prejudices were brought to light and logically stripped away, the theories would appear as the vacuities they are.

Hume's criticism of the contract theory is well known, but most commentators have failed to appreciate the depth of the criticism. The contract theory is a form of false philosophy. Strictly speaking it is no theory of government at all because it does not recognize the independent authority of the political prejudices of common life. Without these, the application of contract theory to the world is entirely arbitrary. Locke argued from the vacuum of the contract to the thesis that absolute monarchy "is inconsistent with Civil Society, and so can be no Form of Civil Government at all."[14] Hume pressed the theory, arguing that, if taken seriously and consistently applied (which it never is), no government has been legitimate. Hume dryly observed that when political principle is entirely cut loose from the original authority of custom, then "the more principle" a man has, the more he can be expected "to neglect and abandon his domestic duties" (H, VI, 513).

Hume does not *disagree* with Locke's theory. His own view of the legitimacy of government is of a logically different type: Hume's theory has the form of true philosophy, Locke's that of false philosophy. It is perhaps worthwhile to observe here that the distinction between true and false philosophy is not the same as the distinction between a philosophical theory that is true and one that is false. The distinction is more like that between the scientific (true science) and the unscientific (false science, i.e., any activity that is not *truly* scientific). Within the class of theories that are truly scientific, some are true (justified) and others are false (unjustified), but all are genuine scientific theories. Likewise, Hume's theory of liberty is a case of true philosophy (genuine philosophy) because it recognizes the independent authority of common life. Hume's theory may be false or in some way inadequate, but it is still a case of true philosophy. The contract theory, not recognizing the independent authority of common life, is not (on Hume's reform of philosophy) a proper philosophical theory at all.

Philosophically false theories may, nevertheless, have some utility. The reason is that philosophical theories, on Hume's view, are instruments for making us conscious of the deeply established prejudices that constitute our common world. There is, then, usually a truth in false philosophical theories which the theories themselves obscure and cannot articulate. Hume finds such a grain of truth in the contract theory. Government, at the very least is instituted to provide security for life and property (understood as the evolving conventions of common life have understood them). When government fails in this task, it loses its title to authority. The theory that the legitimacy of government depends on a contract between the sovereign and the people is at best a symbol of this common experience of government. Locke and others have twisted this truth into the pseudo-rationalistic shape of a contract which, if really taken seriously, alienates the thinker from all the governments of the world. Hume's point is that it is only in the failure to take such theories seriously and to push them all the way that their fundamental emptiness is hidden.

The conceptual destruction of liberty brought on by false philosophy of which the contract theory was the most prominent instance was not merely an affair of the closet. The demand that government have not only moral but *philosophical* legitimacy was coming not merely from closet philosophers but from the vulgar as well. Hume bitterly observed that "no party, in the present age, can well support itself without a philosophical or speculative system of principles annexed to its political or practical one" (E, 465). The philosophical thinking informing these metaphysical parties will typically be false, and, moreover, will be the work of the vulgar who cannot be expected to have the self-critical attitude necessary for true philosophy: The people being commonly very rude builders, especially in this speculative way ... their workmanship must be a little unshapely, and discover evident marks of that violence and hurry in which it was raised" (E, 466).

The presence of false philosophy in politics means that the partizan of a metaphysical political party would undergo the same alienation from common life, with the attendant feelings of resentment and self-disgust, that characterizes the closet philosopher of the *Treatise*. Hume's most thorough discussion of this phenomenon occurs in the *history* with his treatment of the English Civil War which he presents as a uniquely modern and metaphysical war in roughly the way Burke treated the French Revolution. The thoughts and actions of the Puritan party were in the grip of a species of false philosophy, and it is for this reason that Hume finds the war to be *philosophically* interesting: "The gloomy enthusiasm which prevailed among the parliamentary party, is surely the most curious spectacle presented by any history; and the most instructive, as well as entertaining, to a philosophical mind" (H, V, lxii, 519). The philosophic dimension of the war was due mainly to Protestantism which "being chiefly spiritual, resembles more a system of metaphysics" (H, IV, xxxviii, 12). The Protestants were somewhat like "the Stoics," who "join a philosophical enthusiasm to a religious superstition" (NHR, 63).

But political parties informed by philosophy are, Hume thought, unique to modern times: "Parties from principle, especially abstract speculative principle, are known only to modern times, and are, perhaps, the most extraordinary and unaccountable phenomenon that has yet appeared in human affairs" (E, 60). The reason for this is due mainly to the historical merger of philosophy and Christianity in the ancient world. Ancient pagan religion, prior to Christianity, was a civic religion which grew spontaneously with the political community. Just as communities were different but not contrary, so pagan civic religions were not in logical opposition. The result was that pagan religions tended to be pluralistic and tolerant. Ancient philosophical sects, however, were logically opposed and were sources of zeal and fanaticism. Philosophy, however, was divorced from political order which was protected by the civic religion so that the fanaticism of philosophical sects was confined to the private sphere.

When Christianity became the civic religion, the distinction between philosophy and politics collapsed. Christianity is theistic and so necessarily makes an ultimate metaphysical claim: "where theism forms the fundamental principle of any popular religion, that tenet is so conformable to sound reason, that philosophy is apt to incorporate itself into such a system of theology" (NHR, 53). Moreover, adherents of the new sect found themselves in competition with a highly cultivated philosophical opposition and so were obliged to justify their beliefs "with all the subtlety of argument and science" (E, 62). The result was that Christianity became indistinguishable from a highly refined metaphysical system. The alienation from common life characteristic of false philosophy would infect Christianity, and given the union of ecclesiastical and civil authority would infect the state also. The conservative function of the old pagan civic religions served to keep the philosophically threatening force of Christianity (or any other metaphysics) at bay.

But after the reformation and by the 17th century, the demand of philosophical autonomy began to assert itself, though still clothed in the mantle of religion. Hume is very clear that the battle between Crown and Parliament in the Civil War was a battle for the *minds* of men. "The war of the pen preceded that of the sword, and daily sharpened the humours of the opposite parties ... The king and parliament themselves carried on the controversy by messages, remonstrances, and declarations; where the nation was really the party to whom all arguments were addressed" (H, V, lv, 221). Radically free philosophical thinking was a manifestation of a "spirit of innovation with which the age was generally seized" (H, III, xxxi, 204). Central to the conflict was the philosophical question of the foundations of political authority. The "general humour of the time was ... intent on plans of imaginary republics" (H, V, Lix, 334). "Every man had framed the model of a republic; and, however new it was, or fantastical, he was eager in recommending it to his fellow citizens, or even imposing it by force upon them" (H, V, lx, 386).

The end result was a Puritan Republic under the military dictatorship of Cromwell which sought to impose not only a different political constitution but a different social and moral order as well. Hume characterizes the Puritan revolutionaries as "sanctified robbers ... who, under pretence of superior illuminations, would soon extirpate, if possible, all private morality, as they had already done all public law and justice, from the British dominions" (H, lxii, 499). Cromwell ruled, however, in the name of *liberty*. But the concept of liberty was that of false philosophy cut loose from the evolving conventions of common life. When the autonomy principle of false philosophy appears, it "bends every branch of knowledge to its own purpose, without much regard to the phenomena of nature, or to the unbiased sentiments of the mind, hence reasoning, and even language, have been warped from their natural course" (EM, 322). When this happens, liberty may mean anything that power can establish. And so Hume can say, sardonically, of the Puritan republic: "Never in this island was known a more severe and arbitrary government than was generally exercised by the patrons of liberty" (H, V, lix, 365).

By the 18th century, religion had come to have little influence in politics. Metaphysical political parties were now largely secular. Philosophical *reason* not religious piety would be the appeals of public political discourse. In a way Hume thought this was a good thing. When he wrote the first *Enquiry* he saw the growth of philosophy and the stability of modern government as part of the process of civilization, and he hoped that the further spread of philosophy on a popular level would lead to further improvements in political stability and liberty. But all of this depended on whether the philosophy informing popular politics would be the true or the false. False philosophy in politics would yield alienation and instability. By the late 60's with the Wilkes riots (1768–71), the popular sovereignty movement of which they were a part, and the American crisis, Hume had come to think that this was happening.

John Wilkes had written a scandalous article on George III's government and on the Scottish influence in the ministry. His trial for libel and repeated efforts of the House of Commons to unseat him (four times he was elected and four times rejected by the House) led to popular demonstrations. These continued off and on for three years and were often violent. The Wilkes' affair became a symbol around which a number of popular grievances emerged: the demand for a free press, the legitimacy of extraparliamentary political activity, and the rights of electors to send representatives to Parliament. The three-year affair greatly alarmed Hume who interpreted it as a constitutional crisis. Nor was he alone in this. In a letter of October, 1769, Horace Walpole wrote that England "approaches by fast strides to some great crisis, and to me never wore so serious an air, except in the Rebellion." In March of 1770 the city of London drew up a Remonstrance and Petition calling for the dissolution of Parliament and the removal of evil ministers. At this time Walpole wrote: "rebellion is in prospect, and in everybody's mouth."

What especially alarmed Hume was that the government seemed incapable of exercising its legitimate authority, and when after three years the government finally muddled through, Hume could wonder: "if in a case, where popular Complaints had not the smallest Shadow of Pretence, the King and Parliament have prevail'd after a long Struggle and with much Difficulty, what must it be, where there is some plausible Appearance, and perhaps some real Ground of Complaint, such as it is natural to expect in all Government? (L, II, 221). What had weakened the authority of government? Hume did not think there was any legitimate complaint that could have accounted for the riots. The demands of "the Wilkites and the Bill of Rights-men" were "founded on nothing, and had no connexion with any higher order of the state" (L, II, 235, 178). The affair was "without a Cause" (L, II, 210). The Wilkes and liberty affair was the result of a wrong way of thinking about reality. Hume often described it as "Madness" and as a "frenzy."

The victims of this madness are "the London Mob," by which Hume does not mean the classical rabble of antiquity but middle class leaders including the Mayor and Sheriffs of London and that "wicked Madman Pitt" (L, II, 221, 301). But the "Barbarians on the Thames" are only symptomatic of a larger distemper that has infected *English* political thinking: "The Madness and Wickedness of the English (for do not say the Scum of London) appears astonishing, even after all the Experience we have had. It must end fatally either to the King or Constitution or to both" (L, II, 226). The English are a "deluded People" (L, II, 215). In February, 1770, Hume wrote to Gilbert Eliot: "Our Government has become a Chimera; and is too perfect in point of Liberty, for so vile a Beast as an Englishman, who is a Man ... corrupted by above a Century of Licentiousness. The Misfortune is, that this Liberty can scarcely be retrench'd without Danger of being entirely lost" (L, II, 216). These passages are not simply a reaction to English prejudices against the Scots. The "above a Century of Licentiousness" mentioned above refers to the century-long dominance of whig ideology in politics and letters. Hume mentions this dominance "in the state and in literature" again in "My Own Life." Whig ideology is informed by false philosophy, namely the rationalistic contract theory. Hume regretted that something of this theory had infected the first edition of the *History* which was "too full of those foolish English Prejudices, which all Nations and all Ages dis-avow" (L, II, 216). The prejudices are that liberty (the rule of law) is contractual and not a perfection of government but a condition of its legitimacy, prejudices rejected "in every place but this single kingdom..." (E, 487).

Duncan Forbes has criticized Hume for thinking that the contract theory is unique to the English. Leaving aside the fact that Hume recognized a form of the theory in Socrates and in French thinkers (E, 485n, 487), the criticism misses Hume's point. What he finds disturbing is that the contract theory is not simply a bemusing error of closet philosophers but has infected an entire nation. Since the contract theory is a form of false philosophy, the lesson of the "Conclusion" of Book I is applicable: one becomes progressively alienated from common life to the degree that one takes a false philosophical theory seriously. The alienation, resentment, and self-disgust that Hume found characteristic of false philosophy in the closet must now appear in the politics of common life itself. This was something new. Hume observed that "Sects of philosophy, in the ancient world, were more zealous than parties of religion..." (E, 63). But they were controlled by the pagan civil religion. In modern times, critical philosophical reflection has undercut the authority of the Church. There is no institution, except perhaps the state, to restrain the errors of the philosophical intellect. But if the state itself should become a philosophical institution, there would be little question as to whether the philosophy that would dominate it would be the true or the false. The subtle dialectical arguments of the *Treatise* that frame the notion of true philosophy are too refined to have a restraining influence on mass political movements driven by "philosophical enthusiasm" (EM, 343).

The total alienation from common life brought on by false philosophy leads to a paranoid attitude which Hume recognized in the "Conclusion" of Book I: "Every one keeps at a distance ... and can I wonder at the insults I must suffer" (T, 264)? Those caught in the grip of the contract theory may see threats to liberty everywhere. For government to enforce law will give "Pretence for the Cry that Liberty is violated" (L, II, 209). The demands of men caught in the grip of false philosophy are ultimate and autonomous. And since they are cut loose from the prejudices of common life, non-arbitrary distinctions of good and evil can no longer be made, and so "no one can answer for what will please or displease them" (EM, 343). Hume had seen all this before in his examination of what he considered to be the metaphysically motivated Puritan rebellion. The Crown could do nothing to placate "the endless demands of certain insatiable and turbulent spirits, whom nothing less will content than a total subversion of the ancient constitution" (H, V, liv, 163). But there was a difference. The false philosophy informing Puritan thought and action was modified by religion and could not present itself as fully rational. But the Wilkes affair and the constitutional crisis of which it was a symptom was purely secular and all the less excusable. It "exceeds the Absurdity of Titus Oates and the popish Plot; and is so much more disgraceful to the Nation, as the former Folly, being derived from Religion, flow'd from a Source, which has, from uniform Prescription, acquired a Right to impose Nonsense on all Nations & all Ages" (L, II, 197). It seemed to Hume that philosophers in his time were beginning to acquire that unprecedented right in England. In the *Treatise*, he had argued that "Generally speaking, the errors in religion are dangerous; those in philosophy only ridiculous" (T, 272). The errors of religion are dangerous because they infect the public; the errors of philosophy are ridiculous because they merely bemuse and torment the philosopher in the closet. Hume's analysis of false philosophy, his examination of the logic of Puritan rebellion, and his prophetic insight into the metaphysical workings of modern political parties enabled him to view the Wilkes and Liberty affair as a dangerous case of false philosophy in politics.

Hume describes the London mob and the English not only as suffering from a kind of madness but as *barbarians*. The English, he wrote to William Strahan in January, 1773, are "sunk in Stupidity and Barbarism and Faction ..." (L, II, 269). We are apt to read such outbursts as the expression of emotion and as having no descriptive content since we are unlikely to use the term 'barbarian' any but in an emotive way. In Hume's time, however, civilization and barbarism were objects of serious discussion. The term 'barbarism' has descriptive meaning in Hume's works and is a necessary conceptual background for explicating the concept of civilization. For instance, in the *History*, all ages prior to the 15th century are barbarous. The barbarian, as we have seen, is in a state of ignorance. He does not understand the rule of law that makes civilized life possible. Men are freed from barbarism progressively: first by primitive republican institutions and then by critical reflection of the arts and sciences which may flourish equally in republics or monarchies. The perfection of civilization would be the establishment of fully developed republican institutions (the rule of law) and the popular cultivation of philosophy, the highest expression of the arts and sciences. Using these criteria, the English are the most civilized in respect to the rule of law and, on the whole, are equal to any nation in the arts and sciences. Yet Hume thinks that the English are, in some way, "barbarous." Whatever "barbarism" may mean here, it is the sort of thing that can exist only in civilized states.

What he may have had in mind is something like this. The barbarian is one who out of ignorance sees the rule of law as something alien. The 18th century English are barbarous because the rule of law, as embodied in the *conventions* of common life, has, by false philosophical reflection, become an alien system. False *philosophical* thinking has informed British politics, and the English have become alienated from the liberty they actually enjoy. Again, the lesson of the "Conclusion" of Book I of the *Treatise* is that a thinker is alienated from the object of reflection to the degree that a false philosophical theory of it is taken seriously. As a civilized nation, British politics have become necessarily more reflective and philosophical. But the English have taken seriously a false philosophical theory of liberty and so have become alienated from the reality of liberty in common life. Such alienation constitutes a new form of barbarism which is possible only in advanced states where philosophical thinking has become popular.

The mark of such alienation is that the word 'liberty' is thrown into the semantic confusion that false philosophy always brings to the language of common life. Hume recognized that 'liberty' had been cut loose from its semantic moorings in the prejudices of common life and swept into the free play of the autonomy principle of false philosophy. Purged of the semantic constraints of the conventions of common life, 'liberty' could mean anything that power and resentment could establish. And so Hume could wish "that People do not take a Disgust at Liberty; a word, that has been so much profaned by these polluted Mouths, that men of Sense are sick at the very mention of it. I hope a new term will be invented to express so valuable and good a thing" (NHL, 196).

False philosophical thinking was not the only way in which Hume thought the nature and value of the existing constitution of liberty was obscured. False historical thinking had a similar effect. The popular whig view that the present constitution was the sacred reenactment of an ancient constitution which had been maintained over the centuries in spite of unceasing attempts to overthrow it, produces a paranoid view of the present constitution and makes it impossible to understand its actual nature. Catharine Macaulay accepted this Manichean view of the constitution and saw, in her own time, with something of a paranoid eye, the same dark forces at work, forces which would "remove the limitations necessary to render monarchy consistent with liberty ... such a faction has ever existed in this state, from the earliest period of our present constitution." These are "rebels in the worst sense; rebels to the laws of their country, the law of nature, the law of reason, and the law of

God."[15] Instead of viewing the constitution causally (as Hume does), as an *instrument* washed up by historical accidents and human nature, to be understood and cultivated, it is viewed as a *sacred act* of ancestors to be reenacted and protected from desecration. Catharine Macaulay confesses that from early youth, liberty "became the object of a secondary worship" in her "delighted imagination."[16] This worship implied the doctrine of the wickedness of the Stuarts, whose attempts at usurpation were finally overthrown "by the toil and blood of the most exalted individuals that ever adorned humanity," that is, the Puritan party. By comparison with her contemporaries, they "appear more than human."[17] The greatness and perfection of the constitution is in a past world inhabited by heroes. The present is a time of loss.

As Craig Walton has shown, John Baxter's *New and Impartial History of England* (1796), which was a scissors and paste rewriting of Hume's *History* from a radical whig point of view, was chosen by Thomas Jefferson to replace Hume's *History* at the University of Virginia because of its alleged Toryism. Baxter rejected Hume's fundamental thesis about the present constitution, namely that if it was "not the best system of government," it was "at least the most entire system of liberty that ever was known amongst mankind" (H, VI, 531), that it revealed dimensions and possibilities of human nature which could not have been imagined by previous generations, that properly to celebrate and preserve this new system, we must clearly understand its fragile, historical character and its dark, unintended origins. In place of this, Baxter substituted the crudest form of ancient constitutionalism: "Neither can we agree with those who say, the constitution, as it exists at present, is the height of human perfection, improved by time, and sanctioned by experience; for we have pointed out a time when it existed in much greater perfection, and had the universal suffrage of the people."[18]

This misplaced historical thinking produces feelings of paranoia and resentment about the present. But these historical hallucinations are not peculiar to 18th century whigs. They are a feature of liberal progressive ideology generally and are described in Butterfield's classic *The Whig Interpretation of History*. The natural history of the error runs somewhat as follows. A new arrangement evolves spontaneously in society which makes a new value possible. This new value, only vaguely understood, if at all, begins to be established. Once identified by reflection, it is seized upon as a right. The right is then, as in a dream, read back into the past and all previous social orders in which the value was scarcely even conceivable are perceived as having *prevented* possession of the right. The present order, too, is seen as oppressive and threatening – the very order that made the new value possible and in which it was first instantiated. In this way, a liberalizing order is transformed by an act of reflection into an "oppressive" one.

Many 20th century "liberation" movements follow this pattern, especially those that arose under conditions of affluence such as feminist ideology. Spontaneously evolving social and economic conditions such as the gradual establishment of women in the industrial work force and the introduction of more effective means of birth-control brought on changes in social, moral, and political arrangements. These new values and arrangements had to be somehow woven into the tradition. In the nature of the case, no one can know what is to be done. No one can know how far the old utilities may be modified without undoing some important fabric of society nor in what direction the new arrangements may lead. The rationality or irrationality of reform can be understood only *after* an adjustment is established. What is needed for this project, in the meantime, is the good humoured, reconciling genius of the Humean imagination where contraries are somehow brought into unity (as occurs naturally in our belief that we perceive a causally connected external world and rhetorically in Hume's vision, in the *History*, of a new national unity which incorporates the Royalist and Puritan traditions into the Hanoverian regime). Some kind of reconciliation will occur in time, but it is often longer in coming, is made more painful, and is poisoned by 20th century liberal reenactment of 18th century whig historical alienation.

Such a mentality is made popular by a liberal political and literary establishment that suffers the same historical alienation, but, being in power, accepts the misplaced guilt of the present and past. In this way a flourishing liberal regime such as the United States, for example, spawns an ever increasing number of "victims" of oppression. Women, blacks, American indians, orientals, those with Latin surnames (regardless of their past or present wealth, status, or privileges) are conceived as victims and constitute the Affirmative Action group for which special treatment in hiring and promotion is demanded by law. This group comprises around seventy percent of the population and commands over seventy-five percent of the nation's wealth.[19] The spectacle is played out over and over again of the self-confessed guilty oppressor and the protected but accusing oppressed. The one gripped by an unfounded self-disgust, the other by an equally unfounded resentment. Both feed on each other, and both are illusions of a profoundly disordered historical and philosophical imagination. In such a world there are only two categories of existence. To be is to be a victim or the liberator of victims. From the moral point of view, the tragedy here (as Hume recognized in the case of liberty) is that real victims of oppression will be overlooked in favor of philosophically contrived victims or what we might call "conceptual" victims.

Hume saw something of this in the inability of the liberty-loving whig government to punish the self-professed "victim" Wilkes and those who defied its authority. He wrote: "There must necessarily be a Struggle between the Mob and the Constitution; and it cannot come at a more favourable time ... I wish that vigorous Measures will be taken ..." (L, II, 218). Yet Hume despaired of the government's ability to exercise its legitimate authority. Such action would "give a Pretence for the Cry that Liberty is violated" (L, II, 209). He found Lord North's "Timidity towards the London Mob ... unaccountable" (L, II, 244), and observed that the "Country Gentlemen" declared they would not support the Government in any violent measures against the City" (L, II, 224). It seemed to Hume that the whig liberal establishment was superstitiously mesmerized and morally disarmed by the chants of "Wilkes and Liberty."

Whether Hume's assessment of the Wilkes and Liberty riots was reasonable or hysterical cannot be discussed here.[20] The important point is Hume's recognition of how the *conceptual* destruction of liberty by false philosophical and historical thinking can alienate one from the experience and reality of liberty. As in a strange kind of madness, brought on by the *critical intellect* itself, one can disown the liberty one has in the name of liberty. But, paradoxically, such an error is possible only in a civilized society which has become self-conscious of the spontaneously evolved conventions of liberty. In the consciousness of civilized reflective men, a space is opened up between liberty as an object of theoretical reflection and liberty as a pre-reflective form of life in which one participates. An existential tension arises between the thinker as spectator and as participant. It is in this space that the self-destructive errors of the reflective intellect can occur: philosophical and historical alienation. Near the end of his life, Hume thought that this higher sort of critical reflection was beginning, for the first time, to occur in politics on a popular level. He appears to have been the first to recognize it as a threat and the first to appreciate the special philosophical and historical errors to which the liberal intellect is prone – an intellect that Hume cherished as his own.

Abbreviations

Hume's works are abbreviated in the text as follows:

E   *Essays, Moral, Political, and Literary*. Ed. Eugene Miller. (Indianapolis: Liberty Classics, 1985).

EU, EM   *David Hume's Enquiries Concerning Human Understanding* [EU] *And Concerning the Principles of Morals* [EM]. 3rd ed. Ed. L. A. Selby-Bigge, revised by P. H. Nidditch. (Oxford: Clarendon Press, 1975).

H   *The History of England, from the Invasion of Julius Caesar to the Abdication of James the Second, 1688*. 6 vols. Based on the edition of 1778 with the author's last corrections and improvements. (Indianapolis: Liberty Classics, 1983).

L   *The Letters of David Hume*. 2 vols. Ed. J. Y. T. Grieg. (Oxford: Clarendon Press, 1969).

NHL   *New Letters of David Hume*. Ed. Raymond Klibansky and Ernest C. Mossner. (Oxford: Clarendon Press, 1954).

NHR   *The Natural History of Religion*. Ed. H. E. Root. (London: Adam and Charles Black, 1956).

T   *A Treatise of Human Nature*. 2nd edition with text revised and variant readings by P. H. Nidditch. Ed. L. A. Selby-Bigge. (Oxford: Clarendon Press, 1978).

Notes

1. John Stuart Mill, review of Brodie, *History of the British Empire*, in *The Westminster Review* 2 (1824), p. 34.

2. Richard Hiskes, "Does Hume Have a Theory of Social Justice?" *Hume Studies* 3, no. 2 (November, 1977), p. 72.

3. Donald W. Livingston, *Hume's Philosophy of Common Life* (Chicago: University of Chicago Press, 1983). See Chapters 3 and 4.

4. Peter Jones, *Hume's Sentiments* (Edinburgh: Edinburgh University Press, 1982), especially Chapters 1 and 5.

5. I discuss this in *Hume's Philosophy of Common Life*, pp. 329–34.

6. Bernard Bailyn, *The Origins of American Politics* (New York: Knopf, 1968), pp. 17–18.

7. Caroline Robbins, *The Eighteenth-Century Commonwealth Man* (Cambridge: Harvard University Press, 1959).

8. John Locke, *Two Treatises of Government* (New York: Mentor Books, 1963), p. 369.

9. Algernon Sidney, "Discourses Concerning Government," in *The Works of Algernon Sidney* (London, 1772), p. 446.

10. Douglass Adair, "That Politics May be Reduced to a Science: David Hume, James Madison, and the Tenth Federalist," reprinted in *Hume, A Re-Evaluation*, ed. Donald Livingston and James King (New York: Fordham University Press, 1976).

11. "Hume's Early Memoranda, 1729–40: The Complete Text," *Journal of the History of Ideas* (1948): 492–518.

12. Gerald Stourzh, *Alexander Hamilton and the Idea of Republican Government* (Stanford: Stanford University Press, 1970), especially chapters 2 and 3.

13. *Hume's Philosophy of Common Life*, Chapter 1.

14. John Locke, p. 369.

15. Catharine Macaulay, *The History of England* (London, 1763), p. xi.

16. *Ibid.*, pp. vii–viii.

17. *Ibid.*, p. ix.

18. Quoted in Craig Walton, "Hume and Jefferson on the Uses of History," in *Hume a Re-Evaluation*, p. 391.

19. George Gilder, *Wealth and Poverty* (New York: Basic Books, 1981), p. 129.

20. For a discussion of the "Wilkes and Liberty" affair, see G. F. E. Rudé, *Wilkes and Liberty* (Oxford: Clarendon Press, 1962). For a sympathetic, even "whiggish" biography of Wilkes, see O. A. Sherrard, *A Life of John Wilkes* (London: Allen and Unwin, 1930). Most accounts of Wilkes are whiggish; that is, they seek to show how Wilkes is a precursor of certain institutions of liberal democracy. There is room for a study of that part of Wilkes that Hume saw, namely, a self-serving radical dandy made possible by the illusions of a whig ideology which had seized the minds of populace and government, enraging the one and rendering impotent the other. When in power as mayor of London, Wilkes was quite prepared to fire, shoulder to shoulder with George III, into a rioting crowd very like the one that had raised his fortunes. It is instructive to compare Hume's conception of the Wilkes affair with his conception of the American crisis. His reasons for rejecting Wilkes (which to some make him a reactionary) are, at bottom, the same as his reasons for supporting American independence (which to some make him a radical). Hume was the first major British thinker to support total independence for the colonies (as early as 1768). I explore the connection between his views on Wilkes and liberty and the American crisis in "Hume, English Barbarism, and American Independence" in *Scotland and America in the Age of Enlightenment*, edited by Richard Sher and Jeffrey Smitten, forthcoming, University of Edinburgh Press.

JOHN W. DANFORD

HUME'S *HISTORY* AND THE
PARAMETERS OF ECONOMIC DEVELOPMENT

Western observers reacted with enthusiasm to the Chinese announcement
that Peking would loosen the grip of Marxist orthodoxy on its economy.
The Chinese are said to have decided that principles discovered in
nineteenth century Victorian England cannot be expected to work in the
economy of China in the last quarter of the twentieth century, and so
their attachment to Marx's political economy will be qualified. This has
been applauded as a triumph of common sense, and interpreted as
evidence the Chinese are facing up to the obvious. But whatever one
believes about Chinese intentions to "abandon" Marx, it is important to
quarrel with the reason they offered for doing so.

The reason for objecting is the historicist premise embodied in the
claim that the prescriptions of political economy are so time-bound as to
be automatically invalid in times or places other than the ones in which
they are advanced. While this may be true in some cases, and certainly is
true when one is speaking of prescriptions on the most detailed level
(say, the particular requirements of firms which depend on silicon-chip
technology in economies at a specified level of industrialization), it is by
no means established that the general principles of political economy –
involving as they do issues of human psychology or human nature, the
nature of markets, and so on – are limited in their application. This does
not in itself establish that political economy is a timeless science, but
only that we should not casually *assume* it is not.

If political economy is capable of supplying us with timeless principles, oddly enough the principles of economic development seem a
likely candidate for transhistorical validity. All the advanced industrial
economies passed through the early stages of development, by definition,
long ago. All began from roughly similar pre-industrial stages, again by
definition. And the writings of the classical political economists seem a
plausible place to look for an accurate statement of the conditions for the
beginnings of economic development, for at least two reasons: they were

N. Capaldi and D.W. Livingston (eds.), Liberty in Hume's History of England. 155–194.
© 1990 *Kluwer Academic Publishers. Printed in the Netherlands.*

closer to the ages in which early development took place, and – perhaps more important – they were equipped with the requisite theory of a permanent human nature. Without some conception of a genuine human nature, that is, of men and women as having reasonably permanent needs and desires which can account for human activities and institutions, no inquiry into the principles of development could make any sense at all.

Among the giants of classical political economy, David Hume deserves our serious attention, as I shall argue below. Unfortunately the one work among all his writings which bears most on questions of early economic development is generally ignored. Hume's six-volume *History of England, from the Invasion of Julius Caesar to the Revolution in 1688* is rarely read today, though it once adorned the bookshelves of nearly every literate English speaker who professed any interest in political life.[1] Even rarer today is any study of the first two volumes of the *History*, the volumes composed last, tracing English development to the reign of Henry VII. Yet in these volumes are found Hume's remarkable account of the emergence from feudalism. Here are Hume's account of the development of property rights, the emergence of an impartial or at least independent judiciary, and of the political and economic attitudes which accompanied the transformation to a commercial economy. The account in the *History* is complemented by the more famous essays on commerce, which go further to suggest that the *natural* accompaniments of the transition to commercial society are knowledge, industry, and humanity. Moreover, by connecting the *History* and the *Essays* with the *Enquiry concerning the Principles of Morals* it can be shown that Hume's reflections point the way to a deep connection or coincidence between his understanding of a permanent human nature and the political economy of development.

Now, the suggestion that we can look to Hume for a theory of development is likely to raise some eyebrows. Hume is generally thought of as a skeptic and a Tory. He was certainly the former; there are good grounds for doubting the latter, but at any rate it has long been argued whether or to what degree Hume is a conservative.[2] Anthony Quinton includes Hume in his catalog of conservatives in *The Politics of Imperfection*, the title of which expresses forcefully the compelling grounds for doing so: Hume's deep reservations about the "ignorance and weakness of the understanding" (*EHU* 76) or what Burke later called "the fallible contrivances" of human reason, led him to doubt the efficacy of rational schemes for reform in politics, or about the prospects of much political progress altogether. Despite the fact that in most cases such conservatism has been closely tied to some form of religious faith, which is notably absent in Hume's case, it is fair to say that Quinton is correct in his characterization of this side of Hume's political thought.

But it is equally fair to speak of *The Politics of Progress*, as does Hiram Caton,[3] and to include Hume along with Adam Smith and others in a catalog of proponents of the modern commercial republic whose emphasis on trade and commerce, with the attendant virtues of industry and thrift, for example, they believed would improve the condition of mankind. This progressive outlook emphasizes reason, toleration, and peace as the concomitants of enlightened trade and commerce. At the fringes such a view shades into the more radical expectations for equality and liberty associated later with the French Revolution and, at a more distant date, with the millenarian projections of nineteenth century reformers. With the latter, again, Hume has nothing whatever in common. The two sides of his thought, captured by the phrases "politics of imperfection" and "politics of progress," seem difficult to reconcile. As Sheldon Wolin has put it, "to have fathered squabbling children is always something of an embarrassment, but particularly so when one is, like Hume, temperamentally averse to taking sides."[4] Yet both sides are undeniably present in Hume, and neither is adscititious. How can they be reconciled?

The conventional explanation, common to a spate of recent studies, approaches the question historically and presents Hume as standing at the point where the seventeenth century's radical revolt against organicist views of society was itself becoming entrenched as orthodoxy.[5] There is of course something to be learned from such an explanation, but it has the grave defect of all historicist explanations, namely, that it deprives Hume's understanding of things of any possibility of permanent or transcendent significance. Hume's views, on such an account, not only must be studied in historical context, they *only* make sense in the context in which they are presented.[6] Thus Wolin writes that "Hume's position was symptomatic of the change taking place in English liberalism around the middle of the eighteenth century," and later, "Hume was representative of this changing temper, which prized the gains made possible by the upheavals of the previous century, and sought to preserve both the institutional achievements and their social undergirding" (Wolin, pp. 254–55). Hume's forceful defense of the primacy of liberty and property, for example, is understood as a product of his historical position and appropriate to it. But we wish to take seriously the possibility that Hume's understanding of man and society is part of a "science of human nature" meant to be true for all times and places. For reasons which are again outside our focus here, Hume – himself a very great historian – seems a poor candidate for "historicization," for the type of explanation which reduces a set of principles to the level of products of particular historical circumstances. If we are to take Hume's view as a whole seriously, his teaching about the fundamental elements of decent social order must be understood as a recommendation of what is best for human beings simply, not merely in the middle of the eighteenth century.

If we are to approach Hume in this spirit we need an account of the superficial paradoxes of his thought which shows the internal coherence of his understanding both of man and of the conditions and institutions which he recommends as best for such a creature. If Hume teaches the importance of property and liberty, and if his political science is truly a science in his own understanding of the term, we must at least consider the possibility that these are as important in the last decades of the twentieth century as they were in the middle decades of the eighteenth. Is there a teaching valid for all times?

I. The *History of England*

It is not difficult to show that Hume was thoroughly alive to the immense variety of human social and political experience. He devotes an entire essay ("Of National Character") to the question what is the basis of this variety, asking specifically whether moral or physical causes play the greater role. In it he writes that "the manners of a people change very considerably from one age to another; either by great alterations in their government, by the mixtures of new people, or by that inconstancy, to which all human affairs are subject" (*E* 205–6). The *History of England* can be read in fact as the documentary evidence for that claim, since it is a study of precisely such a revolution in the manners of the English during seventeen centuries, tracing all these causes and more. Custom may be "the great guide of human life," but customs change, and are grounded in circumstances and nature. Moreover, "though nature produces all kinds of temper and understanding in great abundance, it does not follow, that she always produces them in like proportions, and that in every society the ingredients of industry and indolence, valour and cowardice, humanity and brutality, wisdom and folly, will be mixed after the same manner" (*E* 203). The challenge to philosophical history – and indeed to practical statesmanship – is to discover the circumstances and institutions which promote industry, valour, humanity and wisdom rather than their opposites, or at least which allow these to predominate in what must inevitably be a mixture of virtues and vices.

In general Hume teaches that English history is the story of progress from conditions in which only one of these virtues – valour – has a place, towards a state of society in which the other three can and often do flourish beside it. The history of any nation, either ancient or modern, if traced back far enough will discover a state of society characterized by ignorance, superstition, and brutality. Hume repeatedly describes such ages as "rude," "turbulent," "barbarous and illiterate," "rough and licentious," "ignorant and barbarous" (*History* I. 14, 24, 17, 185, 51n, 53). "The only virtues which can have place among an uncivilized people, where justice and humanity are commonly rejected," he writes in the volume on the Saxons, are "valour, and love of liberty" (I. 15). This is not yet to judge the issue between the *civilized* nations of ancient or modern times, however, which is a separate and more difficult question.[7]

The *History of England* is first of all a demonstration of the superiority of civilized society over earlier stages of development, but in it Hume also traces the complicated mechanism of progress by which the civilized condition was reached at least in England. In the course of this narration Hume tries to elucidate precisely the social and political institutions and practices in which the excellence of modern civilization is located. That is to say, the *History* shows why inferior social arrangements are inferior, by showing what life was like in earlier ages, materially and morally, even as it explores how earlier modes of life were transformed. Thus by following closely Hume's account of "the gradual progress of improvement" we can also discover the grounds of his claim for the superiority of modern to ancient civilization, or more precisely of liberal commercial society to ancient republicanism. If Hume's teaching in the *History* is a teaching for all times, it may be of more than scholarly interest to us to examine a philosophical defense of the sort of society which is today attacked from many quarters as immoral and inhumane, corrupt and vicious.

The key principle in Hume's *History* seems to be a largely unstated premise, a premise made explicit only once in the entire six volumes, to my knowledge. In it Hume maintains that

the rise, progress, perfection and decline of art and science, are curious objects of contemplation, and intimately connected with a narration of civil transactions. The events of no particular period can be fully accounted for, but by considering the degrees of advancement, which men have reached in those particulars. (II. 519)

But it is wrong to call this a premise, since to do so begs the question of the superiority of developed society. It is, rather, the conclusion of Hume's *History*, and in fact it comes in the concluding pages of the last volume he wrote, the volume which ends with an account of the brief reign of Richard III (1485). It is not merely an artifact of the reverse order in which the *History* was composed. He concludes this second (last-written) volume, in 1762, with a brief essay which begins "Thus we have pursued the history of England through a series of many barbarous ages; till we have at last reached the dawn of civility and sciences, and have the prospect, both of greater certainty in our historical narrations, and of being able to present to the reader a spectacle more worthy of his attention" (II. 518). But in 1759 Hume had written in his discussion of the laws of Henry VII in the first of the Tudor volumes, that "thus a general revolution was made in human affairs throughout this part of the world; and men gradually attained that situation, with regard to commerce, arts, science, government, police, and cultivation, in which they have ever since persevered. Here therefore commences the useful, as well as the more agreeable part of modern annals..." (III. 81–82).[8]

A careful student of the *History* therefore has a double task: he must discover more precisely what the superiority of modernity consists in, and he must unravel Hume's account of the "revolution" in human affairs which led to it. The former is the easier task, because we have the *Essays* and the *Enquiry concerning the Principles of Morals* at our disposal; the latter must depend more on the *History*, and the difficulties are multiplied by the fact that the relevant passages must be found among many hundreds of pages narrating historical transactions of all kinds, from the martial to the marital, involving every aspect of domestic, ecclesiastical and political life. What we seek is a Humean "theory of development," as it would be called today, presenting an orderly account of what Hume termed the "moral cause" which transforms societies, the links which connect certain institutions, such as property ownership, with practices, such as chivalry, husbandry, or entail, with the various virtues and vices which result from these together.

II. The Primacy of War and Arms

The beginning point is that condition of society Hume calls barbarous or savage, that rude state which he does not hesitate to suggest is not even of much interest to us: "the sudden, violent, and unprepared revolutions, incident to Barbarians, are so much guided by caprice, and terminate so often in cruelty, that they disgust us by the uniformity of their appearance" (I. 3–4). It suffices to describe the state of the early Britons. Most were nomadic, "they were clothed with skins of beasts: They dwelt in huts ... they shifted easily their habitation, when actuated either by the hopes of plunder or the fear of an enemy: ... And as they were ignorant of all the refinements of life, their wants and their possessions were equally scanty and limited" (I. 5). The description of these ancestors need detain us no longer than it detains Hume. Successive invasions by Romans and Saxons change the picture but little, despite the Saxon virtues and the rudimentary political institutions they introduced. The almost total lack of security suppressed any progress in other areas. This is a principle which Hume defends as true in all ages. Where no benefit can arise from application or industry, "a habit of indolence naturally prevails. The greater part of the land lies uncultivated" (*E* 261). Men are led in such conditions to apply themselves only to the arts of war, and their rude state allows of very little skill even here. Describing the conditions in Britain in the ninth century, Hume reports that "the Saxons, though they had been so long settled in the island, seem not as yet to have been much improved beyond their German ancestors, either in arts, civility, knowledge, humanity, justice, or obedience to the laws. Even Christianity, though it opened the way to connexions between them and the more polished states of Europe, had not hitherto been very effectual, in banishing their ignorance, or softening their barbarous manners" (I. 50–51).

Even by the time of the Conquest, more than a millennium after the point at which Hume began his *History*, conditions are nearly as dismal as at the beginning, in respect at least to what is beginning to emerge as the cardinal principle of development, which is the rule of law. In his first Appendix, devoted to the "Anglo-Saxon Government and Manners," Hume writes that "among that military and turbulent people, so averse to commerce and the arts, so little enured to industry, justice was commonly very ill administered, and great oppression and violence seem to have prevailed. These disorders would be increased by the exorbitant power of the aristocracy and would, in their turn, contribute to increase it" (I. 166–67). This introduces the next stage of development, which may be considered both a setback and an advance. What prepares the way for the ultimate escape from the cycle of licentious barbarism is actually a step away from the rule of law. "Men, not daring to rely on the guardianship of the laws, were obliged to devote themselves to the service of some chieftain, whose orders they followed even to the disturbance of the government or the injury of their fellow-citizens, and who afforded them in return protection from any insult or injustice by strangers" (I. 167). This is the core of the system Hume calls feudalism, and the crucial stage of Hume's theory of development will be the story of the way its hold on society is broken.

Looked at in one way, the feudal system simply crystallizes the problems of the earlier condition by fixing them institutionally. But the Norman conquest which brought the feudal system also introduced the first glimmerings of civilization to the Anglo-Saxons, whom the conquerors themselves spoke of as barbarians (I. 185). The Anglo-Saxons were "in general a rude, uncultivated people, ignorant of letters, unskilled in the mechanical arts, untamed to submission under law and government, addicted to intemperance, riot and disorder" (I. 185). Despite their "best quality," which was military courage, their conduct was undisciplined, unfaithful, and always marked by a "want of humanity." It was only the Conquest which "put the people in a situation of receiving slowly from abroad the rudiments of science and civilization, and of correcting their rough and licentious manners" (I. 185).

Even before the introduction of feudal system proper, which Hume identified with the Norman Conquest, the problems it institutionalized were present. They stem from one fundamental condition: the paramount importance of war in rude and barbarous times. Speaking of the jurisprudence, if it can be described as such, of the ancient English or Saxons, Hume offers the following characterization:

> Such a state of society was very little advanced beyond the rude state of nature: Violence universally prevailed, instead of general and equitable maxims: The pretended liberty of the times, was only an incapacity of submitting to government: And men, not protected by law in their lives and properties, sought shelter, by their personal servitude and attachments under some powerful chieftain, or by voluntary combinations. (II. 521–22)

In such a condition the want of law is equated with the want of liberty and the radical insecurity of property. In fact property can scarcely be said to exist. In the "antient state of Europe," as Hume puts it, "the far greater part of the society were everywhere bereaved of their *personal* liberty, and lived entirely at the will of their masters" (II. 522). The feudal system institutionalized this by the principle that "the king was the supreme lord of the landed property: All possessors, who enjoyed the fruits or revenue of any part of it, held those privileges, either mediately or immediately, of him; and their property was conceived to be, in some degree, conditional" (I. 461). The barons held their "property" from the king in the same manner as the vassals from the barons (and indirectly from the king). Everything was subordinated to the military requirement, the principle underlying the entire system. If the vassal refused obedience or so much as failed to attend on or do fealty to his lord, "he forfeited all title to his land" (I. 477). Such specious liberty or property is little better than the prefeudal liberty of the Anglo-Saxons, who in fact lived under a system answering to the same military imperative as feudalism though it lacked the terminology of feudalism:

> On the whole, notwithstanding the seeming liberty or rather licentious-ness of the Anglo-Saxons, the great body even of the free citizens, in those ages, really enjoyed much less true liberty, than where the execution of the laws is the most severe, and where subjects are reduced to the strictest subordination and dependence on the civil magistrate. The reason is derived from the excess itself of that liberty. Men must guard themselves at any price against insults and injuries; and where they receive not protection from the laws and magistrate, they will seek it by submission to superiors, and by herding in some private confederacy, which acts under the direction of a powerful leader. And thus all anarchy is the immediate cause of tyranny, if not over the state, at least over many of the individuals. (I. 168–69)

The lack of liberty was not the only deplorable consequence of this principle of the subordination of every consideration to arms and defense. The feudal government was based on that principle no less than the prefeudal Saxon society, and the feudal government was equally prejudicial to "the true liberty even of the military vassal." But "it was still more destructive of the independence and security of the other members of the state, or what in a proper sense we call the people" (I. 463). The greater part of these were, as Hume notes, "*serfs*, and lived in a state of absolute slavery or villainage" (I. 463). The "immense possessions of the nobility" retarded, first of all, any improvements in the arts of agriculture; the "precarious state of feudal property" in general meant that "industry of no kind could ... have place in the kingdom" (I 484). Even the property of the military vassals could hardly be called secure. Compared to the people, the military tenants were "better protected, both by law, and by the great privilege of carrying arms." But even these "were, from the nature of their tenures, much exposed to the inroads of power, and possessed not what we should esteem in our age a very durable security" (I. 476).

The insecurity of property and want of liberty (really two sides of the same coin) precluded the development of trade and commerce, and the lack of economic progress in turn contributed to insecurity.

> The languishing state of commerce kept the inhabitants poor and contemptible; and the political institutions were calculated to render that poverty perpetual. The barons and gentry, living in rustic plenty and hospitality, gave no encouragement to the arts, and had no demand for any of the more elaborate produce of manufactures: Every profession was held in contempt but that of arms: And if any merchant or manufacturer rose by industry and frugality to a degree of opulence, he found himself but the more exposed to injuries, from the envy and avidity of the military nobles. (I. 463–64)

Now, in Saxon times in particular, there was virtually no escape from this condition. Anyone in the lower ranks of society was condemned to remain there. Despite two statutes among the Saxon laws which, as Hume notes, seem to provide an opportunity for change, he suggests that they were ineffective in practice (I. 169). The feudal system did little to improve things, and in fact the right of primogeniture, which came in with the feudal law, added to the problem "by producing and maintaining an unequal division of private property" (I. 486). On the other hand, the feudal system proper, by virtue of its "legalization" of the system of vassalage, land holding by tenure, and primogeniture, introduced the means by which the system would gradually be changed.

III. Hume's Account of the Disintegration of Feudal Order

The permanent significance of Hume's theory of development depends on the fact that the features of society at the time of the Norman Conquest are not peculiar to that age. The conditions marked by lawlessness, insecurity of property, want of liberty, both personal and civil, and suppression of commerce and industry are not unknown in the contemporary world. Hume's account of the means of escape from this deplorable state is of particular interest to us insofar as it does not depend on miracles or on circumstances so singular that they are unlikely to be encountered ever again. At the same time we should be aware, as is Hume, of the essential fragility of all decent civil order and of its dependence on particular circumstances and accidents. His deep appreciation for the framework of English constitutionalism and for the institutions of liberal commercial society is proportionate to the value of these in relation to other forms of social order, and the value of even a form of government is always enhanced by its being rare.

Hume's account of the "gradual progress of improvement" from the dismal condition of feudal society is very complicated. In order to present it intelligibly I will divide his remarks under three headings, and ask the reader to bear in mind that it is impossible to do this tidily: the various explanations shade off into each other at some points and there will be loose ends which cannot be tied up neatly. Nevertheless Hume presents this account with notable consistency despite the fact that in some cases many hundreds of pages separate his comments in different volumes of the *History*. The three parts of his account vary according to their degree of specificity to English circumstances and in the degree to which they are fortuitous, according to the distinction Hume draws in one of the essays: "What depends on a few persons is, in a great measure, to be ascribed to chance, or secret and unknown causes: What arises from a great number may often be accounted for by determinate and known causes" (*E* 112). Thus "to judge by this rule, the domestic and the gradual revolutions of a state must be a more proper subject of reasoning and observation than the foreign and the violent, which are commonly produced by single persons, and are more influenced by whim, folly, or caprice, than by general passions and interests" (*E* 112). The largely domestic revolution we are considering here is not without an admixture of foreign causes, however.

Of the three parts of Hume's account, one has to do with England specifically because it is based partly on the special circumstances of the introduction of the feudal law by the Norman Conquest. A second portion is not specific to England, but dependent nonetheless partly on historical accident, namely, the discovery or recovery in 1130 of the Roman law in the form of the Pandects of Justinian, and the train of events this set in motion. The third is a general "naturalist" explanation of the decline of feudalism based on tendencies in human nature. This last, of course, is universal in its operation, but Hume suggests it was not of sufficient force to overturn feudalism in the absence of other factors.

It may be that Montesquieu's *L'Esprit des Lois* taught Hume to look for circumstances peculiar to English civilization which could explain the development of its remarkable liberal commercial society as early as the eighteenth century. It is certain that Hume found the key in the Norman Conquest. Not that the Normans could be said to have brought the seeds of development with them, though Hume does suggest in one sentence that the Conquest "put the people in a situation of receiving slowly from abroad the rudiments of science and cultivation, and of correcting their rough and licentious manners" (I. 185). Only by contrast with the barbarous manners of the Saxons did the Normans add anything: and even then the Conquest acted only indirectly in the special circumstances of England and combined with other factors, to transform these "military and turbulent people" into something approaching a civilized people or a people capable of civilization. The Normans themselves were, "during this age, so violent and licentious a people, that they may be pronounced incapable of any true or regular liberty; which requires such improvement in knowledge and morals, as can only be the result of reflection and experience, and must grow to perfection during several ages of settled and established government" (I. 254).

What the Conquest served to do was to generate a special kind of tension in English feudalism, as a result of the fact that "England of a sudden became a feudal kingdom" (I. 461). That is, the exigencies arising from the manner in which the feudal system was introduced into England generated a heightened tension between king and barons. Now, a tension between king and barons is inherent in any feudal arrangement, as Hume clearly explains. Indeed in the absence of the principle of hereditary authority which is not "so easily subverted," the most common course for feudal systems is the degeneration "into so many independent [sic] baronies," with the loss of "the political union, by which they were cemented," and the sacrifice to the barons of "both the rights of the crown and the liberties of the people" (I. 464).

There is thus an incipient natural alliance between king and people, and in England special circumstances helped both. The first circumstance was only temporary. "The first kings of the Norman race were favoured by another circumstance, which preserved them from the encroachments of their barons. They were generals of a conquering army, which was obliged to continue in a military posture, and to maintain a great subordination under their leader, in order to secure themselves from the revolt of the numerous natives, whom they had bereaved of all their properties and privileges" (I. 464–65). This result of the Conquest served to help William and his immediate successors to resist the barons, but it ceased to operate after about a century, and its effect was entirely obliterated under the despicable King John, who was compelled by his barons to acknowledge the Great Charter in 1215. In the meantime, however – during the century and a half following the Conquest – the Norman kings were in a position to promote such rudimentary liberties or interests of the people as existed at the time, and thus to move the feudal system down the path to its dissolution.

"If we consider the antient state of Europe," Hume tells us, "we shall find, that the far greater part of the society were everywhere bereaved of their *personal* liberty and lived entirely at the will of their masters" (II. 522). Everyone was either noble or slave; if the latter, one was "sold along with the land: The few inhabitants of cities were not in a better condition" (Ibid.). This condition was the necessary result of the primacy of armed force and the "slender protection" afforded by law or anything else. "The first incident, which broke in upon this violent system of government, was the practice, begun in Italy, and imitated in France, of erecting communities and corporations, endowed with privileges and a separate municipal government, which gave them protection against the tyranny of the barons, and which the prince himself deemed it prudent to respect" (II. 522–23).[9] The granting of a charter to London by Henry I, upon his accession to the throne in 1100, "seems to have been the first step towards rendering that city a corporation," according to Hume (I. 278), although he notes that William at the Conquest itself had "confirmed the liberties and immunities of London and the other cities of England" (I. 192).

If the special powers enjoyed by William and his successors allowed them to promote, however slightly, the liberties of the commons against the villainage practiced by the barons, another specifically English circumstance played its part in this rise of the boroughs; "affairs," as Hume puts it, "in this island particularly, took early a turn, which was more favourable to justice and to liberty." The precise circumstance favoring England was her geography. "Civil employments and occupations soon became honourable among the English: The situation of that people rendered not the perpetual attention to wars so necessary as among their neighbours, and all regard was not confined to the military profession" (II. 522). This has particular relevance to the development of the rule of law, a development owing a great deal to the fortuitous recovery of a code of Roman civil law, the Pandects of Justinian, in 1130 A.D.

IV. The *Pandects* and the beginning of Legal Science

This second part of Hume's account of the rise of the English system of liberty and decline of feudalism owes less to specifically English circumstances. He presents it as part of his account of how the "rise, progress, perfection, and decline of art and science" are "intimately connected with a narration of civil transactions" (II. 519). Hume suggests a sort of cyclical view of history, or the "general revolutions of society," according to which "there is an ultimate point of depression, as well as of exaltation, from which human affairs naturally return in a contrary progress, and beyond which they seldom pass either in their advancement or decline" (II. 519). He cites the Roman age of Augustus as a peak of "the improvements of the human mind," and suggests it was followed by a long descent back into an ignorance and barbarism so profound that they overwhelmed "all human knowledge, which was already far in its decline; and men sunk every age deeper into ignorance, stupidity, and superstition; till the light of ancient science and history had very nearly suffered a total extinction in all the European nations" (Ibid.). The nadir of this cycle, according to Hume, "may justly be fixed at the eleventh century, about the age of William the Conqueror." He sketches the change in the fortunes of Europe in the broadest possible strokes. "From that aera, the sun of science, beginning to re-ascend, threw out many gleams of light, which preceded the full morning, when letters were revived in the fifteenth century." The depredations of the northern pirates ceased gradually as they learned the arts of tillage and agriculture. The feudal governments were gradually reduced "to a kind of system; and though that strange species of civil polity was ill fitted to ensure either liberty or tranquillity, it was preferable to the universal licence and disorder, which had everywhere preceded it" (II. 520). A critical factor in the recovery of civilization, however, was one seldom noticed: "But perhaps there was no event, which tended further to the improvement of the age, than one, which has not been much remarked, the accidental finding of a copy of Justinian's Pandects, about the year 1130, in the town of Amalfi in Italy" (II. 520).

Why was this event so important? The system of law contained in this work answered a pressing need of one sector of the community, and as it spread it undermined the entire feudal order. Hume's description is worth quoting at length:

> The ecclesiastics, who had leisure, and some inclination of study, immediately adopted with zeal this excellent system of jurisprudence, and spread the knowledge of it throughout every part of Europe. Besides the intrinsic merit of the performance, it was recommended to them by its original connexion with the imperial city of Rome, which, being the seat of their religion, seemed to acquire a new lustre and authority, by the diffusion of its laws over the western world. In less than ten years after the discovery of the Pandects, Vacarius, under the protection of Theobald, archbishop of Canterbury, read public lectures of civil law in the university of Oxford; and the clergy everywhere, by their example as well as exhortation, were the means of spreading the highest esteem for this new science. That order of men, having large possessions to defend, were in a manner necessitated to turn their studies towards the law; and their properties being often endangered by the violence of the princes and barons, it became their interest to enforce the observance of general and equitable rules, from which alone they could receive protection. (II. 520).

To appreciate the centrality of this recovery of law in Hume's account of the "gradual progress of improvement" is to locate the key to civilization itself, or the rise and progress of the arts and sciences. The recovery of legal science, however rudimentary, proved to be the decisive factor in breaking out of the feudal system which, with its subordination of all concerns to martial authority, effectively blocked any improvement in commerce, agriculture, and hence in the arts and sciences. Hume speaks quite clearly of the "jealousy entertain'd by the barons against the progress of the arts, as destructive of their licentious power" (II. 523n). Speaking of the rapid spread of the study of the newly recovered Roman law, Hume suggests that "it is easy to see what advantages Europe must have reaped by its inheriting at once from the ancients, so complete an art, which was also so necessary for giving security to all other arts, and which, by refining, and still more, by bestowing solidity on the judgment, served as a model to farther improvements" (II. 521).

The importance of this development can be seen by considering it as a kind of trigger which released tendencies inherent in the "natural course of things" (*E* 260), or in human nature and the physical circumstances of human life, tendencies which were thwarted by the preoccupation of the feudal system with what Hume calls the "military profession" (II. 522). "The gentry, and even the nobility, began to deem an acquaintance with the law, a requisite part of education" (Ibid.). This opened the way for the gradual beginning of the rise of the commons, as men who had earlier been virtual slaves began to achieve some independence. Under the feudal order,

> even the gentry ... were subjected to a long train of subordination under the greater barons or chief vassals of the crown; who, though seemingly placed in a high state of splendor, yet, having but a slender protection from the law, were exposed to every tempest of the state, and by the precarious condition in which they lived, paid dearly for the power of oppressing and tyrannizing over their inferiors. (II. 522)

The "somewhat stricter" execution of the public law, which gradually followed upon the study of this science, "bestowed an independence on vassals, which was unknown to their forefathers. And even the peasants themselves, though later than other orders of the state, made their escape from those bonds of villenage or slavery, in which they had formerly been retained" (II. 523).[10]

V. Property, Law, and Liberty

Precisely how did this liberation take place? Hume offers two clear and general accounts of the feudal system, one dealing with its formation, the other with its disintegration. By considering them together and paying particular attention to the role played by jurisprudence, it is possible to unravel the mechanism of progress more precisely. This brings in what I earlier called the third naturalist component of Hume's account of the deterioration of the feudal system, and it leads directly to the core of his claim of the superiority of modern liberal commercial society.

In explaining how a stable system of "fiefs and tenures" developed, Hume makes use of arguments which are grounded in common sense or common life, to show how, as he puts it, "the idea of property stole in gradually upon that of military pay" (I. 458). Where lands were first distributed as a kind of reward for service in conquest, and held only on condition of continued military service, there is not quite a fixed notion of property. But where lands are cultivated, a kind of natural logic intrudes itself. "The attachment, naturally formed with a fixed portion of land, gradually begets the idea of something like property, and makes the possessor forget his dependant situation … It seemed equitable, that one who had cultivated and sowed a field, should reap the harvest" (I. 458). The result was that fief holdings "at first entirely precarious, were soon made annual" (Ibid.). But the same logic carried men several steps further: "A man, who had employed his money in building, planting, or other improvements, expected to reap the fruits of his labor or expense: Hence they were next granted during a term of years." Since "it would be thought hard to expel a man from his possessions, who had always done his duty," feudal chieftains soon insisted on holding their feudal tenures for life. And the last step follows equally naturally: "It was found, that a man would more willingly expose himself in battle, if assured, that his family should inherit his possessions, and should not be left by his death in want and poverty: Hence fiefs were made hereditary in families …" (Ibid.), and so on. Although there are other imaginable schemes to induce martial loyalty, Hume's account emphasizes the naturalness of this progression; it accords with human nature and the conditions of feudal life.

But the logic which Hume uses here to explain how the feudal property system was stabilized or how "these feudal dependencies" were "corroborated" (I. 459), bears a striking resemblance to the logic which accounts for its later disintegration, which he deals with in his summary of the first two volumes of the *History*. We learn here, as has already been suggested, that the spread of arts and sciences – and particularly the science of jurisprudence – was a general source of liberty, and gradually released feudal villains from their bondage. At first the villains were virtual agricultural slaves to the "military posture" of the chieftain, whose readiness had to be constantly maintained. They were entirely occupied

> in the cultivation of their master's land, and paid their rents either in corn and cattle and other produce of the farm, or in servile offices …. In proportion as agriculture improved, and money increased, it was found, that these services, though extremely burdensome to the villain, were of little advantage to the master; and that the produce of a large estate could be much more conveniently disposed of by the peasant himself, who raised it, than by the landlord or his bailiff, who were formerly accustomed to receive it. (II. 523)

The result was the introduction of the more convenient practice of paying rent instead of services, and later indeed of money rents rather than those in kind; "and as men, in a subsequent age, discovered, that farms were better cultivated where the farmer enjoyed a security of possession, the practice of granting leases to the peasant began to prevail, which entirely broke the bonds of servitude, already much relaxed from the former practices" (II. 524). (The Soviet Union is struggling to resist this lesson today, even as the Chinese are reluctantly learning it.) The system of villenage, as Hume notes, thus "went gradually into disuse throughout the more civilized parts of Europe: The interest of the master, as well as that of the slave, concurred in this alteration" (II. 524). And as the distinction between freeman and villain disappeared, the political aspect of modern Europe began to take shape. "Thus *personal* freedom became almost general in Europe; an advantage which paved the way for the increase of *political* or *civil* liberty" (Ibid.).

How can the same reasoning concerning the convenience of property ownership and inheritance, explain both the formation and dissolution of the feudal land tenure system? The crucial factor is what has already been noted: the development of law following the recovery of the Pandects of Justinian. During the ages when the feudal system was solidifying, as Hume points out repeatedly, military concerns were paramount because there was no effective law. Indeed the "judiciary" itself, such as it was, was constituted largely by the military chieftains; as is "unavoidable to all nations that have made slender advances in refinement," these men "every where united the civil jurisdiction with the military power" (I. 459–60).

> Law, in its commencement, was not an intricate science, and was more governed by maxims of equity, which seem obvious to common sense, than by numerous and subtle principles, applied to a variety of cases by profound reasonings from analogy. An officer, though he had passed his life in the field, was able to determine all legal controversies which could occur within the district committed to his charge; and his decisions were the most likely to meet with a prompt and ready obedience, from men who respected his person, and were accustomed to act under his command. (I. 460)

Since judicial authority was combined with military command and both were attached to an hereditary fief holding, all were together transmitted by inheritance to each chieftain's posterity. The feudal lords were able to "render their dignity perpetual and hereditary ... After this manner, the vast fabric of feudal subordination became quite solid and comprehensive" (Ibid.). The tendencies which acted to solidify this system operated so long as law and justice were virtually identical to the chieftain's word, and this was the natural condition where military considerations were paramount, where "men, not protected by law in their lives and properties, sought shelter, by their personal servility and attachments, under some powerful chieftain; or by voluntary combinations" (II. 521–22).

But the beginning of the development of law as an independent science, which Hume dates in the middle of the twelfth century, acted to break the hold of the military chieftain. The church, for one, was deeply interested in securing its property by other than military force; an independent civil law afforded it the opportunity. In England particularly, as we saw above, affairs "took very early a turn, which was more favorable to justice and to liberty" (II. 522). The study of the law as a science paved the way for the escape from the vicious hold of the feudal system itself, by freeing property from the fief system, or what is more to the point, establishing the security of property *independent of* military vassalage.

It is now possible to assess why Hume's account of the disintegration of the feudal order is so important to an understanding of the general teaching of the *History*: here, at the first origins of the "gradual progress of improvement," the crucial element of liberal commercial order, of civilized or refined society, appear with the greatest clarity, unconfused by the variety of circumstances and institutions which cloud matters when civilized society is more fully developed. The critical first element is the rule of law, or what would today be called an independent judiciary and a science of jurisprudence which separates questions of justice from considerations of military loyalty. When law replaces military force, the security of property – which Hume admits was secure enough before – is no longer dependent on one's loyalty to a chieftain. The results of this development include, most importantly, the beginning of the gradual rise of the commons, which was the natural accompaniment to what Hume calls the "introduction and progress of freedom" (II. 522), and the gradual development of commerce.

He illustrates the connection between these two factors with a story. During the reign of Henry VII, Hume writes, "there scarce passed any session ... without some statute against engaging retainers, and giving them badges or liveries; a practice by which they were, in a manner, inlisted under some great lord, and were kept in readiness to assist him in all wars, insurrections, riots, violences, and even in bearing evidence for him in courts of justice" (III. 75–76). This is of course a remnant of the system of military loyalty just referred to, and "this disorder, which had arisen during turbulent times, when the law could give little protection to the subject, was then deeply rooted in England; and it required all the vigilance and rigour of Henry to extirpate it." He took vigorous steps to eliminate the practice, making it illegal. The story of Henry's severity, Hume suggests, merits praise though it is usually mistakenly taken as an instance of Henry's "avarice and rapacity."

> The earl of Oxford, his favorite general, in whom he always placed great and deserved confidence, having splendidly entertained him at his castle of Heningham, was desirous of making a parade of his magnificence at the departure of his royal guest; and ordered all his retainers, with their liveries and badges, to be drawn up in two lines, that their appearance might be the more gallant and splendid. "My lord," said the king, "I have heard much of your hospitality; but the truth far exceeds the report. These handsome gentlemen and yeomen, whom I see on both sides of me, are no doubt, your menial servants." The earl smiled, and confessed that his fortune was too narrow for such magnificence. "They are most of them," subjoined he, "my retainers, who are come to do me service at this time, when they know I am honoured with your majesty's presence." The king started a little, and said, "By my faith, my lord, I thank you for your good cheer, but I must not allow my laws to be broken in my sight. My attorney must speak with you." Oxford is said to have payed no less than fifteen thousand marks, as a composition for his offence. (III. 76)

This feudal practice of service by personal loyalty, Hume suggests, maintained the common people "in a vicious idleness." He admits that "the increase of the arts, more effectually than all the severities of laws," put an end to "this pernicious practice," but that its gradual disappearance is more than a mere change in manners is very clear. "The nobility, instead of vying with each other, in the number and boldness of their retainers, acquired by degrees a more civilized species of emulation, and endeavoured to excel in the splendour and elegance of their equipage, houses, and tables. The common people, no longer maintained in vicious idleness by their superiors, were obliged to learn some calling or industry, and became useful both to themselves and to others" (III. 76).

The increase in personal liberty, then, was and is directly connected to the growth of commerce, and with it, of the commercial virtues including industry, honesty and thrift. Hume goes further in the *Essays*, where he analyses the effects of "refinement in the arts" with great power and clarity. "In times when industry and the arts flourish, men are kept in perpetual occupation, and enjoy, as their reward, the occupation itself, as well as those pleasures which are the fruit of their labor. The mind acquires new vigour; enlarges its powers and faculties; and by an assiduity in honest industry, both satisfies its natural appetites, and prevents the growth of unnatural ones, which commonly spring up, when nourished by ease and idleness" (*E* 270).

VI. Commerce and the Arts

It must be emphasized that once the feudal system had begun to lose its sway as a result of the spread of legal science or the art of jurisprudence, it is the arts themselves which carry the revolution, or the "gradual progress of improvement" forward. The liberties of even the common people had been, in large measure, secured in theory as early as the Great Charter in 1215, as Hume suggests, but, the effectiveness of the guarantees was nowhere very great in practice. The Charter had included some provisions for free commerce ("Merchants shall be allowed to transact all business, without being exposed to any arbitrary … impositions; … The goods of every free man shall be disposed of according to his will: If he die intestate, his heirs shall succeed to them" etc. (I. 444–45), and Hume speaks of the nobles who extorted it from King John as "those generous barons," and praises them for including clauses which favoured "the interests of the inferior ranks of men …" (I. 445, 444). Nevertheless he is at pains to show that, for example during the reign of Edward III, the provisions of the Charter were not always followed in practice (see II. 275): Why, Hume asks, since "this privilege was sufficiently secured by a clause of the Great Charter … is [it] so anxiously, and, as we may think, so superfluously repeated? Plainly, because there had been some late infringements of it, which gave umbrage to the commons." What succeeded in transforming feudal society was, in the end, the progress of the arts, progress connected to the recovery of the art of Roman jurisprudence, and specifically the spread of a taste for luxury or "refinement in the arts." This is a subject to which Hume devoted considerable thought, and on which he wrote one of his

best and most famous essays.[11] He concludes the report on Henry VII's
reign, quoted above, by insisting that "it must be acknowledged, in spite
of those who declaim so violently against the refinement in the arts, or
what they are pleased to call luxury, that, as much as an industrious
tradesman is both a better man and a better citizen than one of those idle
retainers, who formerly depended on the great families; as much is the
life of a modern nobleman more laudable than that of an ancient baron"
(III. 76–77).

Despite the very great importance Hume accords to commerce and the
close connection he sees between commerce and civilization, at least of
the modern sort, he seems to believe that its spread is partly fortuitous.
At the very least he suggests that attempts to promote commerce by
specific legislation are unlikely to have much success. Speaking still of
Henry VII, whose reign Hume regarded as very important in this regard,
Hume writes that the king's "love of money naturally led him to encourage commerce, which increased his customs; but, if we may judge
by most of the laws enacted during his reign, trade and industry were
rather hurt than promoted by the care and attention given to them" (III.
77). This theme emerges again in the essay on commerce. Hume offers a
number of examples of trade-retarding legislation under Henry VII (III.
77–80), and he makes an important general observation on the relationship between commerce and laws attempting to promote it. Henry VII
was celebrated for his many good laws, and Hume admits that "several
considerable regulations, indeed, are found among the statutes of his
reign, both with regard to the police of the kingdom, and its commerce:
But the former are commonly contrived with much better judgment than
the latter" (III. 74). The reason for this discrepancy is not difficult to see.
A legislator concerned with justice need be guided only by "simple ideas
of order and equity," Hume writes. "But the principles of commerce are
much more complicated, and require long experience and deep reflection
to be well understood in any state. The real consequence of a law or
practice is there often contrary to first appearances" (III. 74). In this
assessment Hume anticipates not only Adam Smith, with whom he
shared so many other views, but also a number of modern economists
who have assembled examples of government policies and legislation
having effects opposite to those intended or anticipated. Hume's catalog
of Henry's misguided attempts at the legislation of economic behavior
aims at showing the futility of resisting what he calls here the "natural
course of improvement."

One law during the reign of Henry VII did have notably beneficial

effects on commerce and indeed on the whole political order, and Hume
even grants that Henry probably intended the results. This law, "the most
important ... in its consequences" of the entire reign,[12] gave the nobility
and gentry the "power of breaking the ancient entails, and of alienating
their estates. By means of this law, joined to the beginning luxury and
refinements of the age, the great fortunes of the barons were gradually
dissipated, and the property of the commons increased in England. It is
probable, that Henry foresaw and intended this consequence, because the
constant scheme of his policy consisted in depressing the great, and
exalting churchmen, lawyers, and men of new families, who were more
dependant on him" (III. 77). Even here, it should be noted, the aim of the
law was not to promote commerce, but to alter the configuration of
power in society. Commerce itself is best promoted indirectly or even
negatively, that is by removing obstacles or by assuring that it is not
subordinated to other considerations, as it was under the feudal system.
Hume believes that if one takes men as they are, given law and liberty,
the "natural course of improvement" will lead to a commercial society in
the absence of distorting factors (the ancient slave system, for example,
or the powerful effects of superstition).

The crucial and original step in Hume's analysis is his claim that legal
property rights should be understood as only an alternative to the feudal
manner of securing property. Such security as property enjoyed under the
feudal system was dependent entirely on personal loyalty and thus on the
subordination of all other concerns to the military. Once the spread of an
independent science of law undermined the hold of feudal chieftains, the
security of property could be combined with justice and personal liberty.
The natural effect of this combination – though over a very long period
of time – is, in Hume's view, the rise of commerce and trade. Hume
suggests that even the principles enshrined in the Great Charter, though
not fully effective in practice for centuries, "involve all the chief outlines
of a legal government, and provide for the equal distribution of justice,
and the free enjoyment of property; the great objects for which political
society was at first founded by men" (I. 445). But he does not equate the
natural course of things, by which human beings flourish, with the
inevitable or even likely course of things: history teaches too many
lessons to the contrary. The study of English history should teach us a
regard for the fragility of the institutions of a decent political order. At
the very end of the second volume of the *History of England*, the last
Hume composed, he writes:

Above all, a civilized nation, like the English, who have happily established the most perfect and most accurate system of liberty that was ever found compatible with government, ought to be cautious in appealing to the practice of their ancestors, or regarding the maxims of uncultivated ages as certain rules for their present conduct. An acquaintance with the history of the remote periods of their government is chiefly *useful* by instructing them to cherish their present constitution, from a comparison or contrast with the condition of those distant times. (II. 525)

It also teaches, he adds, "the great mixture of accident which commonly concurs with a small ingredient of wisdom and foresight, in erecting the complicated fabric of the most perfect government" (Ibid.). This, which is the culmination of lessons about law and justice, liberty and commerce, is the teaching for all times which we find in Hume's *History of England*.

VII. Development Economics Today

The lesson of the *History* as far as economic development is concerned, seems both obvious and simple. In fact it can seem so obvious that I would be reluctant to suggest it as a conclusion of great importance, were not so many nations – including fully half the world's population today – still either groping toward the conditions Hume praised more than two centuries ago or worse, denying the lessons that Hume – and history – teach. In fact the literature of development economics is dominated by what one noted scholar has called the "spurious consensus," a consensus which denies nearly everything Hume teaches about the "gradual progress of improvement."[13] According to Lord Bauer, "since the Second World War, it has been a major axiom of the mainstream development literature that comprehensive central planning is indispensable for the progress of poor countries."[14] This is of course contradicted by the historical experience of the prosperous western capitalist countries, all of which achieved their wealth and "capital infrastructure" without central planning. Bauer traces numerous specific examples of economic progress in the early part of this century, and notes that it "was not the result of conscription of people or the forced mobilization of their resources. Nor was it the result of forcible modernization of attitudes and behavior, nor of large-scale state-sponsored industrialization; nor of any other form of big push." Economic progress was, rather,

> in very large measure the result of the individual voluntary responses
> of millions of people to emerging or expanding opportunities created
> largely by external contacts and brought to their notice in a variety of
> ways, primarily through the operation of the market. These develop-
> ments were made possible by firm but limited government, without
> large expenditures of public funds and without the receipt of large
> external subventions.[15]

Among the reasons Bauer adduces to explain the stubborn reluctance of
economists to admit that human beings can progress economically
without government planning is, ironically (for our purpose here), the
failure of the discipline to pay sufficient attention to history. "The
historical background is essential for a worthwhile discussion of
economic development, which is an integral part of the historical
progress of society. But many of the most widely publicised writings on
development effectively disregard both the historical background and the
nature of development as a process." The neglect of history, he suggests,
"is reflected in the frequent demands for immediate and thoroughgoing
social reform in underdeveloped countries."[16]

The skewed perspective of the "spurious consensus" is connected
partly to the failure of economists to view economic concerns as features
of a human situation common to human beings everywhere, a situation
marked for example by scarce resources the augmenting of which
depends on non-quantifiable characteristics: the attitudes, moral virtues,
and legal and political institutions which facilitate or retard the satisfaction of human wants. The tendency to consider human beings in less
developed countries as somehow basically different from citizens of
liberal commercial ("developed") societies is reflected in the very
terminology of economics, in its distinguishing of "development
economics" from the rest of the discipline. Gottfried Haberler has been
critical of "the notion that there should be one kind of economics for the
less-developed countries and another for the nations that [have] crossed
the threshold to development, whatever that is."[17] A self-described
"monoeconomist," Haberler shares Bauer's view that the principles of
economics have more general application. If personal liberty and the rule
of law (protecting private property and contracts) were essential ingredients in the economic progress of the advanced Western countries,
they may be expected to be equally important in less developed

countries. Critics of the market have argued, Bauer tells us, that "people in less developed countries are unable or unwilling to respond to prices and market signals generally. This is not so." He goes on:

> Within the restrictions imposed by governments and the limits set by mores and customs, decision-making by individuals, families and voluntary groups operates in developing countries much as elsewhere. Indeed, because people are on the whole poorer, and therefore weigh up closely the opportunities open to them, they often respond readily, for example, to small price differences and changes. Buyers of scent in Nigeria deliberate whether to buy a tiny bottle or only a drop on the shoulder, or to buy half a cigarette, a single cigarette, or a packet of ten cigarettes; or whether to buy a bundle of five matches together with a small striking surface, or to buy a whole box.[18]

What is essential for development, it would appear, today as in England during the centuries Hume studied, is the combination of legal practices and institutions, with personal liberty and property, which allow for "the gradual progress of improvement." Perhaps it is too early for optimism, but a recent article describes the works of Hernando de Soto, a Peruvian scholar in law and economics, who seems to have reached conclusions similar to Hume's.[19] He has remarked, according to a commentator, that "the majority of society in less-developed countries is not 'working class' in the Marxist sense, but rather entrepreneurial and "bourgeois" in its interests and world view." He adds a comment which could have come directly from Hume: "Political ideologies, although they operate largely in the realm of values and are thus resistant to empirical falsification, cannot survive for long if they clash continually and fundamentally with lived experience."

We may well ask why the obvious and simple lessons concerning the gradual progress of improvement should have to be relearned today. A number of observers have suggested explanations which revolve around the combination of a rising class of intellectuals and the great increase in the power of the state in our century. Paul Johnson has called this the century of "statism,"[20] and Bauer provides one explanation for the connection between intellectuals and the tendency to favor state planning: "There are in the west certain persons and groups, influential though numerically small, who have come greatly to dislike major institutions of their society, and especially the market system. These people include the many individuals who feel obscurely resentful of a system which does not provide them with the opportunities for directing the affairs of the society and the economic activities of their fellow men, to which they consider their talents entitle them."[21]

But this seems to me to be part of a more general pattern of opposition to the main features of commercial society, at least among Western elites in recent decades. And Hume seems to have confronted something like this opposition in his own advocacy of commercial society two centuries ago. This can be seen most clearly by focusing on his presentation of his understanding of the principles of morals in the second *Enquiry*. Here he takes his bearings not from a philosophical system or what de Soto (above) calls "political ideology," but from "lived experience" ("common life" in Hume's language).

> Are not justice, fidelity, honour, veracity, allegiance, chastity, esteemed solely on account of their tendency to promote the good of society? Is not that tendency inseparable from humanity, benevolence, levity, generosity, gratitude, moderation, tenderness, friendship, and all the other social virtues? Can it possibly be doubted that industry, discretion, frugality, secrecy, order, perseverance, forethought, judgement, and this whole class of virtues and accomplishments, of which many pages would not contain the catalogue; can it be doubted, I say, that the tendency of these qualities to promote interest and happiness of their possessor, is the sole foundation of their merit? *(EPM 277)*

Now this list of virtues, though limited, is easily seen to include, especially in the second and third parts, many qualities which men have little or no opportunity to develop or display in a savage state, or for that matter in conditions which do not include peace, order, security, and a degree of privacy or individual autonomy, in short, the conditions recommended by Hume's account of the "gradual progress of improvement" in the *History*.

Hume seems to regard the list of qualities here as part of the "system" of morals which emerges when human beings are left to their own devices, so to speak, and where they are fortunate in developing appropriate social institutions. It is a moral system consonant with the "natural course of things" (*E* 260). But aren't human beings capable of setting up other systems of morality if they wish? And aren't these to be accorded equal status with what Hume recommends? To the first question we must answer in the affirmative; Hume himself offers an example: "celibacy, fasting, penance, mortification, self-denial, humility, silence, solitude, and the whole train of monkish virtues" (*EPM* 270) have been elevated into a moral system by some. But to the second question Hume answers with a clear negative. Such a "moral system" is a perversion; and could never be received "where men judge of things by their natural, unprejudiced reason, without the delusive glosses of superstition and false religion" (*EPM* 270). The "natural, unprejudiced reason" is of course precisely the capacity which runs into trouble in philosophical systems, and this seems to explain the fact that Hume's account of moral principles is at once so commonsensical and so original: his philosophy is grounded in common life, and eschews the systematizing and distorting inclinations characteristic of so many of his philosophical predecessors. The "monkish virtues" are seen by the ordinary man to "stupify the understanding and harden the heart, obscure the fancy and sour the temper" (*EPM* 270). They properly belong among the vices, when judged by "natural, unprejudiced reason": "nor has any superstition force sufficient among men of the world, to pervert entirely these natural sentiments. A gloomy, hair-brained enthusiast, after his death, may have a place in the calendar; but will scarcely ever be admitted, when alive, into intimacy and society, except by those who are as delirious and dismal as himself" (*EPM* 270).

Hume seems to have believed that an account of morals such as he offered, at once simple, powerful, in accordance with common life, and moreover ratified by the "gradual progress of improvement" in human society, could scarcely admit of serious objections. In the conclusion to the *Enquiry*, he expresses his own conviction in the strongest terms. Despite his aversion to any "positive or dogmatical" tone in philosophy, he says, "I must confess, that this enumeration puts the matter in so strong a light, that I cannot, *at present*, be more assured of any truth, which I learn from reasoning and argument" (*ECPM* 278). Yet he confesses an almost ironical "diffidence and skepticism" because as he puts it, an hypothesis accounting for morals which is "so obvious" must certainly, "had it been a true one, ... long ere now, have been received by the unanimous suffrage and consent of mankind" (*ECPM* 278). What can explain the resistance to it, or the failure to discover it? Indeed what can account for the astonishing degree of resistance, even today, to Hume's account of what constitutes a good society, an account which we have seen to be interwoven with his account of the virtues and with his investigations of English history?

VIII. Misunderstandings of Virtue

It will be instructive to look carefully at several passages in Hume's *Essays* which suggest the lines of his own thought concerning two related sources of resistance to the claim of the superiority of liberal commercial society and its virtues. These antagonists of his position characteristically draw on what might almost be called "myths," the myth of superiority of the ancients and the myth of the viciousness of luxury. What unites them is that both stand in the way of wholehearted approval of the sort of society Hume admires and believes England to be. It should perhaps be added that at least one and perhaps both of these myths continue to be quite powerful today.

First, how is the widespread (in the eighteenth century) belief in the superiority of the ancients connected to this discussion of virtue? The societies in question are of course the ancient republics of Greece and Italy, famous not only for letters but for their virtue. Hume admits that the ancient republics were quite different from modern ones. Ancient republics "were free states, they were small ones; and the age being martial, all their neighbors were continually in arms. Freedom naturally begets public spirit, especially in small states..." (*E* 259). Their chief and most splendid virtue seems indeed to have been (an apparently selfless) public spiritedness, or what Hume calls "this *amor patriae*," which made their republics powerful and helped to protect their free and non-commercial way of life, their arts and civility. An admiration for ancient republics is evident in many eighteenth century writers, most notably Rousseau, and it was widely understood that the ancients' greatness was connected to their contempt for the merely commercial (as opposed to military) pursuit of wealth. The form in which this admiration emerged most often was in claims about the superior populousness of the ancient world.

We have already mentioned E.C. Mossner's brilliant article showing that Hume's longest essay, "Of the Populousness of Ancient Nations," constitutes Hume's contribution to the controversy between ancients and moderns. Hume himself explains why this apparently demographic issue has a far greater importance: "in general, we may observe, that the question with regard to the comparative populousness of ages or kingdoms, implies important consequences, and commonly determines concerning the preference of their whole police, their manners, and the constitution of their government" (*E* 381). Hume calls attention to the ubiquitous human tendency to venerate what is ancient ("the humour of blaming the present, admiring the past, is strongly rooted in human nature" (*E* 464), but suggests that such veneration is in this instance misplaced. Since in general "every wise, just, and mild government, by rendering the condition of its subjects easy and secure, will always abound most in people, as well in commodities and riches" (*E* 382), Hume's conviction of the superiority of modern commercial society requires that he show the belief in the greater populousness of ancient nations false or at least doubtful. In the course both of his lengthy and ingenious analysis of the available figures on population, and in other essays, Hume introduces two related criticisms of ancient republicanism. The defects to which he calls attention, though not fully separable, are the ancient republics' reliance on slavery, and the unnaturalness of their political institutions when considered in the light of natural human inclinations. Both of these are due in part at least to an external circumstance: the primacy of war and the resulting overemphasis on martial qualities.[22]

"The chief difference," Hume writes, "between the *domestic* economy of the ancients and that of the moderns, consists in the practice of slavery, which prevailed among the former" (*E* 383). This practice is itself unjust, and Hume castigates admirers of the civil liberty and virtue of the ancients for inconsistency: "whilst they brand all submission to the government of a single person with the harsh denomination of slavery, they would gladly reduce the greater part of mankind to real slavery and subjection" (Ibid.). Any reasonable analysis will show that "human nature, in general, really enjoys more liberty at present, in the most arbitrary government of Europe, than it ever did during the most flourishing period of ancient times" (Ibid.). Hume's argument depends on his inclusion – suggested by the use of the term *human nature* – of all human beings, masters and slaves, in the calculation. He shows that the modern practice of service for wages is both more equitable and produces superior virtue. In the ancient system there were no "checks" on the master, "to engage him in the reciprocal duties of gentleness and humanity"; even slave masters are corrupted by slavery. "In modern times, a bad servant finds not easily a good master, nor a bad master a good servant; and the checks are mutual, suitably to the inviolable and eternal laws of reason and equity" (*E* 384). Claims about the superior virtue of the ancients require turning a blind eye to the destructive influence of domestic slavery on virtue, and not only with regard to slaves themselves.

In the essay "Of Commerce" Hume examines the question whether commerce can properly be said to contribute to the strength and greatness of a state. The question arises because admirers of the ancient republics maintain that their greatness was connected to their suppression of commerce, a suppression undertaken with the aim of maintaining a fit and ready military force. According to the ancient view, private wealth and even happiness are in conflict with public spirit and civic virtue. In the course of refuting this view Hume comments that "ancient policy was violent, and contrary to the more natural and usual course of things" (*E* 260). In fact, he says, with reference to the "peculiar laws" by which Sparta was governed, "were the testimony of history less positive and circumstantial, such a government would appear a mere philosophical whim or fiction, and impossible ever to be reduced to practice." Sparta will seem a "prodigy" to anyone "who has considered human nature, as it displayed itself in other nations, and other ages" (*E* 259). Though Roman principles were "somewhat more natural," even they could prevail only because an "extraordinary concurrence of circumstances," including above all considerations of survival in an age when a number of small states were continually in arms, made citizens "submit to such grievous burdens" (*E* 259).

> A continual succession of wars makes every citizen a soldier: he takes the field in his turn: and during his service he is chiefly maintained by himself. This service is indeed equivalent to a heavy tax; yet it is less felt by people addicted to arms, who fight for honor and revenge more than pay, and are unacquainted with gain and industry, as well as pleasure. (E 259; see Hume's note to this passage)

But this is not the usual course of things, and "the less natural any set of principles are, which support a particular society, the more difficulty will a legislator meet with in raising and cultivating them" (*E* 260). Even sovereigns, Hume suggests, "must take mankind as they find them." The best policy for a wise legislator is "to comply with the common bent of mankind and give it all the improvements of which it is susceptible." As we will see below, this often involves, according to Hume, balancing *vices* and not merely promoting virtue. A moral system, just as much as a legislator, must take human nature as it is. "Now, according to the most natural course of things, industry, and arts, and trade, increase the power of the sovereign, as well as the happiness of the subjects; and that policy is violent which aggrandizes the public by the poverty of individuals" (*E* 260). Mossner summarizes Hume's case against the ancient republics and their conception of virtue with the assertion that ancient manners "were unfavorable to the general welfare: these manners include the misunderstanding of liberty, the precariousness of property rights, the inhuman maxims of politics ... the inferiority of ancient manufactures and commerce did not contribute to the growth of luxury nor the general well-being of the masses of people" (Mossner, 1949, p. 151). This brings us neatly to the second of the myths Hume examines and explodes.

IX. Luxury

There is among moral and political thinkers a widespread antipathy, amounting to a prejudice, against luxury. Hume seems to see this prejudice as a deplorable kind of moralism, an ignorant moralism which is unwilling to scrutinize carefully the genuine and solid morality of common life. The prejudice against luxury continues to operate today on both left and right sides of the political spectrum. It has roots both in secular egalitarianism, from which come calls for confiscatory taxes on the rich, and in some religious teachings which see commerce and especially capitalism or free enterprise commerce to be sources of evil and exploitation.

There is a peculiar and mystifying tendency to attack luxury as the source of greed and avarice, a relationship which common sense would reverse. The prejudice is fed by the strong historical association of ostentatious luxury with ages of stultifying social stratification and oppression. The luxury of magnificent palaces and the pomp and ceremony of a corrupt nobility, however, are looked at very carefully by Hume in their relation to commerce, as we have seen. And his advocacy of commercial society is based on his conclusion that stratification and nobility – not luxury – are obstacles to commerce, which in itself has a tendency to promote liberty and the rise of the commons; and thus to dissolve the stratification. (Consider the story about Henry VII fining the Earl of Oxford on account of his "retainers.") Especially virulent strains of complaint about the viciousness of luxury are connected to religious fundamentalism, as may be seen from a consideration of the ratings of the Ayatollah Khomeini or the more moderate warnings of decadence of Aleksandr Solzhenitsyn.[23]

These complaints and warnings are very close in spirit to the eighteenth century prejudice against luxury which Hume examined in the essay originally introduced under the title "Of Luxury." The essay (whose name he changed to "Of Refinement in the Arts") begins as follows: "Luxury is a word of an uncertain signification, and may be taken in a good as well as a bad sense. In general it means great refinement in the gratification of the senses; and any degree of it may be innocent, or blamable, according to the age, or country, or condition of the person" (*E* 268). He undertakes to examine luxury dispassionately, noting that since luxury may be either innocent or blamable, "one may be surprised at those preposterous opinions which have been entertained concerning it." Some men "of libertine principles" go so far as to praise even vicious luxury, while others represent luxury in any degree "as the source of all the corruptions, disorders, and factions incident to civil government" (*E* 269). The former, in their praise of luxury, "represent it as highly advantageous to society." Hume says his intention is to "endeavor to correct both these extremes," though by the end of the essay the reader finds that however evenhanded Hume's analysis, he has undercut the moralist position far more than the view of those who praise luxury. He will proceed, he says, by proving "*first*, that the ages of refinement are both the happiest and most virtuous; *secondly*, that wherever luxury ceases to be innocent, it also ceases to be beneficial; and when carried a degree too far, is a quality pernicious, though perhaps not the most pernicious, to political society" (*E* 269). The last clause contains the catch: Hume will suggest, at the end, that even vicious luxury is preferable to the alternatives. Though he is neither libertine nor severe moralist, and though he stops short of praising vicious luxury simply, Hume suggests that until all vices are eliminated from the human condition – an eventuality he does not look for – the vice even of vicious luxury may justly be endorsed as beneficial by its overall effect.

Hume undertakes his first task, the proof that ages of refinement are happiest and most virtuous, by considering the effects of luxury in two aspects of life, private and public. He begins by asserting it is generally agreed that human happiness consists of three ingredients (action, pleasure, and indolence), concerning which it is possible to disagree only about the proper proportions. Now, "in times when industry and the arts flourish, men are kept in perpetual occupation, and enjoy, as their reward, the occupation itself, as well as those pleasures which are the fruit of their labour" (*E* 270; unless otherwise noted, all references are to this and the following ten pages). If in an attempt to prevent luxury one were to banish or discourage the refined arts, "you deprive men both of action and of pleasure," since indolence must fill the empty place, men will be less happy because even indolence, which may be enjoyable, can only be enjoyed as a respite from action and employment. Thus refinement in the arts contributes to happiness by promoting *industry*.

Not only are men encouraged to be active and enjoy the satisfaction of active employment, but industry itself and the naturally concomitant refinements in mechanical arts "commonly produce some refinements in the liberal." Thus knowledge is promoted by refinement in the arts: "The spirit of the age affects all the arts, and the minds of men being once roused from their lethargy, and put into a fermentation, turn themselves on all sides, carry improvements into every art and science. Profound ignorance is totally banished, and men ... cultivate the pleasures of the mind as well as those of the body." Thus refinement or luxury contributes to both industry and knowledge. And Hume notes a third beneficial effect: men become more sociable, and with more sociability comes humanity. Only in "ignorant and barbarous nations" are men content to live in solitude or at a distance. When the arts flourish, "they flock into cities; love to receive and communicate knowledge; to show their wit or their breeding; their taste in conversation or living, in clothes or furniture." Whether from motives of curiosity, which "allures the wise," or vanity or pleasure, men are drawn together, and meet in an increasingly "easy and sociable" manner. The result is that, "beside the improvements which they receive from knowledge and the liberal arts, it is impossible but they must feel an increase of humanity, from the very habit of conversing together, and contributing to each other's pleasure and entertainment." Hume's summing up brings all three effects together: "Thus *industry*, *knowledge*, and *humanity*, are linked together by an indissoluble chain, and are found, from experience as well as reason, to be peculiar to the more polished, and, what are commonly denominated, the more luxurious ages" (*E* 271). To those three good effects Hume adds a fourth, almost as an afterthought: men will indulge less in excesses as they become more refined, since "nothing is more destructive to true pleasure than such excesses." Thus luxury or refinement in the arts, contrary to what severe moralists assert, actually promotes moderation.

In terms of public life, the effect of refinement in the arts is to contribute to the strength and power of society as a whole. "The increase and consumption of all the commodities, which serve to the ornament and pleasure of life, are advantageous to society; because, at the same time that they multiply those innocent gratifications to individuals, they are a kind of *storehouse* of labour, which, in the exigencies of state, may be turned to the public service." This is of course the real answer to the charges that luxury and commerce are incompatible with public spiritedness: they supply a kind of *alternative* to the sort of direct public spirit which the ancients promoted at such enormous cost; the public spirit of a commercial society exists in reserve only, but though less splendid it is preserved much more easily and is always there to be drawn on. Ancient public spirit was maintained only at great cost in terms of natural human inclinations, and was thus fragile and not entirely reliable. Without refinement in the arts, according to Hume, that is, "in a nation where there is no demand for such superfluities, men sink into indolence, lose all enjoyment of life, and are useless to the public, which cannot maintain or support its fleets and armies from the industry of such slothful members." In addition to increasing the strength of the society, luxury and commerce contribute to *wiser* government by promoting improvements in the knowledge of "laws, order, police, discipline," which "can never be carried to any degree of perfection, before human reason has refined itself by exercise." By combating superstition and prejudice, advances in arts and sciences promote political decency. "Knowledge in the arts of government begets mildness and moderation, by instructing men in the advantages of humane maxims above rigour and severity, which drive subjects into rebellion." Hume was no doubt thinking here of the violent religious strife he was to write about so eloquently in the Stuart volumes of the *History*.[24] The spread of refinement or luxury softens the tempers of men, improves their knowledge and promotes humanity even in public life, and thus conspicuous humanity "is the chief characteristic which distinguishes a civilized age from times of barbarity and ignorance" (*E* 274).

Hume maintains that commerce and the arts need not diminish a nation's "martial spirit" even though they tame men's ferocity; honor is a principle which becomes more important with civility, politeness and refinement, and a sense of honor may promote courage just as well as does the anger characteristic of more brutal and savage ages. He denies the claim that the decline of Rome was due to an effeminacy brought on by its embrace of luxury and refinement: though "all the Latin classics whom we peruse in our infancy are full of these sentiments, and universally ascribe the ruin of their state to the arts and riches imported from the East," Hume writes, "it would be easy to prove, that these writers mistook the cause of the disorders in the Roman state, and ascribed to luxury and the arts, what really proceeded from an ill-modelled government, and the unlimited extent of conquests" (*E* 276). He might have added that the decline of Rome seems to strengthen his claim that the ancient republics had to distort human nature in order to achieve that public spirit which distinguished them, gloriously but briefly.

The final and perhaps most important claim concerning the effects of refinement in the arts is also the most general: "if we consider the matter in a proper light we shall find, that a progress in the arts is rather favourable to liberty, and has a natural tendency to preserve, if not produce a free government" (*E* 277). This is the core of the argument we have traced in detail from the *History*. In "rude unpolished nations" almost all labor is necessarily devoted to cultivation of the ground (or to fighting), with the result that there are invariably two classes of men: peasants or serfs, who are often slaves, and are fitted only for subjection, and a class of proprietors, or nobles, whom Hume calls "petty tyrants."

> But where luxury nourishes commerce and industry, the peasants, by a proper cultivation of the land, become rich and independent; while the tradesmen and merchants acquire a share of the property, and draw authority and consideration to that middling rank of men, who are the best and firmest basis of public liberty. These submit not to slavery, like the peasants, from poverty and meanness of spirit; and having no hopes of tyrannizing over others, like the barons, they are not tempted, for the sake of that gratification, to submit to the tyranny of their sovereign. They covet equal laws, which may secure their property, and preserve them from monarchical, as well as aristocratical tyranny. (*E* 277–78)

Hume expresses amazement at the violent blame attached to luxury or refinement, in view of the role it has played in transforming English society by contributing to the rise of popular government. The lower house of Parliament is the mainstay of that government, and "all the world acknowledges, that it owes its chief influence and consideration to the increase of commerce, which threw such a balance of property into the hands of the commons."

What though of the effects of luxury or refinement when it ceases to be "innocent"? The argument Hume offers here is almost devious, but it is so elegantly simple that one scarcely notices the real force of his conclusion. He has already warned the reader of its bearing by noting, and now repeating, that even vicious luxury, while a quality pernicious in itself, is "perhaps not the most pernicious, to political society." "Vicious luxury" is taken to mean a "gratification" which "engrosses all of a man's expense, and leaves no ability for such acts of duty and generosity as are required by his situation and fortune." That virtue is desirable and superior to vice Hume readily acknowledges. But if we are to speak of removing a vice – for example, the indulgence of a desire for some vicious luxury – is the alternative some virtue? If for example by banning a vicious luxury we could be assured that a man would employ the saving on "the education of his children, the support of his friends, and in relieving the poor," then the benefit is self-evident. But what if by removing one vice we simply promote another: if by banning a luxury we encourage a man to give way to indolence? "To say that, without a vicious luxury, the labour would not have been employed at all, is only to say, that there is some other defect in human nature, such as indolence, selfishness, inattention to others, for which luxury, in some measure, provides a remedy; as one poison may be an antidote to another." Of course, as Hume admits, "virtue, like wholesome food, is better than poison, however corrected" (*E* 279).

The comparison invites us to ask what course is open to us as reformers. Aside from bodily sickness, Hume suggests, "all other ills spring from some vice, either in ourselves or others; and even many of our diseases proceed from the same origin." To deny this is to maintain that this is the best of all possible worlds, a view to which Hume is no subscriber. Since our ills proceed from vice, he says, "remove the vices, and the ills follow. You must only take care to remove all the vices. If you remove part, you may render the matter worse. By banishing *vicious* luxury, without curing sloth and an indifference to others, you only diminish industry in the state, and add nothing to men's charity or their generosity" (*E* 279–80). Hume leaves the reader to draw the conclusion, and in fact immediately obscures the issue by arguing against those who assert vice to be beneficial to society, which he calls a contradiction in terms. And rightly, for Hume is not praising vices. All he does is to show that they stand in a complex relation to one another. With delightful irony he calls attention to the fact that he is contributing to a *philosophical* question and not a *political* one, and so underlines the irrelevance of his fastidious refusal to endorse a vice.

> I call it a *philosophical* question, not a *political* one. For whatever may be the consequence of such a miraculous transformation of mankind, as would endow them with every species of virtue, and free them from every species of vice, this concerns not the magistrate, who aims only at possibilities. He cannot cure every vice by substituting a virtue in its place. Very often he can only cure one vice by another; and in that case he ought to prefer what is least pernicious to society.

Luxury, when excessive, is the source of many ills; but it is in general preferable to sloth and idleness, which would commonly succeed in its place, and are more hurtful both to private persons, and to the public. *(E 280)*

The proper understanding of luxury, like the understanding of economic progress, requires a comprehensive understanding of human nature and of the physical and moral circumstances of human life. Hume's account has the advantage of its close agreement with common life, or as he put it here, with a political perspective rather than the narrowly philosophic.

Notes

1. The *History of England* went through editions numbering well into the hundreds; there is no standard edition. Even the placement of appendices can vary from edition to edition. References in this paper are to the Liberty Classics edition, which follows the 1777 edition and incorporates Hume's last changes. For an account of the changes, see Duncan Forbes, *Hume's Philosophical Politics* (Cambridge, 1975), esp. 233–324; for some of the vicissitudes of publication, see Ernest Cambell Mossner, *The Life of David Hume* (2nd edition, Oxford, 1980), 301–318. Mossner is the standard biographical source on Hume, and a rich mine of detail.

As for the ubiquity of Hume's *History*, even well into the nineteenth century, I should mention anecdotal evidence. While touring the home of famous children's authoress Beatrix Potter in Sawrey, in England's lake district, I stopped to look at her "library," or what was on display. It consisted of one bookcase, and in it was a nineteenth century edition of Hume's *History*.

Other works by Hume will be cited according to the following convention:

Essays, Moral, Political, and Literary (Liberty Classics edition, ed. Eugene Miller, 1984), cited as *E* followed by page number, as: *(E 211)*.

Enquiry concerning Human Understanding, from *Hume's Enquiries,* edited by L.A.Selby-Bigge, 3rd edition revised by P.H. Nidditch (Oxford 1975), cited as *EHU* followed by page number.

Enquiry concerning the Principles of Morals, in *Ibid.,* cited as *ECPM* followed by page number.

2. See, for example, Sheldon Wolin, "Hume and Conservatism," in Donald K. Livingston and James T. King, *HUME: A Re-evaluation* (New York, 1976), 239–256; Craig Walton, "Hume and Jefferson on the Uses of History," in *Ibid.,* 389–403.
3. This is the title of a work in progress, parts of which I have seen as a result of private correspondence with Professor Caton, who teaches in Brisbane, Australia.
4. Wolin, *Op. cit.,* p. 239.
5. See, for example, D.F. Norton, *David Hume,* (Princeton, 1982), *passim.*; Wolin, *Op.*

cit., Forbes, *Op. cit.*.

6. An especially clear case of this reasoning is found in Mossner, *Op. cit.*, p. 318: "Although Hume's *History* is not for our times, it is proper to turn to it for either of two reasons: to enjoy it as literature, or to learn from it how the greatest mind of the Enlightenment interpreted the past for his age." It should go without saying that the approach taken here is quite different.

7. An excellent discussion of the issue between ancients and moderns, and Hume's position in that controversy, is E.C. Mossner, "Hume and the Ancient-Modern Controversy, 1725–1752: A Study in Creative Skepticism," (University of Texas, *Studies in English*, XXVIII (1949), 139–53.

8. See *The Letters of David Hume*, ed. J. Y. T. Grieg (Oxford, 1932; 2 volumes), Vol. I, 249: Hume writes to publisher Andrew Millar that he is writing the history beginning with the reign of Henry VII, and adds "It is properly at that Period modern History commences. America was discovered: Commerce extended: The Arts cultivated: Printing invented: Religion reform'd: And all the Governments of Europe almost chang'd." See also *Letters* I, 251.

9. In a note to this passage Hume writes that "the kings, to encourage the boroughs, granted them this privilege, that any villain, who had lived a twelvemonth in any corporation and had been of the gild, should be thenceforth regarded as free" (II. 523n). Cf. I. 469–470.

10. The process of liberation which follows or accompanies the development of the arts and sciences is contrasted by Hume with the course of events in Greek and Roman times, when the progress of the arts "seems ... to have daily increased the number of slaves." The difference, he teaches, results "from a great difference in the circumstances" (II. 523): where the Roman lords were interested in opulence and displays of wealth, and hence in domestic services of all kinds, the feudal barons, "being obliged to maintain themselves continually in a military posture, and little emulous of elegance or splendor, employed not their villains as domestic servants, much less as manufacturers, but composed their retinue of freemen, whose military spirit rendered the chieftain formidable to his neighbours" (*Ibid.*).

11. "Of Refinement in the Arts" (*E* 268–280). This essay comprises the second of the set of essays generally read today as political economy (see Mossner, *Op. cit.*, 269–71). It was originally entitled "Of Luxury" in the first edition of "Political Essays." The essay will be used to extend the argument of this essay (below).

12. It is instructive to compare Hume's estimation of the importance of this change with the account offered by Tocqueville of the centrality of inheritance laws: "I am surprised that ancient and modern writers have not attributed greater importance to the laws of inheritance (fn.) and their effect on the progress of human affairs.... they should head the list of all political institutions, for they have an unbelievable influence on the social state of peoples..." (Tocqueville, *Democracy in America* (New York: Anchor, 1969), 51–52).

13. P. T. Bauer, "The Spurious Consensus and its Background," chapter 9 of *Dissent on Development* (Cambridge, Mass.: Harvard University Press, 1972). See also Bauer's *Reality and Rhetoric: Studies in the Economics of Development* (Cambridge, Mass.: Harvard University Press, 1984). For a brief introduction to other economists whose work Bauer criticizes, see *Pioneers in Development*, ed. Gerald Meier and Dudley Seers (New York: Oxford University Press, 1984). This study itself contains an article by Bauer.

14. Bauer, *Reality and Rhetoric*, 19. Cf. Bauer, *Dissent on Development*, 31-49; 69-82.

15. Bauer, *Reality and Rhetoric*, 4–5.

16. Bauer, *Dissent on Development*, 324, 325.

17. I cite here from an article on the man and his work: "Why the Less-Developed Nations May Go on Laying Eggs," by Lindley H. Clark, Jr., *Wall Street Journal* (March 12, 1985), 31. See also Gottfried Haberler, *Selected Essays of Gottfried Haberler*, edited by Anthony Y.C. Koo, (Cambridge, Mass.: M.I.T. Press, 1985), especially 495–527.

18. Bauer, *Reality and Rhetoric*, 30.

19. Mr. de Soto's book, *El Otro Sendero*, (*The Other Path* – a reference to the Peruvian Maoist group "Shining Path"), has not yet been translated or released in the U.S.. See "A New Latin Hero Has a Message for Capitalists," by George Melloan, *Wall Street Journal* (March 17, 1987), 35.

20. Paul Johnson, *Modern Times: The World from the Twenties to the Eighties* (New York: Harper & Row, 1983), 729. The discussion in the Chapter "The Bandung Generation" bears in many respects on the argument here.

21. Bauer, *Dissent on Development*, 322–23.

22. Views similar to Hume's (in favoring commercial republics over ancient martial republics) are found in John Adam's *A Defence of the Constitutions of Government of the United States of America* (New York: Da Capo Press, 1971), esp. vol. I., pp.113–114, 212, 256–57. A careful reading of Montesquieu's *Spirit of the Laws* will find powerful coincident arguments. See Pangle, *Montesquieu's Philosophy of Liberalism* (Chicago: University of Chicago Press, 1973).

23. For Solzhenitzyn's views see his celebrated Harvard commencement address in 1978, "A World Split Apart," published in *National Review*, (July 7, 1978, 836–55). But the view that commerce or capitalist society is hopelessly decadent is very widespread today among political commentators. See Henry Fairlie's lament for the disappearance of public spirit (civic virtue) under Reagan, in "Citizen Kennedy" (*The New Republic*, February 3, 1986, pp. 14–17). Fairlie complains that "With the idea of citizenship all but submerged in appeals to private pursuits, private satisfactions, the private sector, the most Reagan could hope to lead against a real enemy would be a herd of the Gadarene swine."

24. The paradox that severity in government drives subjects to rebellion is treated analytically in one of Hume's *Essays*. See "Of the Liberty of the Press" (*E* 9–13).

NICHOLAS CAPALDI

THE PRESERVATION OF LIBERTY

Introduction

In writing his *History of England*, David Hume had more than one purpose in mind. Philosophically, Hume argued that the emergence of liberty was a unique event for which it was not possible to specify necessary and sufficient conditions. That is, the emergence of liberty could not be deduced from human psychology or the laws of economics or the dialectic of history. What was demanded was a new understanding of how norms emerged and functioned. Historically, Hume labored to expose the Whig illusion of an appeal to a definitive ancient constitution. Politically, Hume's objective was to bring together both Whigs and Tories in a new consensus or coalition that taught men to cherish civil liberty by revealing the political liberty which supported it. This political liberty rested on the recognition that the only basis of government is the established practice of the age.

If I were to risk one sweeping generalization it would be that Hume was primarily concerned with preserving liberty and that the account of its origin was subordinate to that purpose. Certainly, Hume thought that he had accounted for its origins in a natural-historical fashion, and certainly he thought it was important to refute false and illusory accounts of that origin, but even here he was intent on arguing that misperceptions about origins constituted a threat to preservation.

What Hume was doing was making a distinction between the origin of liberty and the preservation of liberty. In his *History of England*, during a discussion of the importance of executive patronage and the necessity for a two party system, Hume remarked that when liberty was a novel phenomenon men did not develop those maxims which protect it. Here we have Hume's main focus, the guarding and regulating of liberty. It is also important to point out that what Hume stressed was the formulation of maxims, not the formulation of universal principles.

N. Capaldi and D.W. Livingston (eds.), Liberty in Hume's History of England. 195–224.
© 1990 *Kluwer Academic Publishers. Printed in the Netherlands.*

The fact that liberty emerged from the existence of unique events is also important. If there are unique events then there is no atemporal perspective from which we can rationalize those events. This is what necessitates a peculiarly historical approach. Moreover, what emerged from a series of unique events could just as easily disappear back into the stream of events. Not only was it possible for something like the Dark Ages to return but evil itself could not be discounted. On the other hand, once a practice has been initiated or once we become aware of the norms that structure our practice we can self-consciously maintain and extend that practice. This, I take to be the grand design of Hume's *History of England*, preserving liberty through a proper understanding of liberty.

In setting out to show Hume's case for the preservation of liberty as he articulated it in the *History of England*, we are naturally led to ask if this bears on Hume's other discussions of political philosophy, especially in the *Treatise of Human Nature* and in the essays. I think it does, and the main philosophical parallel I would draw is the following. In the *Treatise*, Hume distinguishes between the origin or first motive to justice and the subsequent motive or obligation to maintain justice. He is primarily concerned to account for the latter. In the *History of England*, Hume likewise distinguishes between the origin of liberty and the present conditions necessary to sustain liberty. Not unexpectedly, the sustaining conditions enunciated in the *History* are precisely the conditions that Hume had elevated to a more general status in his political, economic, and social essays.

In what follows, we shall see that Hume stressed four general sets of conditions for sustaining liberty. First, he stressed the *legal* foundations of liberty, specifically the importance of due process. Second, he stressed the *political* foundations of liberty, specifically what we have come to call the system of checks and balances. Third, he stressed the *economic* foundations of liberty, specifically defending what we know as a free market economy (private property, market exchange, and the sanctity of contracts). Finally, he stressed the intellectual foundations of liberty, what we would recognize as Hume's peculiarly secular and conservative understanding of the social world.[1]

Law and Liberty

We have drawn a parallel between justice and liberty, namely, a parallel between accounting for the preservation of justice in Hume's *Treatise* and accounting for the preservation of liberty in the *History*. The relationship between justice and liberty is even tighter in Hume's view. There is an important sense in which Hume equates liberty with justice or the rule of law. *Liberty*, for Hume, is the absence of *arbitrary* coercion. One of the things for which Hume criticized the Whigs is their confusion of liberty with (a) the absence of constraint, (b) the transition from barbarism to civilization and (c) the emergence of a free constitution. All three of these states were lumped together by Whigs and spoken of as "liberty". But, as Hume argued, there is all the difference in the world among a state of lawlessness, a state of order imposed by tyranny, and a state of constitutionally recognized freedoms. The kind of liberty about which Hume was concerned was the third kind, the liberty that arises from justice.

On the whole, notwithstanding the seeming liberty or rather licentiousness of the Anglo-Saxons, the great body even of the free citizens, in those ages, really enjoyed much less true liberty, than where the execution of the laws is the most severe, and where subjects are reduced to the strictest subordination and dependence on the civil magistrate. The reason is derived from the excess itself of that liberty. Men must guard themselves at any price against insults and injuries; and where they receive not protection from the laws and magistrate, they will seek it by submission to superiors, and by herding in some private confederacy, which acts under the direction of a powerful leader. And thus all anarchy is the immediate cause of tyranny, if not over the state, at least over many of the individuals.[2]

Put more precisely, a state of civil liberty exists when law or authority is tempered by justice. Hume sought to transcend intractable controversies about the combat of liberty and authority by showing that liberty had to be grounded in authority. "In all governments, there is a perpetual intestine struggle, open or secret, between authority and liberty; and neither of them can ever absolutely prevail in the contest."[3] It would be simplistic to say that Hume's point is that liberty may subvert other values such as order. Rather, he is arguing that without order there is no liberty. The purpose of government is to increase the liberty of the individual by replacing "natural liberty" with "*civil liberty*."[4] Where government is absent or ineffective we have a state of *natural liberty* or licentiousness. If government becomes too powerful, then liberty disappears. The proper salutary balance is achieved when civil liberty is supported by law and justice.

Two questions are raised by Hume's implicit notion that liberty is the absence of arbitrary coercion. The first question concerns how we determine when coercion is arbitrary. As we shall see in greater detail later in the paper, Hume defines "arbitrary" as what is in conflict with custom and tradition.

A second question concerns the distinction between natural liberty and civil liberty. "How does the transition take place?" Certainly not through the Whig notion of an original contract. Hume denied both the historical existence and the normative force of the so-called original contract. The "people", as Hume showed in his *History*, had never been consulted except in a government that had already been established. Hume also rejected the normative passive obedience theory of the Tories. All authority originated in force, so it is only longevity and tradition that legitimated authority. Here, at last, we come to the beginning of an answer. The law and justice that serve as a necessary condition of civil liberty come into existence when all parties concerned give their allegiance to established practice. It is this allegiance to custom that legitimates authority and elevates it to the status of due process.[5]

In a sense, both the Whigs and Tories were correct to think in terms of a social process (i.e. a contract or an implicit commitment or promise) by which citizens legitimate a political structure. Where the Whigs were incorrect was in thinking that (a) the contract was an actual historical event and (b) that the parties to the contract could negotiate in an ahistorical vacuum. The Whigs had contradicted themselves by using normative social concepts to account for the origin of a normative social context. The Whigs were thus mistaken on both historical and philosophical grounds. Where the Tories were incorrect was in thinking that the status quo legitimated itself. "Passive obedience" is the response of a subject, not the moral condition of a citizen. Something had happened historically that changed the way in which people thought of themselves. In both the case of the Whigs and of the Tories we had been given a false historical view of how law and justice had emerged. If liberty depends upon law, and if we have a false view of how law emerged, then we shall have a false view of how liberty emerged. A false view of how liberty emerged jeopardizes liberty itself.

Already implicit in Hume's view is the notion that in order to understand a concept we must understand the historical development of the concept and that the structural transformations of the concept become part of the meaning of the concept. Whereas Locke had always stressed throughout his philosophy the original experience, Hume on the contrary stressed the repeated experience. In the *Treatise of Human Nature* and in his political essays Hume had exposed in an abstract way the philosophical errors of both the Whigs and the Tories. In the *History of England* what Hume provided was what he thought was the correct historical account of the evolution of the concept of liberty.

In his *History of England*, Hume cited several examples of how liberty fared without due process. One example is the infamous Star Chamber under Elizabeth I. The Star Chamber possessed unlimited discretionary authority so that all customary exercises of liberty ceased to exist. A second example comes from Hume's discussion of Strafford's trial. Strafford was accused of a crime as yet undefined by law and sentenced without due process. In the case of Strafford, Commons had discovered a form of treason "entirely new and unknown to the laws", and, further, had "invented a kind of accumulated or constructive evidence" by which any unguarded action or word "assisted by the malevolent fancy of the accuser, and tortured by doubtful constructions is transmuted into the deepest guilt."[6] A third example can be found in Hume's treatment of Cromwell, which shows us that without due process both the despot and his subordinates will act despotically. Hume's fourth example concerns *habeas corpus*. He claims that *habeas corpus* "seems necessary for the protection of liberty in a mixed monarchy; and as it has not place in any other form of government, this consideration alone may induce us to prefer our present constitution to all others."[7]

Due process has one very subtle effect on rulers. It minimizes the abuse of discretionary power. In his discussion of Cromwell, Hume stressed how "irresistible" the temptation to crime is when one wields power.[8] The existence of due process causes rulers to take an immediate interest in every execution of justice as opposed to a remote attitude towards acts of injustice.[9] It is not only in mixed monarchies that due process is important. It is even more important in republican forms of government, because the discretionary powers granted to the chief magistrate in a republican form of government may be greater than those granted to a monarch.

It should be stressed that due process is not to be confused with legalism or bureaucratization. Due process is the legitimation of customary practice. Due process underscores the contention that *liberty is also a product of self-imposed rules derived from past practice.*[10]

Politics and Liberty

Consistent with Hume's emphasis on due process in the law is his advocacy in politics of a division of power. Hume supported a mixed constitution or mixed monarchy in which power is shared by an independent executive (the monarch) and a parliament. All legislative power resides in Parliament. The division of power functions as a system of checks and balances. Hume also advocated annual parliaments and, in his discussion of the Godwin case of 1604, that Commons needed the power to judge their own election returns.

Hume's attitude toward an independent executive power is interesting. On the one hand, Hume not only recognized the dangers of an all powerful executive but he delighted in pointing out how the Tudors had exemplified this danger. In their haste to castigate the Stuarts' alleged abuse of executive power, the Whigs had created a myth about government under the Tudors. On the contrary, Hume pointed out how close the English had come during the reign of Henry VIII to placing all of their burdens on the government instead of upon themselves and even would have tolerated a large standing army. Henry had been so confident that he had not felt the need to formalize his power. The threat under Elizabeth I was even greater, for her prerogatives were so extensive as to be "incompatible with an exact or regular enjoyment of liberty."[11] In addition to his fear of the abuse of executive power in the case of a large standing army, usually mercenary, Hume cited the dispensing power, the power of imprisonment, the power of exacting loans, and the power of creating monopolies as "directly opposite to the principles of all free governments."[12]

On the other hand, Hume was equally adamant that the executive must have some countervailing power in dealing with Commons. Specifically, Hume stressed the positive importance of patronage in supporting the constitutional balance and liberty. Crown patronage consisted largely of appointing magistrates and conferring honors such as titles. Hume insisted upon the difference between a royal pension and a royal bribe. Hume maintained that Britain enjoyed more liberty under this system than it would have under a pure republic where, presumably, there is no check on legislative power. Parenthetically, it is worth pointing out that in one respect the U.S. constitution and some others embody this notion of checks and balances to a greater degree because the U.S. President, for example, does not owe his election to the majority party in Congress.

The other check on legislative power is the two party system. Accord-

ing to Hume, in a mixed constitution there will inevitably develop two
parties divided on principle.[13] Paradoxically, this division of parties
helps to sustain liberty. Hume also envisioned this division as something
to be exploited to enhance executive power. It was Hume's firm belief
that a constitutionally limited monarchy was a better guarantee of liberty
than a democracy infected by political enthusiasms.

It is useful to note the parallels to Montesquieu in Hume as well as
Hume's influence on Madison.[14] Madison used Hume's arguments to
defend the viability of large commercial commonwealths and indirect
elections as a means to their proper functioning. Indirect elections serve
as a check on unbridled democracy, and it is the threat of unbridled
democracy to liberty that Hume always has in mind. Hume maintained
that a system of indirect elections is better because only those who are
close to a situation can judge it best. This is not unlike the classical
liberal economic argument against a centralized economy based on the
contention that individuals are best left to judge their own affairs rather
than being directed by a remote authority.

In the light of this position, it seems clear that it was not Hume's
affection for Hanoverians or monarchy that was crucial but rather his
belief that liberty requires a system of checks and balances as well as the
belief that in the relevant historical context Britain had developed as a
mixed monarchy. In refashioning a political system, Hume advocated
that we adopt the perspective of a legislator who "*transmits* a system of
laws and institutions to secure the peace, happiness and liberty of future
generations."[15]

The difficult problem raised by Hume's insistence on a respect for
customary practice in politics is the question,"When do unconstitutional
practices become hallowed by custom?" This is a problem from which
Hume does not shrink in the *History of England*. In his discussion of the
king's dispensing power, Hume claimed that in "the irregular nature of
the old English government" one could discern "the existence of such a
prerogative, always exercised and never questioned till the acquisition of
real liberty discovered at last the danger of it."[16]

A clearer way of putting this question is, "What do we do when we
discover conflicting customs?" It is here that Hume's general philosophical orientation is helpful. Hume maintained that philosophy is common
sense methodized and corrected. Political philosophy functions
analogously to resolve conflicts that emerge when an on-going or
evolving system confronts novel circumstances.

In general it is easy to say that when a conflict surfaces the conflict is to be resolved by appeal to some conception of what is more consistent with the implicit norms of the practices that constitute a system. What is not easy is to say who adjudicates or resolves disputes over what constitutes the implicit norms. Hume offered no formal answer to this question. It was clear to Hume that an appeal to the mythical social contract would not do the job, and the entire *History of England* evidences the inadequacy of such an appeal. In retrospect, we can see that this function is now performed in Great Britain by the appeal to the unwritten British Constitution. Elsewhere, different systems have been formulated such as the arrogation of this role by the U.S. Supreme Court, that is by the judiciary. What Hume lacked, but consistent with his views, was the notion of an independent judiciary as a third countervailing force. It should also be clear that a third countervailing force is not just a political requirement but a philosophical one dictated by the need to identify implicit norms in our customary practices. What is important in this context is not who or what performs the function but that the function itself be recognized.

In the *History of England*, Hume is content to argue in specific cases, much along the lines of an advocate, when he thinks that implicit norms have been violated or need clarification. His general principle is that the system has to be preserved. Therefore, at different times different responses are required. For example, the "liberties" of the Saxons are described as barbaric and lawless, whereas certain authoritarian feudal practices create the "liberty" of security. At the same time, neither of these previous kinds of "liberty" are to be confused with the "liberties" of a free constitution. Hence, what would have been justified in the name of liberty for a feudal king, might be a violation of liberty in a modern commercial society.

In dealing with specific cases, Hume's principle seems to be that whatever maximizes the liberty and independence of citizens so long as it is compatible with public order and survival of the system is to be preferred over all other considerations. This should explain why his treatment of the early Stuarts differs so markedly from his treatment of the later Stuarts. Whereas the early Stuarts were innocent of the charge of expanding the prerogatives of the crown, the later Stuarts were adamantly condemned. According to Hume, Charles II and James II erred in not understanding the implicit norms of the system they had inherited, namely peace, security, and the new plan of liberty. They had learned nothing from the events which transpired among the early Stuarts. The early Stuarts were victims of novel events beyond their comprehension, but the later Stuarts were guilty of ignorance and blind ambition about prerogatives. It was the later Stuarts who were attempting to destabilize the system.

Economics and Liberty

When it comes to discussing the economic conditions that sustain liberty, Hume was at his most unequivocal. The preservation of liberty requires a free market economy of trade, commerce and industry. It is the commercial free market society that produces that "middling rank" of person who both requires and fosters liberty. As Hume put it in the *History of England*, the tradesman is a better man and a better citizen than an idle retainer. The growth of both civilization and commerce produced that "middling rank" no longer willing to tolerate either anomalies in the Constitution or an overly broad discretionary power on the part of the executive (monarch).

Hume offered three arguments for the claim that the preservation of liberty requires a free market economy. Hume's first argument is historical, namely, that both commerce and liberty emerged jointly from the decline of feudalism. According to Hume, feudalism had three major drawbacks: no liberty, no civic virtue, and no inducement for capital formation. First, there was no real liberty. "If the feudal government was so little favorable to the true liberty even of the military vassal, it was still more destructive of the independence and security of the other members of the state, or what, in a proper sense, we call the people."[17] Second, feudal arrangements, by their emphasis on personal loyalty, discouraged the formation of that sense of civic virtue that both jealously guards liberty and encourages individuals to participate actively and positively in the running of their own communities. In feudal governments individuals are more anxious to secure their private property than to share in the public administration. Consequently, the execution of the laws is left largely to the discretion of the sovereign.

The third great liability of feudalism is its discouragement of capital formation. In feudalism there was a vicious economic and political cycle. There was little commerce because there was little liberty and security, and there was little liberty because there was little commerce. The peasants were too impoverished to save or to accumulate capital; the idle landed gentry was so bent upon consumption that it too failed to accumulate capital. With no savings available, interest rates were prohibitively high and commerce at a standstill.

In the *History of England*, Hume argued that the vicious cycle was broken with the establishment of corporate communities endowed with privileges and protection from the tyranny of the barons. The English kings adopted this policy in imitation of continental European princes. King Edward I's need for money led him to grant such charters to the burgesses, and it was during his reign that we see the commencement of the House of Burgesses during the Parliament of 1295.[18] The new merchant class saved its money, which in turn encouraged the love of gain, which in turn encouraged frugality and thereby lowered interest rates. The creation of a middle class was also the creation of a group with a positive interest in public administration. Subsequently, Henry VII allowed the nobility and gentry to alienate their estates.[19] This led to a decline in "villeinage" and to a growth in personal freedom. Ultimately, this paved the way for an increase in civil liberty. The symbiotic relationship between luxury and the growth of commerce was a kind of secret or unnoticed and unplanned revolution that caused the decline of the nobility and the rise of the middle class.

The importance of private property as a locus of consumption, savings, and security, helps to explain Hume's critique of Henry VIII's power to impose taxes without consent of parliament. Those who see Hume's attacks on the Tudors as a mere red-herring defense of the early Stuarts fail to notice that Hume always attacked the Tudors for adopting economic policies that threatened the rise of the middle class who were to prove so important for the new plan of liberty. Hume's *History of England* is such a massive collection of facts and commentary that it is often difficult to see the connecting thread. Moreover, those who interpret the *History* from a primarily political point of view fail to notice how important a stress Hume placed on the economic foundations of liberty.

Hume's second argument for the importance of a free market for the preservation of liberty is his contention that the only alternative to a free market society is a society based upon status. A monolithic status society, that is one where there is but a single and centrally determined status system, obstructs the development of liberty. Absolute governments discourage commerce by fostering a social system based on birth, titles, or public function and in which status is difficult to earn by independent means, such as commercial success.

It has become an established opinion, that commerce can never flourish but in a free government; and this opinion seems to be founded on a longer and larger experience than the foregoing, with regard to the arts and sciences. If we trace commerce in its progress through TYRE, ATHENS, SYRACUSE, CARTHAGE, VENICE, FLORENCE, GENOA, ANTWERP, HOLLAND and ENGLAND we shall always find it to have fixed its seat in free governments. The three greatest trading towns now in Europe, are LONDON, AMSTERDAM, and HAMBURG; all free cities, and protestant cities; that is, enjoying a double liberty.[20]

Hume raises the case of the apparent exception, namely, the rise of commerce in Absolutist France. However, Hume counters the exception with the following response:

> ...there is something hurtful to commerce inherent in the very nature of absolute government, and inseparable from it....Commerce, therefore, in my opinion, is apt to decay in absolute governments, not because it is there less *secure*, but because it is less *honourable*. A subordination of ranks is absolutely necessary to the support of monarchy. Birth, titles, and place, must be honoured above industry and riches. And while these notions prevail, all the considerable traders will be tempted to throw up their commerce, in order to purchase some of those employments, to which privileges and honours are annexed."[21]

The third argument for the importance of a free market economy to liberty is a psychological one made more explicit in the *Treatise* and in the essay "Of Refinement in the Arts". Hume contends that liberty is not only prized but jealously guarded by people who are proud of liberty. He further contends that the circumstance that most induces pride is property. The "relation which is esteemed the closest and which of all others produces most commonly the passion of pride is *property*."[22] Pride, in Hume's account of human nature, is an indirect passion. An indirect passion is an impression produced by a preceding idea. Property would be such an idea capable of causing the indirect passion of pride. As an indirect passion, pride also gives rise to the impression of self. Hence, our idea of who we are, our self-identity, is vitally determined by what causes us to feel pride. Hume is thus making the case in the *Treatise* that the social institution of private property is a major determinant of our sense of personal autonomy. *In his essays and in the*

History, Hume is arguing that the transition from feudalism to modern commercial societies was a major factor in the evolution of our sense of personal identity and in the value we attach to liberty as autonomy. It should be noted that since property is not a natural relation but a moral one based upon artifice, Hume's account of property is not time bound. That is, his theory leaves open the further evolution of this notion. Hence, it would be inappropriate to saddle Hume with a static conception of what constitutes property, and it would be a misrepresentation to see him simply as an apologist for the rising middle classes.

In the essay "of Refinement in the Arts", Hume elaborates on this point in his discussion of what gives human beings a sense both of meaningful striving and of fulfillment. In that essay, Hume claims that the major causes of labor are consumption, action, and liveliness. If you eliminate luxury then you undermine the motive of consumption. Left only with action and liveliness, human beings would seek more socially disruptive forms of action both internal and external (e.g. wars, crusades, etc.) In commercial societies with a free market economy the pursuit of luxury becomes a positive force for social stability as well as international order, and it channels human striving in a direction that is personally more satisfying and likely to encourage a sense of personal identity associated with liberty.

Both in the *History* and in his economic essays, Hume drew from these events and from his thesis of the evolution of liberty out of the demise of feudalism a number of specific economic policy lessons about how best to preserve the economic foundations of liberty.[23] Generally speaking, whatever encourages the growth of commerce is to be preferred. Among other things, this explains (1) Hume's approval of luxury and consumption. It also explains (2) Hume's approval of free international trade which he thought expanded domestic growth and that "spirit of industry" which spurs competition and diversification. The favoring of international trade explains (3) his rejection of mercantilism and his specific refutation of mercantilism by noting the self-correcting mechanism of the balance of trade. His approval of competition explains (4) his opposition to price fixing and to monopoly. Hume was especially critical of monopoly under Queen ELizabeth I which he claimed undermined domestic industry and in turn foreign trade. Finally, the importance of savings for low interest rates and of low interest rates for economic growth explains (5) Hume's opposition to inflationary policies, among which is a large national debt, and (6) Hume's critique of Edward I's expulsion of the Jews allegedly for charging interest.[24]

In closing our discussion of Hume's views on the economic foundations of liberty, we should also note Hume's discussion of equality in
both the *History* and in the *Enquiry Concerning the Principles of Morals*.
In the *History*, Hume brings up equality in the following context:

> One John Ball also, a seditious preacher...inculcated on his audience
> the principles of the first origin of mankind from one common stock,
> their equal right to liberty and to all the goods of nature, the tyranny of
> artificial distinctions....These doctrines so agreeable to the populace,
> and so conformable to the ideas of primitive equality, which are
> engraven in the hearts of all men, were greedily received by the
> multitude....[25]

In the second *Enquiry*, Hume interrupted his discussion of justice in
order to excoriate those who advocated equality of possession as enemies
of liberty. The attempt to impose and maintain equality of possession
undermines economic growth and encourages the rise of tyranny. On
both counts, liberty is threatened.

> ...these ideas of perfect equality...are really, at bottom, impracticable;
> and were they not so, would be extremely pernicious to human
> society. Render possessions ever so equal, men's different degrees of
> art, care and industry will immediately break that equality. Or if you
> check these virtues, you reduce society to the most extreme in-
> digence....The most rigorous inquisition too is requisite to watch
> every inequality on its first appearance....so much authority must soon
> degenerate into tyranny."[26]

Intellectual Foundations of Liberty

Nothing is more important for the preservation of liberty than the climate
of opinion that surrounds it. The preservation of liberty requires that we
understand both its origins and supporting conditions. The explication of
liberty calls into play the entire apparatus of Hume's philosophy.

Hume's ethical, social, and political philosophy exemplify the practice
of explication. In explicating, Hume tries to clarify that which is
routinely taken for granted, namely, our ordinary understanding of our
practices. The point of explication is to extract from our previous

practice a set of norms that can be used reflectively to guide future practice. Explication presupposes that efficient practice precedes the theory of it. Explication attempts to specify the sense we have of ourselves when we act and to clarify that which serves to guide us. We do not change our ordinary understanding but rather come to know it in a new and better way. Explication seeks to arrive at a kind of practical knowledge that takes human agency as primary.

When Hume criticized the Whigs for having distorted the history of England, his criticisms were of two kinds. First, the Whigs were often mistaken about the facts. The most egregious Whig error was the contention that ancient liberties were violated by Stuart claims of absolutism. Over and over again, Hume was able to show "how absolute the authority was which the English kings then possessed, and that the Stuarts did little or nothing more than continue matters in the former track, which the people were determined no longer to admit."[27] The more Hume worked on the *History*, the more he was able to document his critique of the Whigs. "In above a hundred alterations which further study, reading, or reflection engaged me to make in the reigns of the first two Stuarts, I have made all of them invariably to the Tory side."[28] Hume was particularly harsh in his criticism of the Whig attempt to present a portrait of Elizabeth I that ignored her claims to absolutism as well as her arbitrary practices.[29]

Hume's second kind of criticism of the Whig history or account of past practice was more theoretical. Hume claimed that the Whigs had imposed upon the history of England a peculiarly distorting framework. By the eighteenth century, the Whig appeal to the concept of the ancient constitution was no longer an appeal to the binding force of custom. Custom could certainly not legitimate an anti-monarchical stance. What the Whigs put in place of custom and tradition was the Lockean theory or hypothesis of natural law and the original contract. The theory of natural law is ahistorical. That is, natural law cannot be read directly off from tradition. The Whig position thus amounted to an anti-historical theory about the underlying conditions or structures behind historical events. Hume's *History* is a sustained rebuttal that exposed the countless distortions to which such a theory gave rise, items like the myth of an immemorial Parliament.

The notion of a social contract as an external and distorting framework was attacked by Hume in both the *Treatise* and in his essays. The social contract doctrine is an exploratory hypothesis about the underlying or hidden structure of our everyday practice. As an exploratory hypothesis, not an actual historical event, it is subject to the charge that there is no way of distinguishing the difference between an alleged violation of the contract and a misunderstanding of what is the content of the contract. As a consequence, the notion of a social contract licenses conflicting views that are irreconcilable, encourages resistance instead of dialogue, and is thus a destabilizing factor in the social polity. Exploratory hypotheses about underlying structure lead to mythical justifications of the right of resistance. Hume pointed out that no "theory" of revolution is possible since such a theory would have to appeal to an authoritative framework, and a mythical event cannot be an authoritative framework precisely because there is no rational way to choose among competing interpretations of that mythical event.

Hume's ironic criticism of the Whigs is that their pursuit of the perfection of civil society was the greatest present danger to the preservation of Liberty. Those who had inaugurated the new plan of liberty were about to undermine it. A second irony is that Hume used the position of the Tories, who had originally opposed the new plan of liberty, to protect the new plan. The Tories, Hume noted, "maintained those maxims that are essential to [liberty's] very existence."[30] The entire *History of England* is an attempt to salvage the historical truth so distorted by Whig historians. As expressed in his essay "The Coalition of Parties", Whig talk about recovering ancient liberty simply shows that even Whigs admit that innovation is dangerous and that the only rule of government is established practice. Hume dwells on the irony of how even those who think they are going beyond history by appealing to abstract ahistorical structures nevertheless feel compelled to offer some kind of historical and narrative account. The shortcoming of the latter kinds of historical accounts is that they are mythical. Failure to get the story straight is to misconstrue what was done, to misconstrue what we are doing, and to misconstrue what can and must be done in the future.

What good history accomplishes is the raising of our consciousness about prior social practice and its inherent logic. This is the conservative theme in Hume's social philosophy. Philosophy explicates the implicit norms rather than standing outside of those norms and pretending to judge them from a super-rational perspective. A proper understanding of custom and a respect for it carries with it the responsibility to use custom both to defend and to criticize custom. Rather than being a mere rationalization for the *status quo*, this Humean understanding of custom can serve as an active basis for responsible social criticism. In the *History*, for example, Hume criticized the docile Parliament of

James II.[31] It was, moreover, precisely because the later Stuarts failed to respect custom in the form of the new plan of liberty that Hume was compelled to criticize them. Again it is worth noting that Hume was prepared to risk the ire of the Tories when he felt they were wrong. Finally, Hume attacked the Tory theory of passive obedience because passive obedience, like the social contract, referred to no historical reality and was an exploratory hypothesis rather than an explication of historical practice.

Since traditions are historical products, and since there are no absolute frames of reference for understanding traditions, Hume would deny that traditions can have a closure, i.e., a teleological endpoint beyond which they no longer can evolve. Traditions must be read as fertile sources of adaptation and reconstruction. One can explicate a tradition, but one cannot circumnavigate it. We cannot totally conceptualize or definitively state its hidden essential structure. For Hume, this is not only a truth about custom but a general philosophical or ontological truth about everything. Understanding a tradition is a matter of practical, not theoretical knowledge. Practical knowledge is not inferior to theoretical knowledge and is not to be rejected by appeal to theoretical criteria. On the contrary, as Hume argued in his philosophical works such theoretical criteria are themselves meaningless and destructive unless grounded in practical knowledge.

Social understanding always carries with it an historical or temporal dimension. Timeless theoretical standpoints are not only external to custom but dangerous because they feed the illusion of total comprehension that breeds fanaticism. Sometimes, it is even important not to try to state too definitively what is behind a practice. As Hume put it in the *History*, "perhaps the English is the first mixed government where the authority of every part has been very accurately defined; and yet there still remain many very important questions between the two houses, that, by common consent, are buried in a discreet silence."[32]

Perhaps the most important immediate practical problem to which Hume applied his understanding of history was the issue of the role of political parties. Whereas Rapin and Bolingbroke had argued that the rise of opposing political parties was an unfortunate consequence caused by James I's appeal to the divine right theory, Hume argued that parties based upon principle were built into the very fabric of the British Constitution. Parties of interest, parties of affection, and parties of principle were now a major part of the practice of parliamentary government. But it was especially parties of principle, a peculiarly modern phenomenon, that according to Hume constituted one of the greatest dangers to liberty.

Specifically, Hume argued that the pursuit of liberty leads to tyranny when that pursuit was inflamed by doctrinaire and fanatical beliefs. Hume thought his *History* had amply demonstrated that the dispute between king and Parliament could have been resolved if it had been conducted in purely secular terms. However, when religion and enthusiasm aided by the appeal to philosophical absolutes were injected into the disputes, civil war became inevitable. This point, by the way, should put Hume's general critique of religion in a new light. In his own time, Hume identified the continuation of the problem as the threat of fanatical and doctrinaire beliefs about key historical events. The misperception of the past mediated by speculative principles is one of the "touchstones of party-men."[33]

Why was it so important to Hume that we have a correct understanding of the history of Great Britain? The answer is that social and political institutions cannot be understood apart from custom and that custom is the product of evolution. This point is reflected in Hume's philosophical contentions that the natural state of human beings is a social state, that the uniformities we observe in human action result from the fundamental features of human nature as revealed in society, and that these features justify political policy maxims. We should recall that in Hume's science of politics what we discover are maxims, not timeless truths. Human beings cannot understand and practice their social and political roles without an understanding of how those roles have evolved.

Philosophical Foundations of Hume's History

In our previous section entitled "Intellectual Foundations of Liberty" we have begun the process of explaining not only what norms Hume advocated but how he understood those norms and his own rationale for them. By focusing on liberty in Hume's *History of England* we have touched on the core of Hume's philosophy as a whole. Our treatment thus far raises two important questions. First, is our discussion of the preservation of liberty consistent with Hume's philosophy as a whole? Second, does our discussion of the preservation of liberty provide a new dimension for the understanding of Hume's philosophy?

There was a time when the first question would have seemed important to the historian but unnecessary to the philosopher. For some time,

Hume's work as a historian was viewed by philosophers as having no connection with his philosophy, as constituting in a sense a separate career. This lack of connection or the appearance of a lack of connection was abetted by interpretations of Hume that viewed him as a positivist or a forerunner of positivism. Armed with positivist preconceptions about both Hume in particular and what constituted worthy intellectual consideration in general, it hardly seemed necessary even to read Hume's *History*. Historians or historically oriented thinkers, on the other hand, could take a broader view of Hume's published works and look at least for methodological continuities in them and for some assurance that they were reading the *History* correctly. It was the pursuit of this latter course that raised questions about what really constituted Hume's philosophical orientation. This leads naturally to the second question about how the *History* helps to throw light on Hume's philosophy as a whole. Finally, all of this created a context for mutual illumination, so that in the end both questions necessarily overlap. It is my contention that the more we distance Hume from positivism the more the philosopher and the historian begin to merge. *The end result is that Hume's concern for preserving liberty by writing the History* is not only a microcosm of his thought as a whole but its very core.

What kind of explanation was Hume offering when he wrote the *History of England*? To begin with, it is anachronistic as well as misleading to read back into Hume any conception of a covering law model of explanation. Hume would deny the appropriateness of explaining social and historical phenomena in terms of an hypothesis about an underlying law-like structure. Social and historical explanations are not deductions from first principles.

Specifically, Hume's explanations are not deductions from psychological first principles. To be sure, Hume appeals to crucial psychological forces like the association of ideas and sympathy, but these forces do not on their own explain the individual or society. Hume rejected the notion of an original social contract in part because contract theory presupposes atomic human beings in a state of nature. The natural state of a human being is social, and this claim is an empirical one. Whereas Locke had focused on the "motion of one single body alone", Hume focused on the "communication of their motion...their attraction and mutual cohesion."[34] Nor does Hume maintain that there is a natural and fundamental drive for self-preservation, as can be seen by anyone who reads his essay on suicide. Nor does Hume maintain that there is a contextless self-interest in terms of which we calculate the utility of social arrangements.

The *Enquiry Concerning the Principles of Morals* makes clear that there has to be an explanation for why utility pleases us in the first place. "Though men be much governed by interest, yet even interest itself, and all human affairs, are entirely governed by opinion."[35]

In the *Enquiry Concerning Human Understanding*, Hume does assert that there is a uniformity to human nature. But a closer examination of the passage in which this comment appears and the surrounding context reveals a deeper meaning. let us quote the passage in full:

> It is universally acknowledged that there is a great uniformity among the actions of men, in all nations and ages, and that human nature remains still the same, in its principles and operations. The same motives always produce the same actions. The same events follow from the same causes. Ambition, avarice, self-love, vanity, friendship, generosity, public spirit: these passions, mixed in various degrees, and distributed through society, have been, from the beginning of the world, and still are, the source of all actions and enterprises, which have ever been observed among mankind. Would you know the sentiments, inclinations, and course of life of the Greeks and Romans? Study well the temper and actions of the French and English: You cannot be much mistaken in transferring to the former *most* of the observations which you have made with regard to the latter. Mankind are so much the same, in all times and places, that history informs us of nothing new or strange in this particular. Its chief use is only to discover the constant and universal principles of human nature, by showing men in all varieties of circumstances and situations, and furnishing us with materials from which we may form our observations and become acquainted with the regular springs of human action and behaviour. These records of wars, intrigues, factions, and revolutions, are so many collections of experiments, by which the politician or moral philosopher fixes the principles of his science, in the same manner as the physician or natural philosopher becomes acquainted with the nature of plants, minerals, and other external objects, by the experiments which he forms concerning them. Nor are the earth, water, and other elements, examined by Aristotle and Hippocrates, more like to those which at present lie under our observation than the men described by Polybius and Tacitus are to those who now govern the world."[36]

What Hume is telling us is that history provides us with the data from which we may draw generalizations about human nature. The function of these generalizations is to form part of a framework from which we can extract norms for guiding future practice. These generalizations have the same status as scientific causal generalizations, that is they are based on constant conjunction. However, just as there is no necessary connection or essence in the physical world, so there is no essence or necessary connection in the human world. As a result, all generalizations are provisional and subject to revision in the light of later experience or history. Hence, any generalization we make about human nature is a generalization relative to social and historical circumstances. Perhaps the most important word in the quotation above is Hume's italicized word "most". In our world we never have complete closure so that the *ceteris paribus* clause of any causal claim cannot be definitively specified. In the light of this logical limitation, it would be no exaggeration to say that for Hume *history is the intellectually fundamental discipline.*[37] If so, then Hume the historian and Hume the philosopher cannot be separated.

Neither do we find in Hume the view that there are timeless general laws of a social dimension, either historical, political, or economic, that serve as first principles. For Hume, human affairs may not be explained without reference to the conscious understanding we as individuals have of those affairs.[38] Keep in mind that for Hume a conscious understanding does not connote a reductive view about psychological forces. That is why we stressed in the previous paragraph that in Hume's philosophy there are no psychological first principles which on their own explain either the individual or the social world. Totally impersonal forces alone would not constitute an adequate explanation. Our understanding of social events is an integral part of the meaning of those events. In this sense, social order arises from within society as opposed to being imposed from without. Both social structure and changes within that structure depend upon the conceptions that social agents have of those structures and not just the structures themselves. All of this underscores why it is so important to write a correct historical account of our practices. What we believe to be our history becomes part of the meaning of who we are.

It is sometimes claimed that Hume, no doubt as a product of his age, subscribed to a cyclical view of history.[39] The chief evidence for this assertion is a solitary passage in the *History*.

...as almost all the improvements of the human mind had reached nearly to their state of perfection about the age of Augustus, there was a sensible decline....But there is a point of depression, as well as exhalation, from which human affairs naturally return in a contrary direction, and beyond which they seldom pass either in their advancement or decline."[40]

The important things to notice about this statement are, first, that it is carefully qualified by the word "seldom", and, second, that it is therefore an instance of an historical generalization rather than a meta-historical statement. Therefore, the foregoing passage does not serve as evidence that Hume subscribed to a cyclical view of history. As an historical generalization the foregoing passage is subject to all of the limitations Hume specifies for any historical generalization. In addition to the limitations on all causal-historical generalizations, we may note other qualifications Hume introduced on historical statements. For instance, Hume said that "no prudent man, however sure of his principles, dares prophesy concerning any event, or foretell the remote consequences of things."[41] Hume also cautioned us that it is not fully known what degrees of refinement, either in virtue or vice, human nature is susceptible of, nor what may be expected of mankind from any great revolution in their education, custom, or principles. Both of these qualifications should also reinforce our contention about the limitations of all causal generalizations about human beings.

It is clear that Hume did draw some generalizations from history and that these generalizations are crucial to his understanding of the social world. The justification for this is that history is all of the evidence that we have. It is past experience to which we must always appeal in any rational assessment. That we may misperceive what is going on does not by itself point to another and stronger source of evidence. Rather, this underlines the caution that must be employed in handling historical data. It should be clear that history teaches us about anomalies, but the only policy we can base on that evidence is one of caution. The claim that we have been mistaken in the past and might be mistaken in the future is itself a generalization from history.

Although Hume buttressed his historical accounts with appeals to economic generalizations, it remains the case that economic generalizations have the same status as other generalizations. Hence, there are in Hume no eternal economic laws. There is not in Hume, as there is in Harrington for example, a simple relationship between property and power. Moreover, Hume, unlike Adam Smith and Karl Marx, did not adhere to any rigid hypothesis about stages of economic growth. Despite his stress on the importance of economics (e.g. the rise of the middle class, stabilizing property relations, etc.), Hume was not an economic determinist. That is, he did not subscribe to the view that all social and political phenomena are the product of underlying economic causes. To be sure, there are many instances where Hume asserted that economic changes produced social changes, but then there are also instances where social changes produced economic changes, where social and cultural developments led to changes of political structure and vice versa. This is precisely where the historical record can be useful in calling into question simplistic hypotheses about hidden structure underlying historical events.

History remains, for Hume, the evidence for testing generalizations. Consequently, there cannot be a rational hypothesis about the hidden structure behind history, economic or otherwise. Such hypotheses are in principle unverifiable because they put at risk the very realm which constitutes the realm of evidence.

Let us examine one example in Hume of the mutual interaction of economic causes with other kinds of social causes. In the essay "Refinement in the Arts", Hume says that progress in the industrial and commercial arts "is rather favourable to liberty, and has a natural tendency to preserve, if not produce a free government."[42] Having established that there can be economic causes to social and political phenomena, we can raise the question of what are the causes of the economic phenomena. That is, upon what does the progress in the arts depend? In the *History of England*, Hume tells us that "the rise, progress, perfection and decline of art and science are ...intimately connected with a narration of civil transactions. The events of no particular period can be fully accounted for, but by considering the degree of advancement which men have reached in those particulars."[43] Clearly then there can be political, social, and intellectual causes for economic forces.

As a further elaboration of the complex interaction between intellectual, economic, political, and social factors consider another of Hume's claims. According to Hume, in modern times progress in the industrial and commercial arts led to liberty, but among the classical Greeks and Romans such progress daily increased the number of slaves. Why should there be a difference? The Humean answer is that other political and intellectual factors were absent. Specifically, those conditions that allowed for the development of the "middling rank" were inhibited by both a jealous aristocracy and a turbulent, factious, tyrannical democracy that combined to banish "every merchant and manufacturer."[44] It is this sense of how the same factor can function differently in different contexts that enabled Hume to appreciate the importance of the historical evolution of institutions. It permitted Hume to see the difference between ancient republics and modern republics, that modern republics were only possible in the context of large commercial societies, and hence how different was modern liberty from ancient liberty. The difference between ancient and modern liberty was not lost on Hume the historian who exploded the myth and the dangers of the doctrine of an ancient British Constitution.

One final element in the complex interaction is worth noting. Political institutions help to mould human beings so that the conception that agents have of themselves is partly a reflection of the institutions to which they belong. It is because of this political structure and its influence that Hume can make generalizations in his science of politics. Hence, it would be misleading according to Hume to explain political virtue solely in terms of religion, or manners and morals, or abstract philosophy. Political virtue, for example, can exist apart from moral virtue as it did in the Roman Republic. The conclusion that Hume drew from this was that the cause of Rome's decline was not its immorality or its pursuit of luxury, that is moral causes, nor even any inevitable decline of some cyclic process. Rather, the decline of political virtue in Rome was the result of poor political institutions and continuing foreign conquests.

So far in this section we have been concerned to stress our opposition to familiar ways of trying to grasp Hume's notion of how to comprehend the social world. Can we say anything positive? As a first approximation to stating Hume's view of social dynamics we can say that the relationship among social, intellectual, political and economic factors is *organic*.[45] It is not possible to separate out an individual factor and study it in isolation from all of the others. In this sense, saying that Hume's social dynamics is organic is merely to assert that it is not mechanical. Hume's social dynamics is organic in a further sense, namely that as a result of the interaction of each of these factors qualitative transformations take place within each of them. That is, later stages of economic or political activity, for example, cannot be understood without reference to the previous history of interaction.

The importance of continuity was stressed by Hume in his essay on the original contract. There, Hume maintained that each generation did not go off the stage at once...as in the case with silk-worms and butterflies", rather "human society is in a perpetual flux, one man every hour going out of the world, another coming into it."[46] Because our world is organic, human beings cannot be fully understood apart from or outside of it. There are no contextless rights held apart from society. Just as we cannot step outside of ideas and impressions and find things-in-themselves, so we cannot step outside of society and find individuals-in-themselves. As Hume put it, man's "very first state and situation may justly be esteemed social."[47] This is also why the dichotomy between the natural and the artificial is ultimately unsound, and when it is jettisoned by Hume it is jettisoned in favor of the artificial.

This leads us to another dimension of Hume's social dynamics, namely the *historical* dimension. The configuration of political, economic, intellectual, and social factors at any given time transforms itself in such a way that later configurations are dependent upon earlier configurations. The configuration is qualitatively transformed through time. In moving from a strictly organic and biological metaphor to the metaphor of history Hume avoided the temptation to think in terms of adaptation to the environment. Adaptation is always limited to individuals. The danger in applying the concept of adaptation to the social level is that it gets transposed into a form of progressive social evolution. The real historical development, however, is much more precarious and in so sense unilinear. It evolves but it does not progress to an endpoint. To postulate a teleological envelope is to over-rationalize and at the expense of historical truth.

Hume's history, like his philosophy as a whole, is anti-foundational. We would look in vain for a uniform model of temporality. There are no simple cause and effect sequences and no simple timeless grid into which all factors fit neatly. There is no straight line development. On the contrary, Hume dwells on the importance of discontinuities like the revolution as well as chance occurrences. To understand an event is to look for the multiple processes and levels that constitute that event, not a single mechanism.

If a community is an organic and historical entity, then it is senseless to talk about establishing a community. That is a pseudo problem. On the other hand, it is always meaningful to ask what sustains a community, and this was a rather pertinent question for a post-revolution Britain. However, the question of what sustains a community cannot be answered by reference to the pseudo-question of how the community originated. Hume would no doubt have agreed with Adam Ferguson that there are social phenomena that result from human action but not from human design. In fact, there are a number of sources from which Hume inherited the doctrine of unintended consequences, namely, Pufendorf's *The Law of Nature and Nations*, Montesquieu's *Spirit of the Laws*, and Mandeville's *Fable of the Bees*.

It is "spontaneous order" that accounts for the origin of a system. But the further elaboration of that order in the face of new circumstances demands an explication of the implicit norms that have evolved historically. The historian plays a crucial role here, for in determining that an event is historically significant he or she is consciously including the implicit norms of that event into "our" narrative. It would appear, therefore, that for Hume the true historian must see himself or herself as a potentially engaged agent in an on-going drama. This is also what permits the historian to draw moral lessons from history. This is also why in his axiological writings Hume keeps insisting that any attempt to clarify the norms of our social practices necessarily involves an internal historical account of those norms. Finally, in Hume's view, it is custom that bridges the theoretical gap between spontaneous order and sustaining motive.

As a second approximation to stating Hume's view of social dynamics we can characterize the organic and historical configuration of the social world as *conservative*. That is, all norms are contextual and cannot be grasped from an external perspective. For Hume, the function of social and political philosophy is to explicate the implicit norms of our past or historical practice. These norms are not objective structures but rather a sense of what we have been trying to do. It is important that these norms not be construed as symbols of a supernatural or teleological historical process, that these norms not be construed as forming a neat deductive system that can be definitively conceptualized. It is important that we be sensitive to the potential conflicts our implicit norms are always capable of engendering, that we try to smooth the way for the negotiation of those conflicts, and that we see implicit norms or custom as a fertile source of adaptation to new conditions.

Liberty is just such an implicit norm. Historically, according to Hume's *History of England*, liberty emerged as a natural but unintended by-product of justice. Although justice can be established, it has to be sustained over time in order to produce liberty. Thus if our concern is to guard liberty, the critical rational question becomes how to sustain justice. That is one of the key questions that the *History of England* tries to answer. Justice is sustained, according to Hume, by an evolving sense of social obligation, a sympathetic "communication of sentiments and passions."[48]

The two greatest dangers to the evolving sense of social obligation are an unauthentic account of the evolution of our polity and misguided intellectual speculation about the alleged abstract and timeless hidden structure behind our historical practice. Hume's *History* is an attempt to avoid the first danger. Hume's epistemological and metaphysical works are an attempt to avoid the second danger. Those who seek to guard or to produce liberty by discovering its necessary and sufficient conditions are among the greatest threats to liberty. We can even go so far as to suggest that if Hume is correct then his thesis about the preservation of liberty and the danger to liberty represented by certain kinds of intellectual speculation has consequences far beyond this one historical context and for all axiological discussions.[49]

The term "conservative"[50] has many connotations, so perhaps it would be helpful to indicate Hume's unique for his time version of conservatism.[51] Let's contrast Hume with Blackstone and the common lawyers. The latter opposed the divine right theory of monarchy and supported Parliament during the revolution. They could not accept the idea of the Norman Conquest because, in their view, it made the King the ultimate owner of all property in England. Hence, when they invoked the ancient constitution they either ignored this whole period of English history (as in Rapin) or they proposed ingenious *ad hoc* fabrications such as Lyttleton's notion that William was a tyrant or Blackstone's view that William conquered Harold and not England. The intellectual danger of the common law tradition is that it always ends up making of tradition a metaphysical absolute. Hume, on the contrary, could argue that the British Constitution evolved, that our cherished liberty could spring in part from religious fanatics such as the Puritans, that the Norman Conquest was indeed modified by Magna Carta but also by inherent peculiarities in English feudalism.[52]

Failure to perceive Hume's special version of conservatism leads to the following kind of misunderstanding. In his work on Hume, Greig asks: "How could the same man, and at the same time, be both, Edmund Burke and George III? How could he defend the colonists in North America for their resistance to the arbitrary power of king, ministers, and venal House of Commons and yet attack the old Whigs, and Patriots, and Wilkites, and democratic radicals of every sort for trying to resist the same agencies at home?....In metaphysics, theory of knowledge, economics, ethics and religion, and in politics as far as they concerned Americans, he deserved rather to be dubbed a Radical: he depended not upon authority, but upon his own reasonings...he disintegrated and destroyed many settled notions by an acid logic of his own. Why therefore did he fail to bring the same acid logic to the politics of Charles I and Cromwell, George II and John Wilkes?"[53]

Greig's question is misdirected. Hume's revolution was conservative, a restoration of custom and common sense. Contrary to Greig, what Hume's epistemology shows is that logic left to its own devices will undermine itself.[54] Rationality has nothing to do with that sort of logic. On the contrary, being rational means explicating the implicit norms that inform our logical practice. Those norms are social and historical. The enemies of rationality are those who seek to read into our cultural norms a ready-made hypothesis, a doctrine of necessary and sufficient conditions, a magisterial archimedean point from which to pontificate.

I close with a quotation from Hayek that I think captures the intellectual spirit of Hume's conservatism.

> Thought seems to have made little advance since David Hume and Immanuel Kant....It was they who came nearer than anybody has done since to a clear recognition of the status of values as independent and guiding conditions of all rational construction. What I am ultimately concerned with here...is that destruction of values by scientific error which has increasingly come to seem to me the great tragedy of our time – a tragedy, because the values which scientific error tends to dethrone are the indispensable foundation of all our civilization, including the very scientific efforts which have turned against them. The tendency of constructivism to represent those values which it cannot explain as determined by arbitrary human decisions, or acts of will, or mere emotions, rather than as the necessary conditions of facts which are taken for granted by its expounders, has done much to shake the foundations of civilization, and of science itself, which also rests on a system of values which cannot be scientifically proved."[55]

In this last section of the paper, we have tried to show how Hume's discussion of the preservation of liberty in the *History of England* is a consistent application of Hume's political and social philosophy and at the same time how the discussion of liberty in the *History* raises methodological questions which help to shed light on Hume's philosophy as a whole.

Notes

1. See Donald W. Livingston, *Hume's Philosophy of Common Life* (Chicago: University of Chicago Press, 1983).
2. David Hume, *The History of England*, ed. W.B. Todd (Indianapolis: Liberty Classics, 1983), vol. I, pp.168–69. Hereafter, this work will be referred to as *History*.
3. David Hume, *Essays: Moral, Political, and Literary*, ed. Eugene Miller (Indianapolis: Liberty Classics, 1985), p. 40 ("Origin of Government"). Hereafter this work will be cited as *Essays*.
4. Duncan Forbes, in *Hume's Philosophical Politics* (Cambridge: University Press, 1975), and others, have suggested that Hume's case would have been clearer if he had distinguished more sharply between civil liberty and political liberty as Montesquieu had done.
5. I have argued elsewhere that Hume rejected natural law. See Nicholas Capaldi, *David Hume: The Newtonian Philosopher* (Boston: Twayne, 1975) and *Hume's Place in Moral Philosophy* (New York: Peter Lang, 1989). The attempt to generate a natural law theory out of Hume by studying natural passions in their social setting fails to recognize the extent to which the social setting is historically evolving and therefore not capable of being definitively conceptualized. It is difficult to see what natural law would mean here.

For the foregoing reasons, I do not think that Hume would have been sympathetic either to Grotius or to Pufendorf. Hume's concern was with justice, not law per se. The rules of justice become binding because sympathy creates social bonds which collectively legitimate authority.

For a clear presentation of an opposing argument see the work of Knud Haakonssen, especially *The Science of a Legislator. The Natural Jurisprudence of David Hume and Adam Smith* (Cambridge: University Press, 1981).
6. David Hume, *The History of England*, *op.cit.*, V, pp. 315–16.
7. *Ibid.*, VI, p. 367.
8. *Ibid.*, V, p. 450.
9. David Hume, *A Treatise of Human Nature*, ed. Selby-Bigge (Oxford: Clarendon Press, 1968), p. 537. Hereafter this work will be cited as *Treatise*.
10. I believe that Hume is employing several different but related notions of liberty. It is clear that, following Hobbes and Locke, Hume understands liberty as the absence of arbitrary external constraint (i.e. negative liberty). But it is also clear that Hume was beginning to develop a sense of positive liberty as autonomy, somewhat in the Kantian sense. We shall see some indication of this when we get to Hume's discussion of property and personal identity. The two senses of liberty are related in that the latter or positive sense subsumes the former. As a consequence, great weight will be put on what "arbitrary" means. None of this is completely worked out in Hume, but the rudiments of the discussion are undoubtedly there.
11. *History, op.cit.*, IV, p. 364.
12. *Ibid.*, V, p. 126.
13. For an interpretation of Hume's *History* that stresses the crucial importance of political parties in his thinking, see Nicholas Phillipson, *Hume* (New York: St. Martin's, 1989), in the series Historians on Historians.
14. See the articles by Douglass Adair, "'That Politics May Be Reduced to a Science': David Hume, James Madison, and the Tenth Federalist," and Craig Walton, "Hume and

Jefferson on the Uses of History", in *Hume: A Reevaluation*, ed. Donald W. Livingston and James T. King (New York: Fordham University Press, 1976).

15. *Essays, op.cit.*, p. 54. Italics are mine.

16. *History, op.cit.*, VI, p. 476.

17. *History, op.cit.*, I, p. 463.

18. *Ibid.*, II, pp. 99–110.

19. *Ibid.*, III, p. 76.

20. *Essays, op.cit.*, "Of Civil Liberty", p. 92.

21. *Ibid.*, pp. 92–93.

22. *Treatise, op.cit.*, p. 309.

23. For further discussion of Hume's economic views consult Tom Velk and A.R. Riggs, "David Hume's Practical Economics," in *Hume Studies* (1985), pp. 154–165; David Levy, "David Hume's Invisible Hand in The Wealth of Nations – The Public Choice of Moral Information," *Hume Studies Tenth Anniversary Issue* (1985), pp. 110–149; Eugene Rotwein, ed., *David Hume, Writings on Economics* (Madison: University of Wisconsin Press, 1955).

24. *History, op.cit.*, I, pp.76–77.

25. *Ibid.*, II, pp. 289–90.

26. David Hume, *Enquiry Concerning Human Understanding* and *Enquiry Concerning the Principles of Morals*, ed. Selby-Bigge (Oxford: The Clarendon Press, 1972), "Of Justice", Part II, p. 194.

27. Hume letter to Dr. Clephane in J. Hill Burton, *Life and Correspondence of David Hume* (Edinburgh, 1846) II, pp.38–39.

28. *Ibid.*, p. 73.

29. See *History, op.cit.*, IV, appendix III, pp. 454–486.

30. *Ibid.*, VI, p. 533.

31. *Ibid.*, VI, pp. 468–69.

32. *Ibid.*, V, p. 573 (note BB to chap. 55).

33. *Ibid.*, IV, p. 395 (note M to chap. 39).

34. *Treatise, op.cit.*, p. 399.

35. *Essays, op.cit.*, p. 51.

36. *Enquiry Concerning Human Understanding, op.cit.*, pp. 83–84.

37. The affinity between Hume and Collingwood is striking, despite Collingwood's unsympathetic reading of Hume.

38. See Nicholas Capaldi, "Hume as Social Scientist," *Review of Metaphysics* (1978), pp. 99–123.

39. John Laird, on p. 270 of his book *Hume's Philosophy of Human Nature* (New York: Dutton, 1931), claims that Hume had a cyclical view of history. He refers to a passage in the *Dialogues Concerning Natural Religion* and a passage in the *Natural History of Religion*. I doubt if either passage will sustain such a thesis, but I shall quote both of those passages for readers. In the *Dialogues*, Cleanthes says: "Empires may rise and fall; liberty and slavery succeed alternately; ignorance and knowledge give place to each other; but the cherry tree will still remain in the woods of Greece, Spain, and Italy, and will never be affected by the revolutions of human society." (Part VI; p. 173 of the edition edited by Norman Kemp Smith, London, Nelson, 1947). In the *Natural History of Religion*, part VIII, Hume says: "...men have a natural tendency to rise from idolatry to theism, and to sink again from theism into idolatry."

40. *History, op.cit.*, II, p. 519.

41. *Essays, op.cit.*, p. 47.

42. *Essays, op.cit.*, p. 277.

43. *History, op.cit.*, II, p. 519.

44. *Essays, op.cit.*, p. 419, in the essay "The Populousness of Ancient Nations".

45. This reading of Hume would tend to support those who place him in the tradition of classical republicanism or civic humanism as defined originally by J.G.A. Pocock and applied to Hume and the Scottish Enlightenment by Nicholas T. Phillipson. See especially, J.G.A. Pocock, *The Machiavellian Moment. Florentine Political Thought and the Atlantic Republican Tradition* (Princeton: University Press, 1975); Nicholas T. Phillipson, "Towards a Definition of the Scottish Enlightenment," in *City and Society*, ed. P. Fritz and D. Williams (Toronto: University Press, 1973), pp. 125–47; and by the same author, "Hume as Moralist: A Social Historian's Perspective," in *Philosophers of the Enlightenment*, ed. S.C. Brown (Brighton, 1979), pp. 140–61. See also J. Moore, "Hume's Political Science and the Classical Republican Tradition," *Canadian Journal of Political Science* (1977), pp. 809–39. For a critique of the civic humanist reading of Hume see Knud Haakonssen, "Natural Law and Moral Realism: The Scottish Synthesis," in *Oxford Studies in the History of Philosophy*, ed. M.A. Stewart, vol. I, *The Philosophy of the Scottish Enlightenment* (Oxford: University Press, 1989).

I am myself inclined not to want to place Hume or characterize him strictly within the confines of either civic humanism or the debate between civic humanists and natural law adherents. It is easy to say, but I would prefer to see Hume as the first modern secular conservative theorist in his political theory, and in his philosophy in general as subscribing to the Copernican Revolution. See N. Capaldi, *Hume's Place in Moral Philosophy, op.cit.*

46. *Essays, op.cit.*, p. 476.

47. *Treatise, op.cit.*, p. 493.

48. *Treatise, op.cit.*, p. 592.

49. This is what Donald Livingston is attempting, in part, to show in his article in this collection.

50. I think that Sheldon Wolin is incorrect when he asserts that "Hume cleared the way for political romanticism" ("Hume's Conservatism" in Livingston and King, *op.cit.*, p. 243). This might be true of Burke but not of Hume.

For a different reading of Hume's conservatism see David Miller, *Philosophy and Ideology in Hume's Political Thought* (Clarendon Press: Oxford, 1981).

51. In another context, I would argue that Hume's twentieth-century followers include Ortega, Hayek, and Oakeshott among others.

52. Alan MacFarlane, in his *Origins of English Individualism*, argues that England had in the 13th century a market economy without factories. This not only minimized the effects of Norman feudalism but shows how a market economy could arise out of unique English property relations. As a result, there is much more to the development of individualism than Protestantism.

53. J.Y.T. Greig, *David Hume* (London, 1931) pp. 375–76.

54. See Nicholas Capaldi, *David Hume*: The Newtonian Philosopher (Boston: Twayne, 1975); *Hume's Place in Moral Philosophy* (New York: Peter Lang, 1989).

55. F.A. Hayek, *Law, Legislation, and Liberty*, vol. I, *Rules and Order* (London: Routledge and Kegan Paul, 1973), pp. 6–7.

INDEX